The Bare Truth...

Stars of Burlesque

From the '40s & '50s

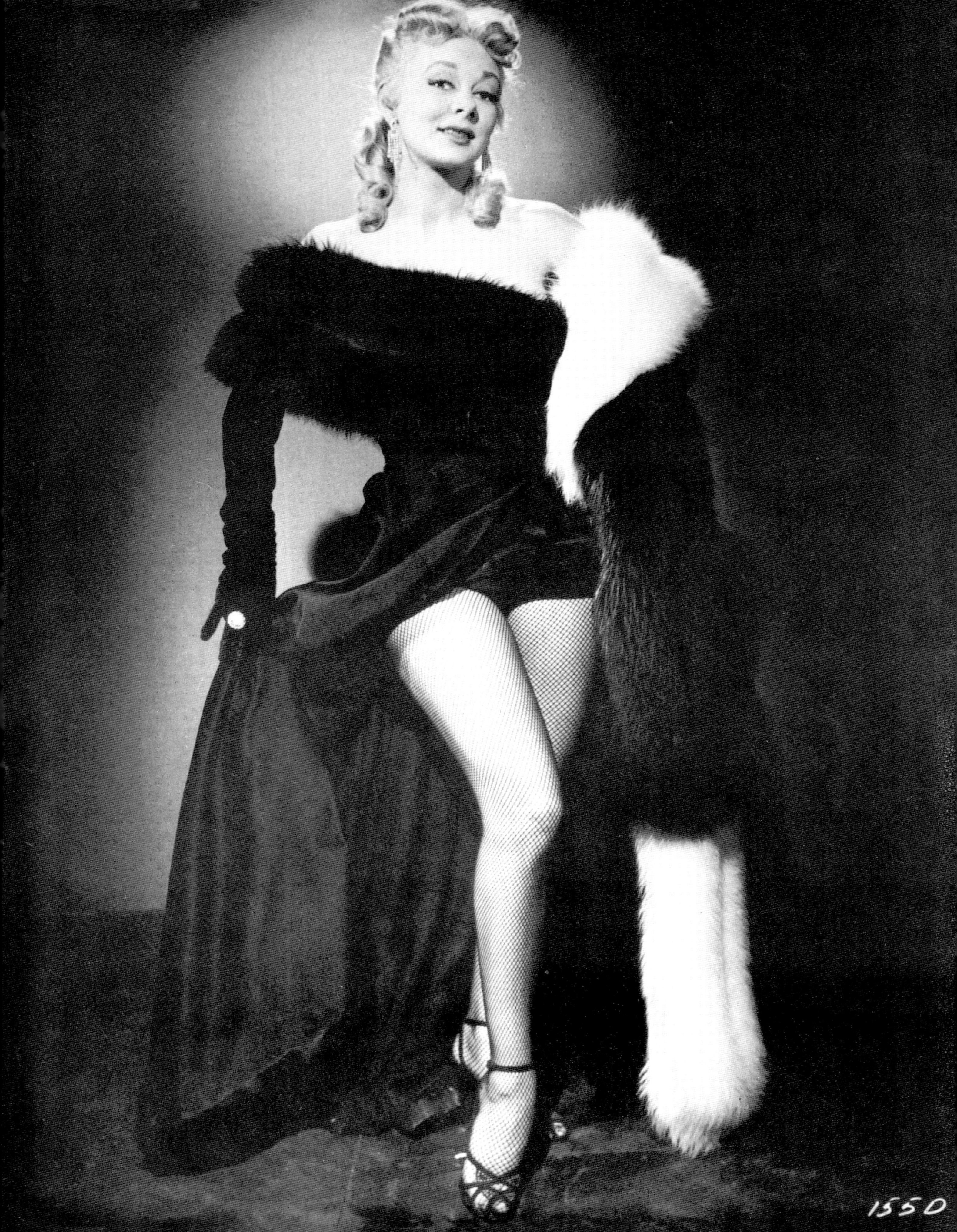
1550

THE BARE TRUTH...

Stars of Burlesque

of the '40s & '50s

Len Rothe

Schiffer Publishing Ltd

4880 Lower Valley Road, Atglen, PA 19310

Dedication

This book is dedicated to the four special women in my life, not one of whom is in my books on Burlesque. First to my most understanding wife,
Babs
and to my three daughters,
Laurie,
Lisa, and
Hilary.
All four allowed me to live my life the way I wanted (which I am sure, at times, was not easy for them) and still encourage me to do so while waiting for me to decide what I want to be when I grow up.

Library of Congress Catalog Card Number: 98-84528

Book design by Blair R. Loughrey
Typeset in Geometri 231 BT/Souvenir Lt Bt/Kabel Bk Bt

ISBN: 978-0-7643-0603-7
Printed in China

Schiffer Books are available at special discounts for bulk purchases for sales promotions or premiums. Special editions, including personalized covers, corporate imprints, and excerpts can be created in large quantities for special needs. For more information contact the publisher:

Published by Schiffer Publishing Ltd.
4880 Lower Valley Road
Atglen, PA 19310
Phone: (610) 593-1777;
Fax: (610) 593-2002
E-mail: Info@schifferbooks.com

For the largest selection of fine reference books
on this and related subjects,
please visit our web site at **www.schifferbooks.com**
We are always looking for people to write books on new and related subjects. If you have an idea for a book please contact us at the above address.

This book may be purchased from the publisher.
Include $5.00 for shipping.
Please try your bookstore first.
You may write for a free catalog.

In Europe, Schiffer books are distributed by
Bushwood Books
6 Marksbury Ave.
Kew Gardens
Surrey TW9 4JF England
Phone: 44 (0) 20 8392-8585;
Fax: 44 (0) 20 8392-9876
E-mail: info@bushwoodbooks.co.uk
Website: www.bushwoodbooks.co.uk

Contents

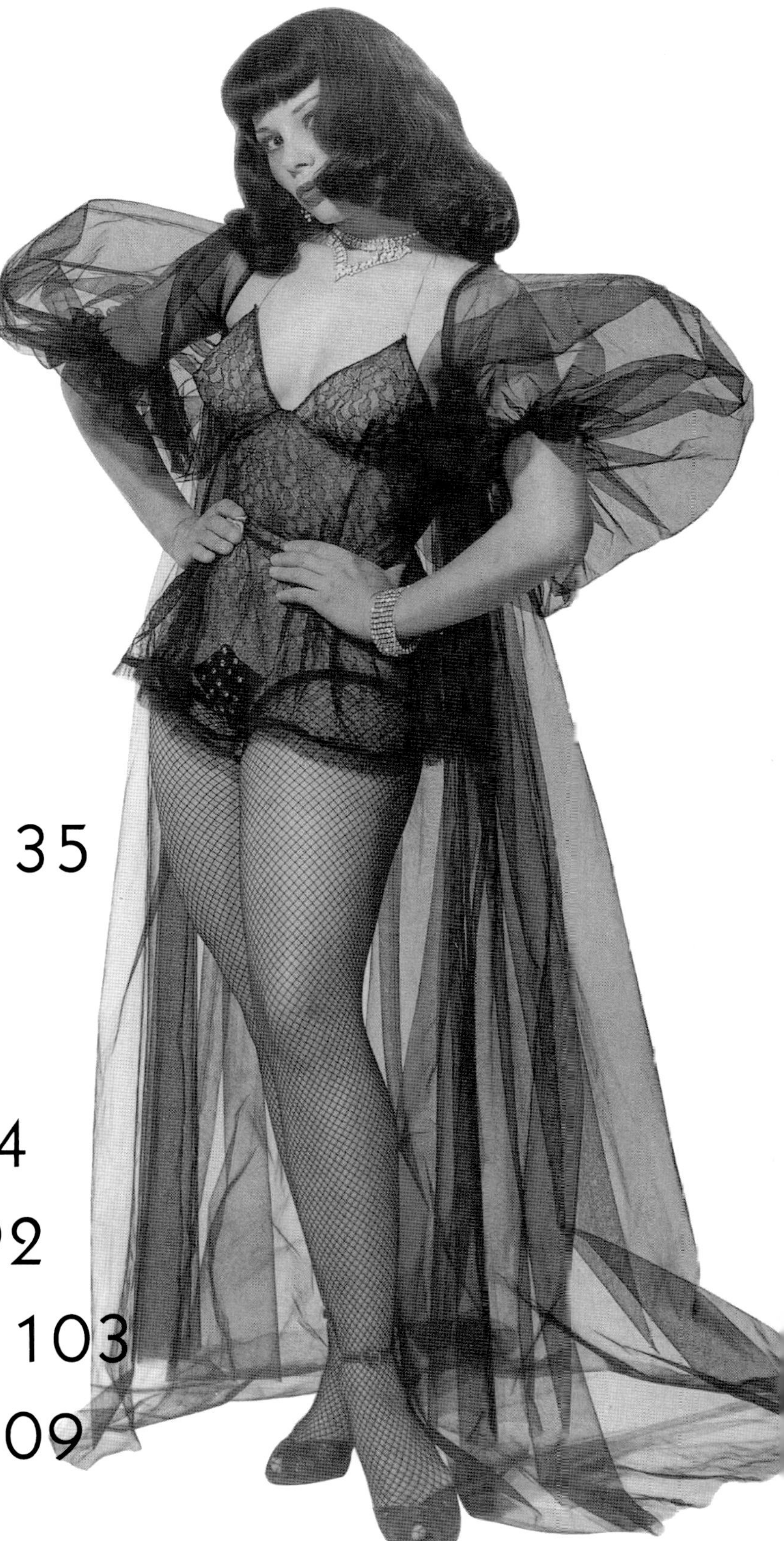

Introduction

As the former owner of an exhibit and display studio, which in by-gone days of the 1940s and 1950s created photo displays for Broadway theaters, movie palaces, and burlesque houses, I could not bear to throw out those rare, old, original, black and white photos from which the photo enlargements and murals were made. Over a period of time my collection grew to number in the thousands, all of which I neatly boxed and stored.

Not until Daniel, my teen-age grandson, discovered my hidden "treasure" did I realize the interest that photos of burlesque queens held for today's generation. His comments about the pictures were unexpected, as he spoke little about the nudity but was more interested in knowing about the burlesque as a form of entertainment. Once the meaning of the word "burlesque" was explained -- a situation where the serious is treated lightly and the frivolous seriously -- he began to appreciate how important a part humor and satire played in it. The names the strippers had chosen brought knowing grins; he chuckled at the brilliant satire evident in the titles of the acts and he broke into laughter when I told him about some of the comedians' humorous sight gags and "bits."

His mother, hearing his gales of laughter, came to see what so amused him. At first, she was appalled to learn that I had allowed an impressionable teen-age boy to look at pictures that she perceived to be "naughty." Yet, after looking at them and listening to some of the stories being told, she began to realize how innocent burlesque really was, when measured by today's entertainment standards. As she continued to rifle through the photos, she expressed amazement about how contemporary these gorgeous women with their striking bodies were (most are grandmothers today). She also developed greater appreciation for how timeless beauty really is, especially when there are few articles of clothing from which to identify the era in which the pictures were taken.

Seeing the keen interest in burlesque shown by two generations that wanted to know more about it, I came to realize there are countless others like them. Some have never seen a burlesque show and are curious to learn about this lost art form. Others remember burlesque fondly and want to be reminded of what they actually saw. Still others are interested in seeing beautiful women in different stages of undress... for whatever reason. As with my first book, *Queens of Burlesque*, I present this volume for your enjoyment, understanding, and entertainment.

Len Rothe
February, 1998

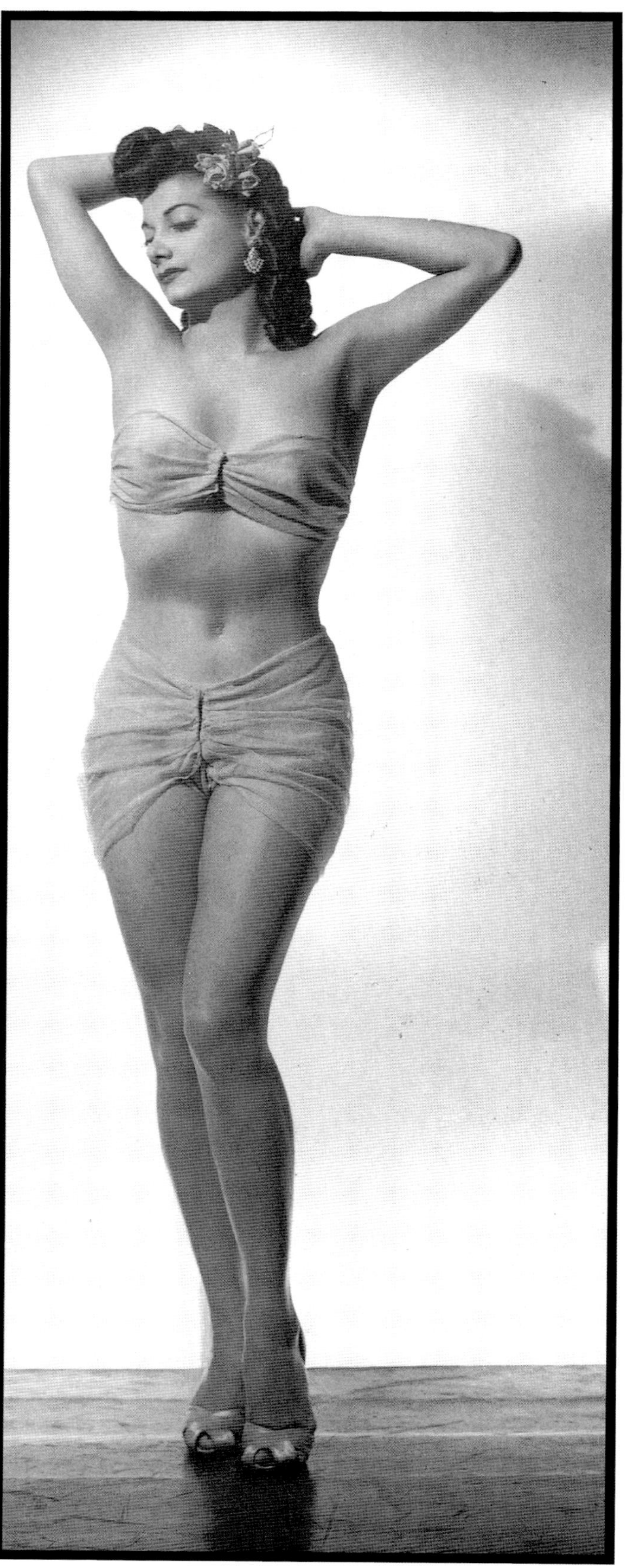

Andrea

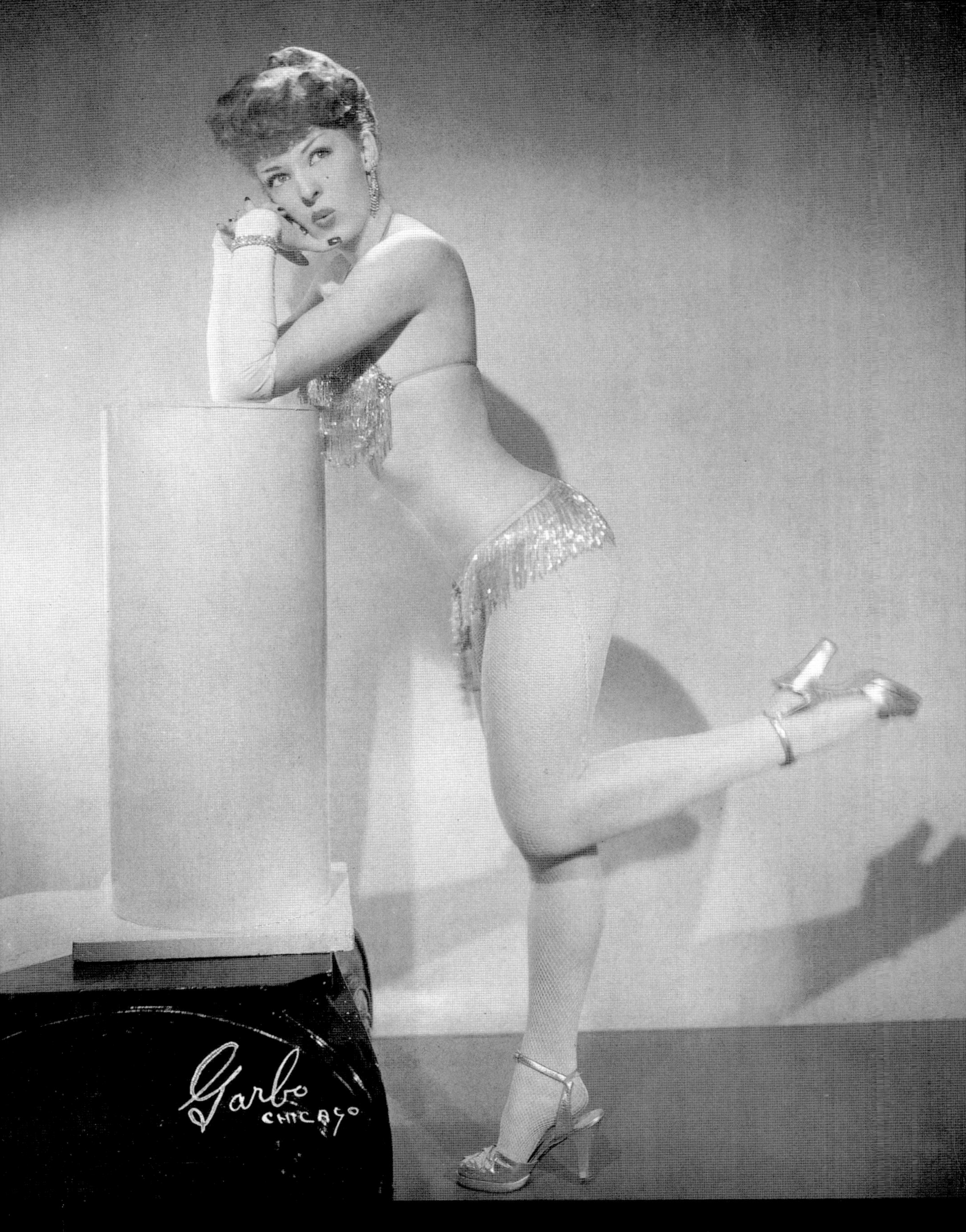

Ann "Bang Bang" Arbor

The Million Dollar Figure

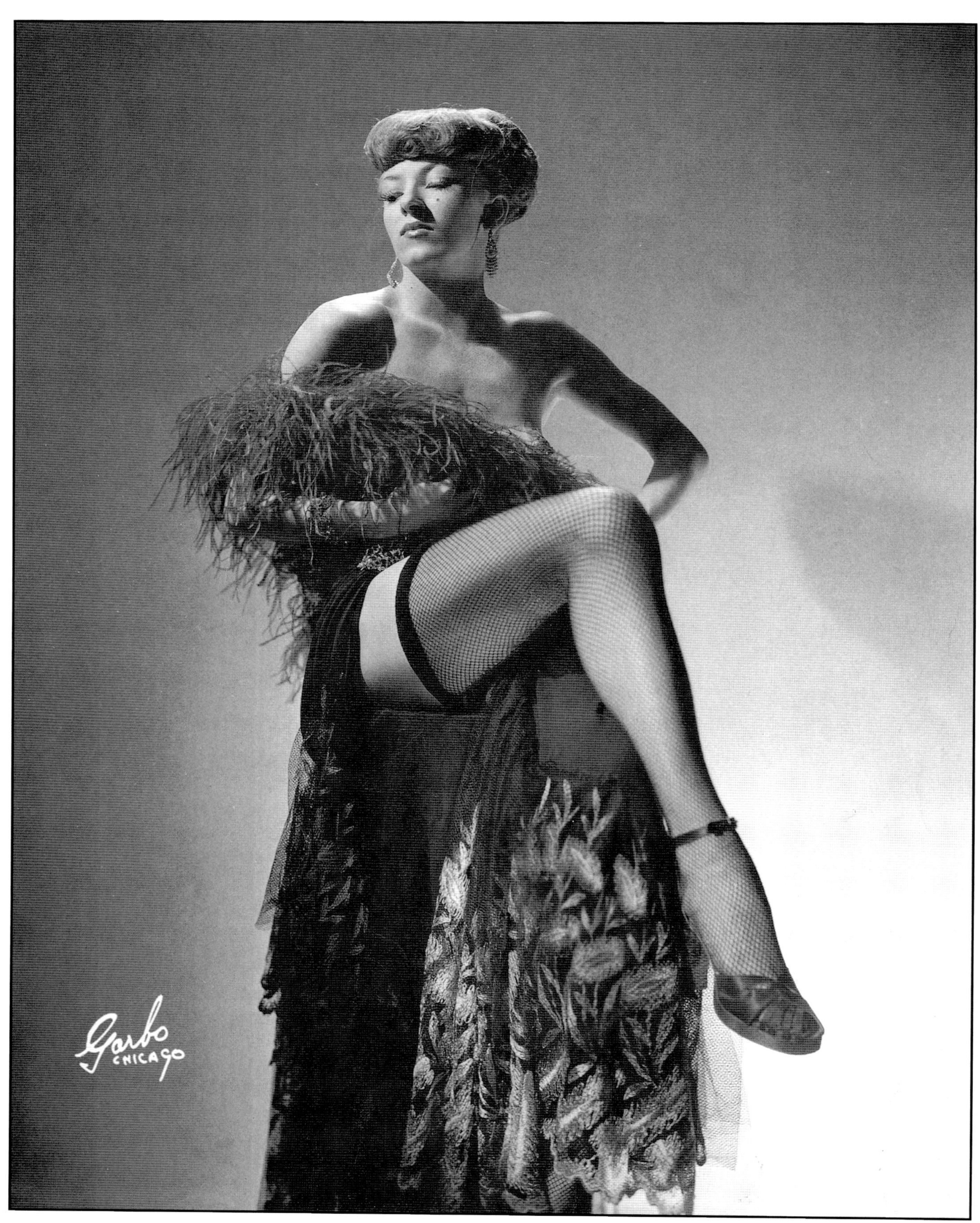

Ann "Bang Bang" Arbor
The Million Dollar Figure

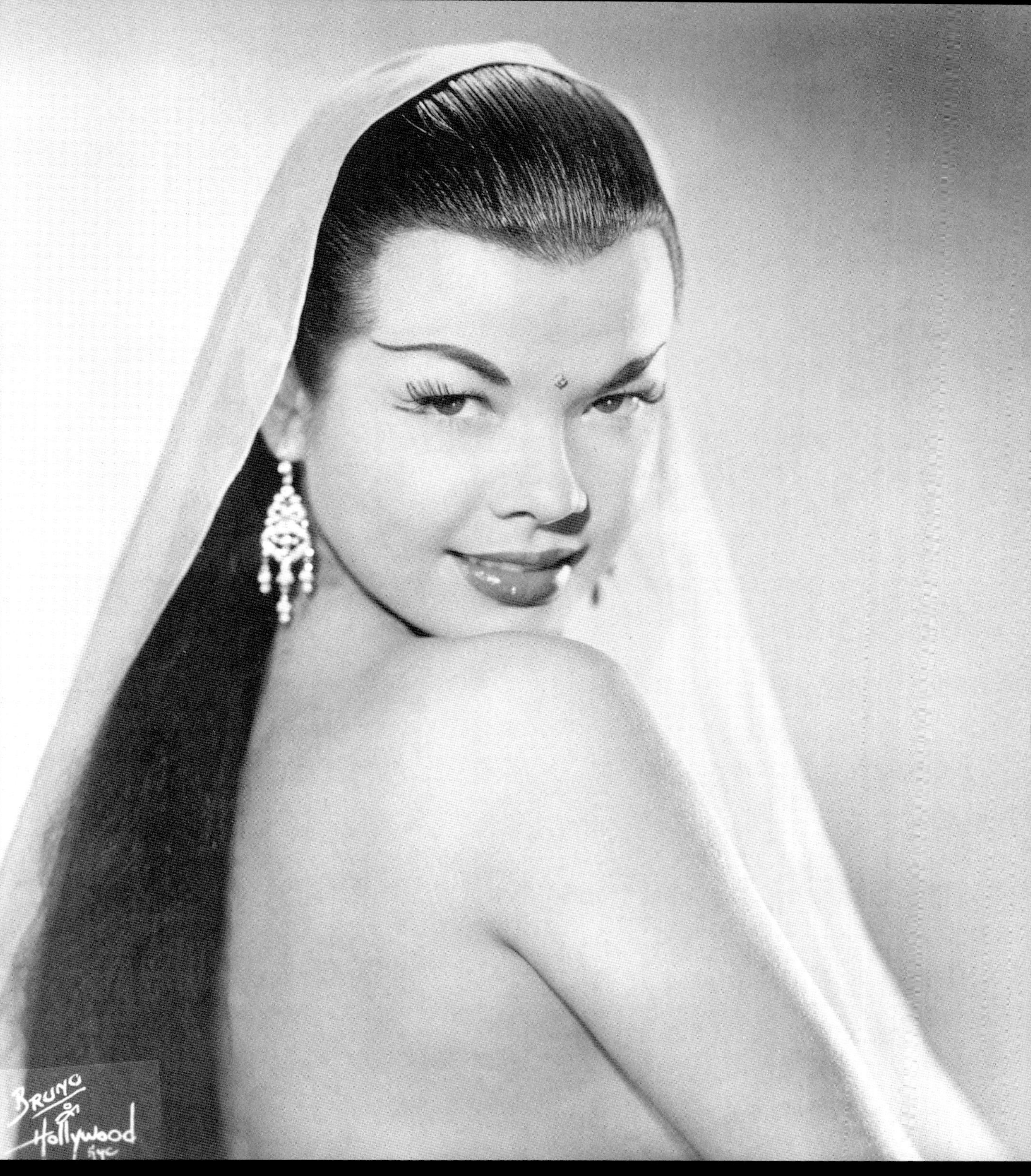

Nejla Ates
The Exquisite Turkish Delight

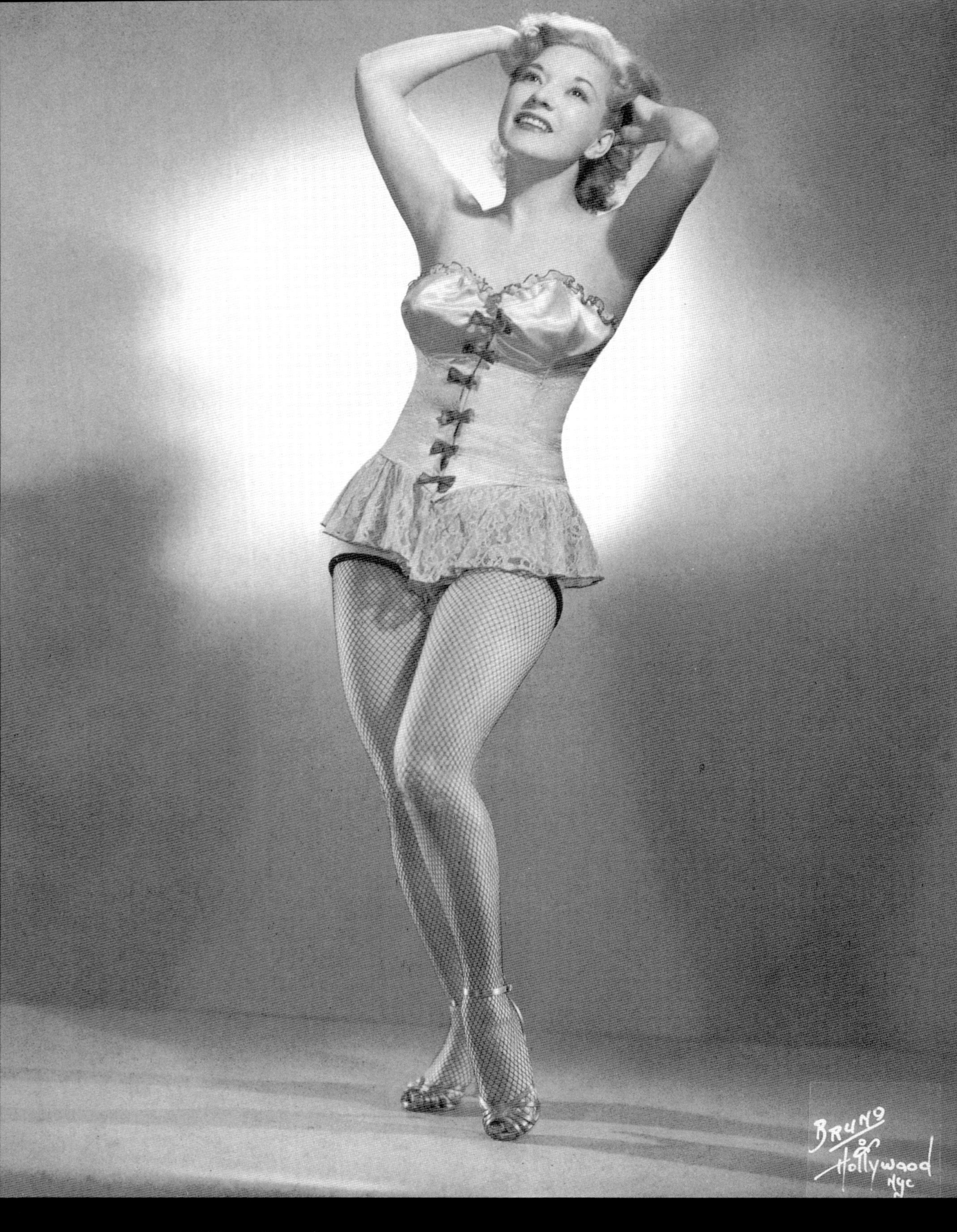

Elisa Barri

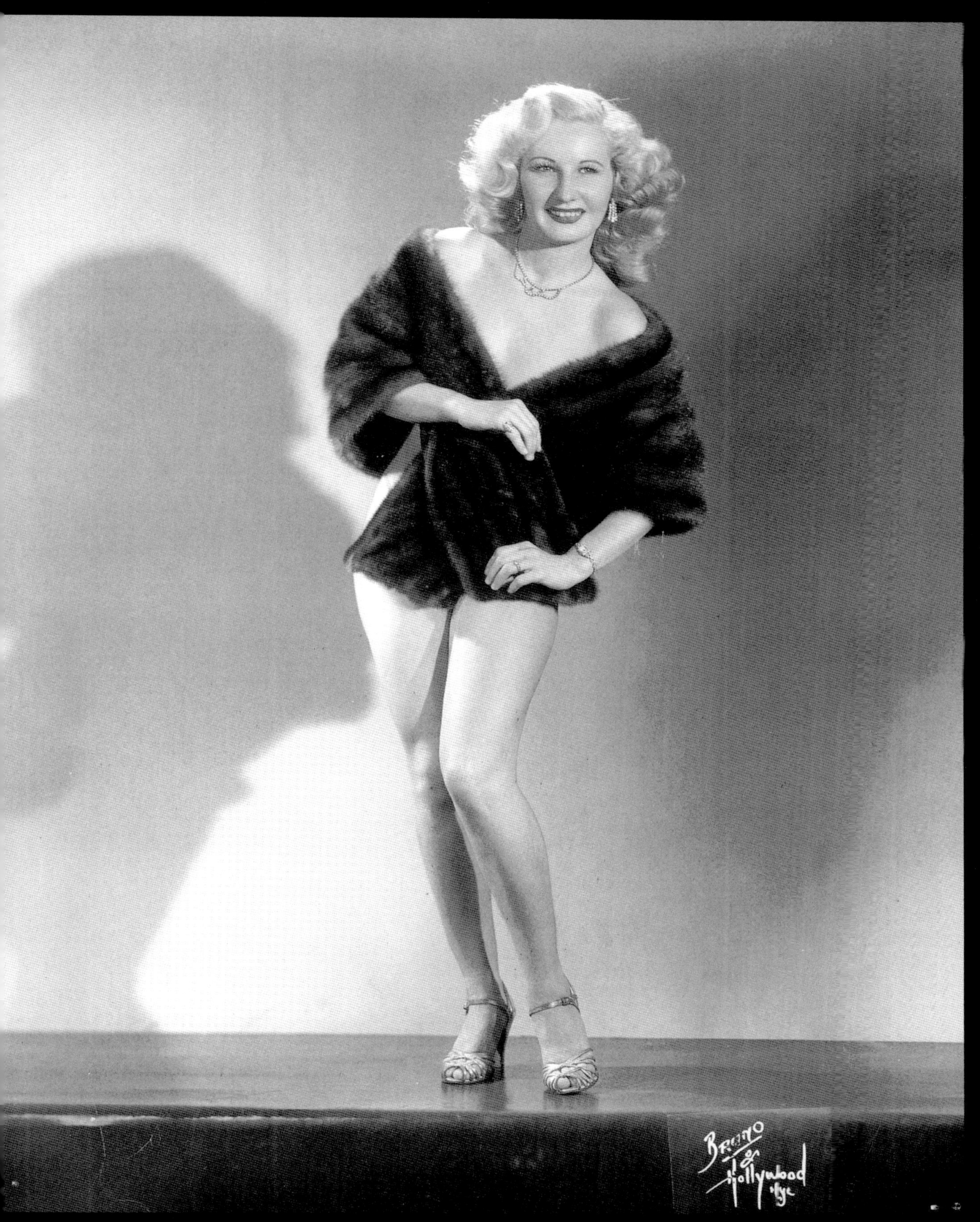

Betty Biddle

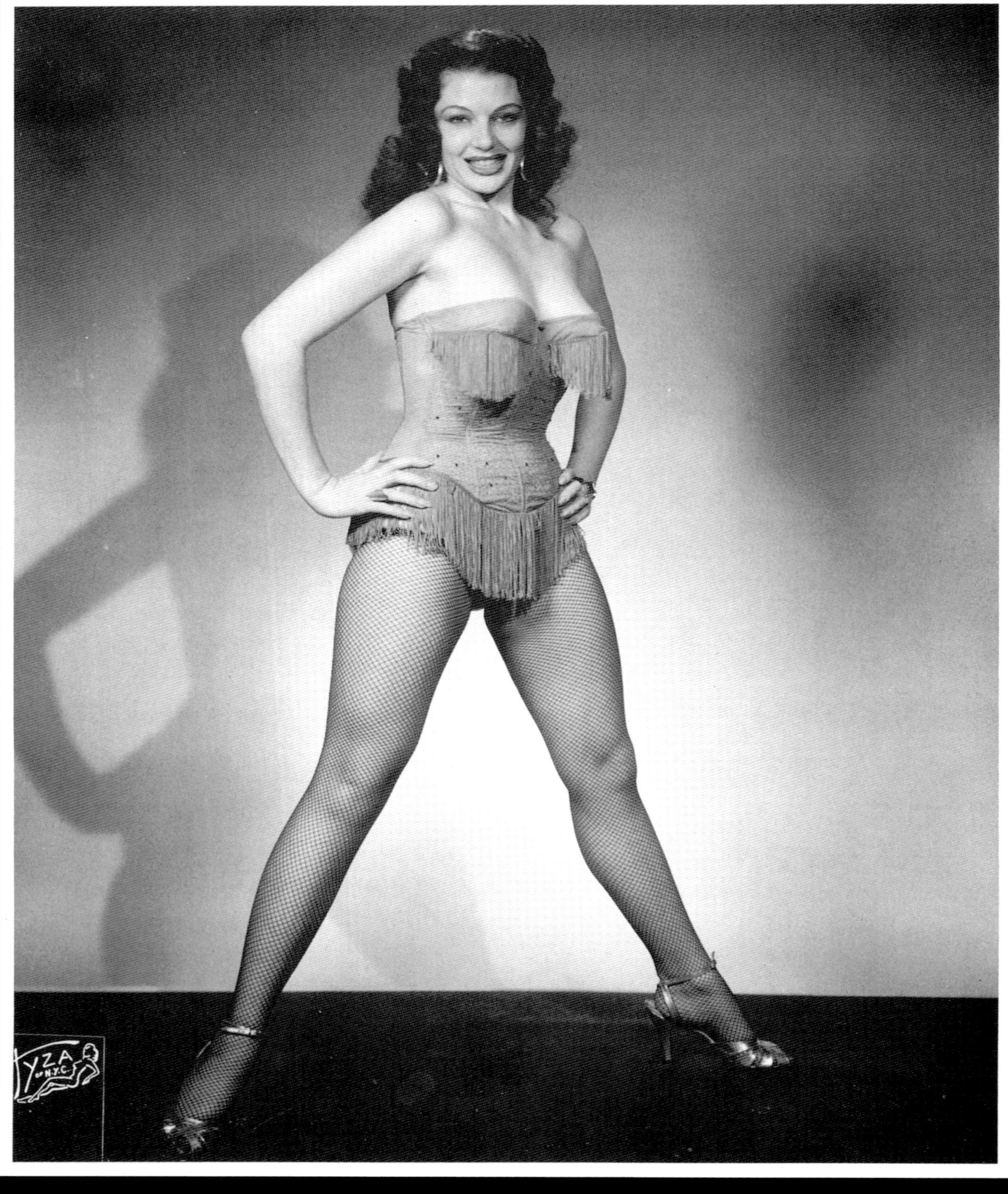

Camille

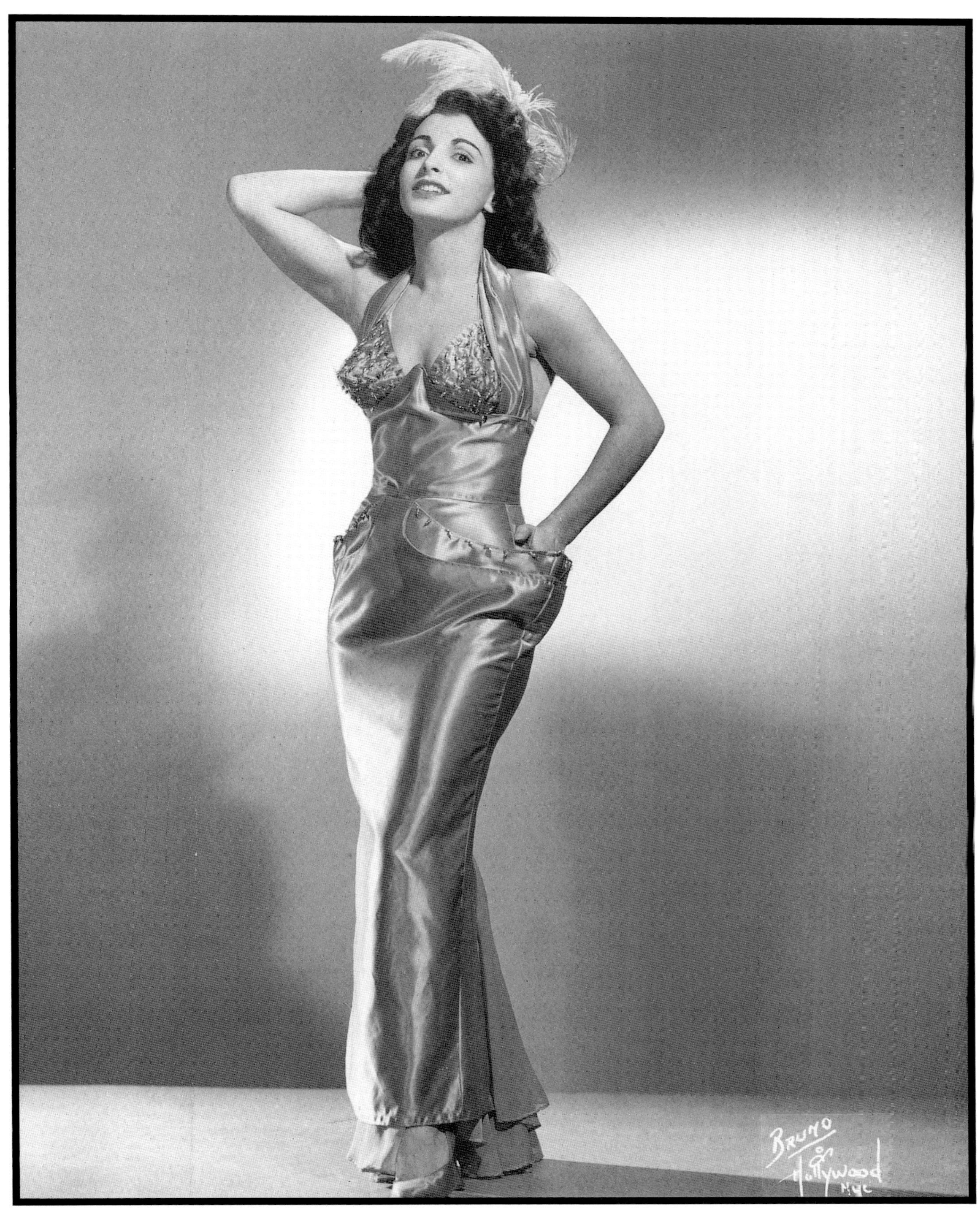

Carmila

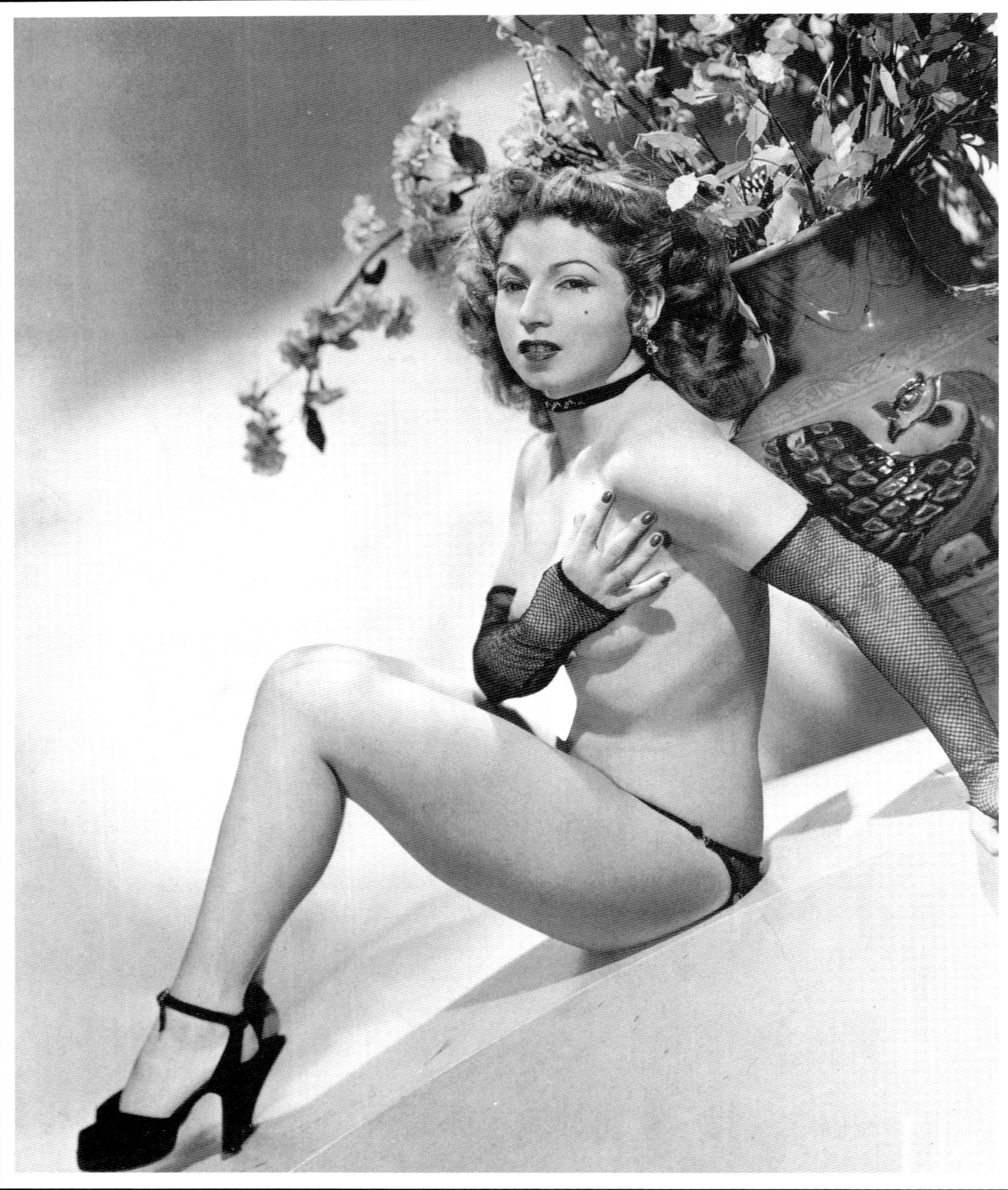

Chiki
Dancing Venus

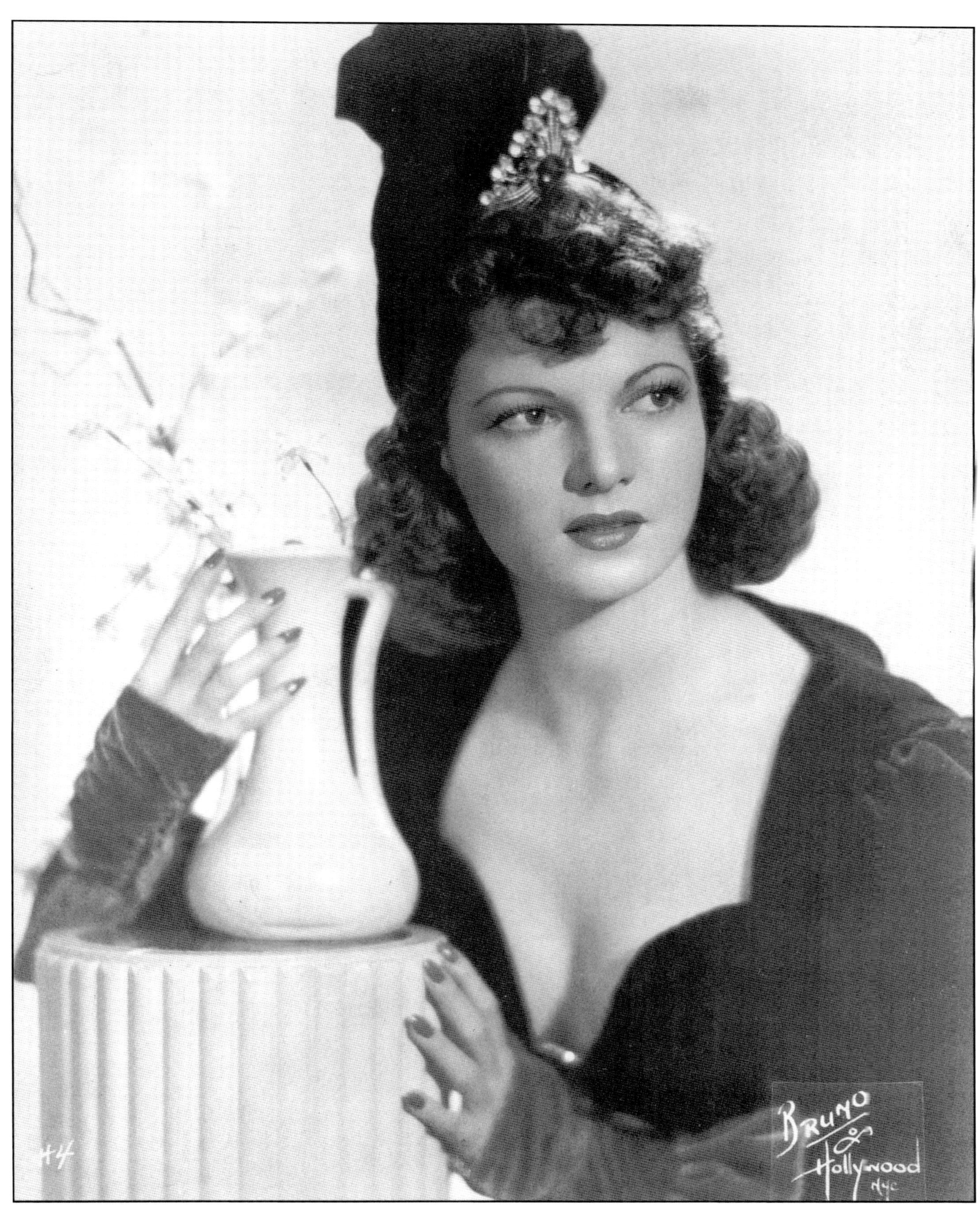

Ann Corio

History

To provide *The Bare Truth* about burlesque, we must begin in 1868 when Lydia Thompson's *British Blondes* daringly presented a chorus line of girls in tights for the first time to a New York audience. The show was quickly branded "wicked." However, it had so much audience appeal it continued to develop in one form or another until the 1890s when it became what we now call a variety show. Comedians did sketches (bits), "wicked" girls sang and danced, and acrobats thrilled the audience with feats of daring.

When the Chicago World's Columbian Exposition opened in 1893, Little Egypt, an exotic belly dancer, became the sensation of the midway. American entertainment would never be the same. The belly dancer eventually evolved into the uniquely American strip dancer (the *tease* would come later). However, it was not until 1914 that four brothers from New York, the Minsky brothers, decided, "If the people want it, we'll give it to them." And thus was born the "burleycue," "leg show," "bawdy show," also known as "burlesque." At that time, Minsky dancers wiggled, jiggled and bumped to classical, exotic and oriental music. Brooks Atkinson, a highly respected theater reviewer for the *New York Times,* advised his readers, "What the Follies Bergere is to Paris the Minsky shows are to a lucky New York." Perhaps taking his cue from the review, Minsky's ads began to read:

Burlesque as you like it —
The Poor Man's Follies!
Not a Family Show!

With this disclaimer you would think that no one who would be offended by burlesque would expose themselves to this type of theater, but some people apparently attended just to be shocked and demanded that the show be closed. In fact, the most vociferous opponents were people who never attended a burlesque show. Furthermore, Minsky is quoted as saying, "I call my shows burlesque, so that people who don't like it will be warned away. If I called them stage shows or vaudeville it wouldn't be right." No one under 18 years of age was ever knowingly admitted to a Minsky burlesque show.

It was not until 1920 that a Minsky performer began to strip (disrobe) in time to music, a performance described in the press as "daring and sensational." The Poor Man's Follies became an instant success. The Minsky Theater was on the Lower East Side of New York City in an area inhabited by poor immigrants who paid 75 cents to see the Minsky shows. Minsky's was a place where "hoity-toity, uptown bluenoses" rarely ventured.

Burlesque became a popular form of entertainment with gals, gags and music performed in a language so broad and slapstick it was easily understood, even by people who did not yet fully understand the English language.

Other variety shows were offered in New York on Broadway, which attracted the society crowd that rarely ventured down to the dangerous Lower East Side. On Broadway, *Florenz Ziegfield and his Follies* presented naked girls all over the stage, some hanging from the drapes, others swinging from the chandeliers. Also, *George White's Scandals* and *Earl Carroll's Vanities* were no less risqué, displaying nude girls bathing in champagne or wine, in a transparent tub, for an uptown admission price of $4.40. Whereas nudity was considered "art" uptown, it was considered indecent and immoral downtown, where the patron could see more skin in his newspaper than at Minsky's.

The time eventually came in 1935 for an attorney for the Minskys to ask the New York City License Commissioner, "Could you explain why exposed breasts are decent north of Fourteenth Street but indecent south of it?" The answer he received was, "the difference is movement. On Broadway unadorned female figures are used to artistic advantage in tableaux. They do not move. Minsky's, although also nude from the waist up, did move." Apparently, there would forever continue to be a geographic distinction between uptown and downtown nudity and humor.

The 1920s were already considered the "Sexy Decade" as skirts had risen from ankle length to knee length, causing panic in many areas of the country. In Philadelphia, a law was passed making it illegal to wear a skirt more than 7½" off the floor; in Utah skirts could be no more than 3" above the ankle; in Virginia, dresses could show no more than 3" of throat, and in Ohio a dress could show no more than 2" of throat.

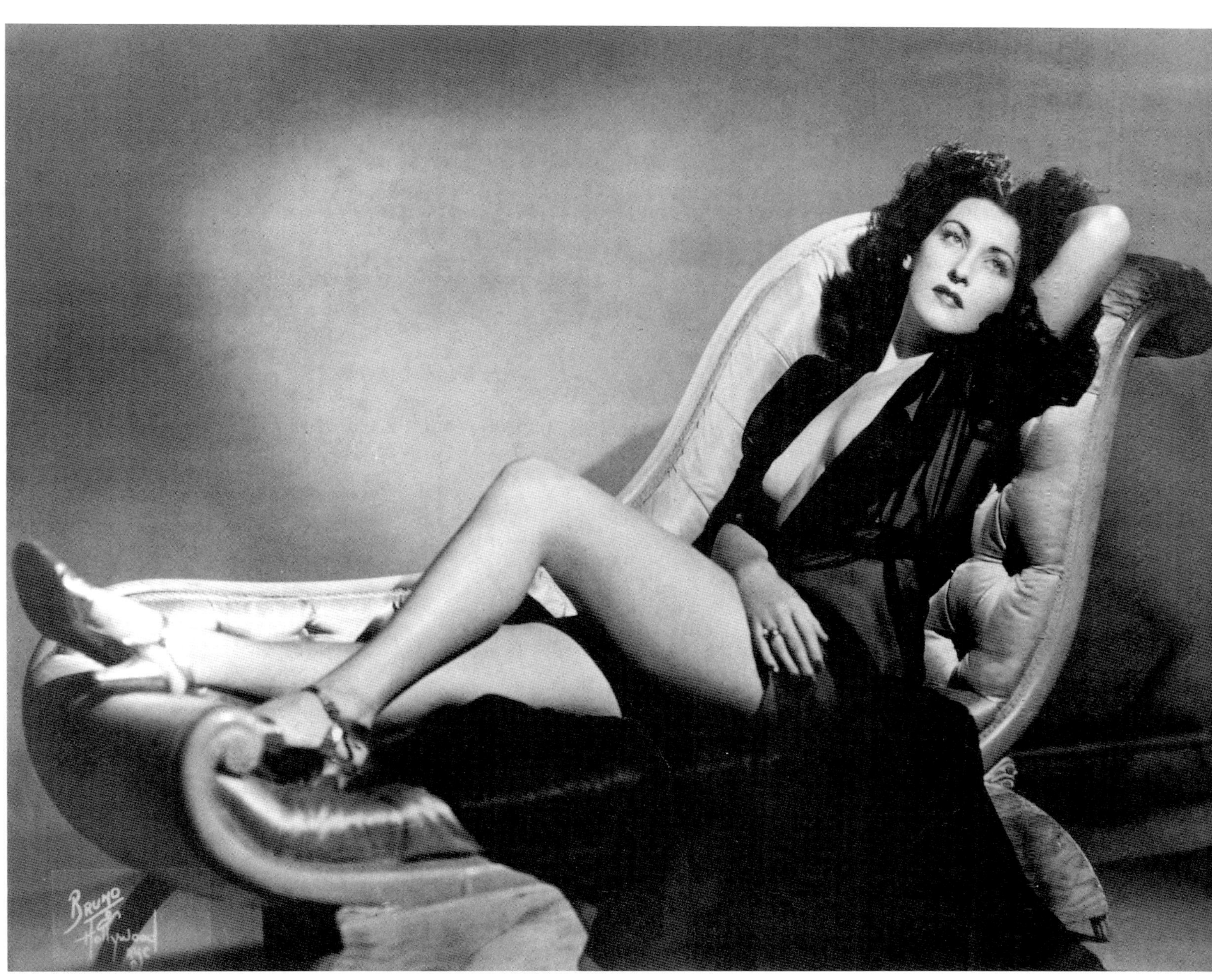

Debra Dante
Hottest Thing Since Chicago Firre

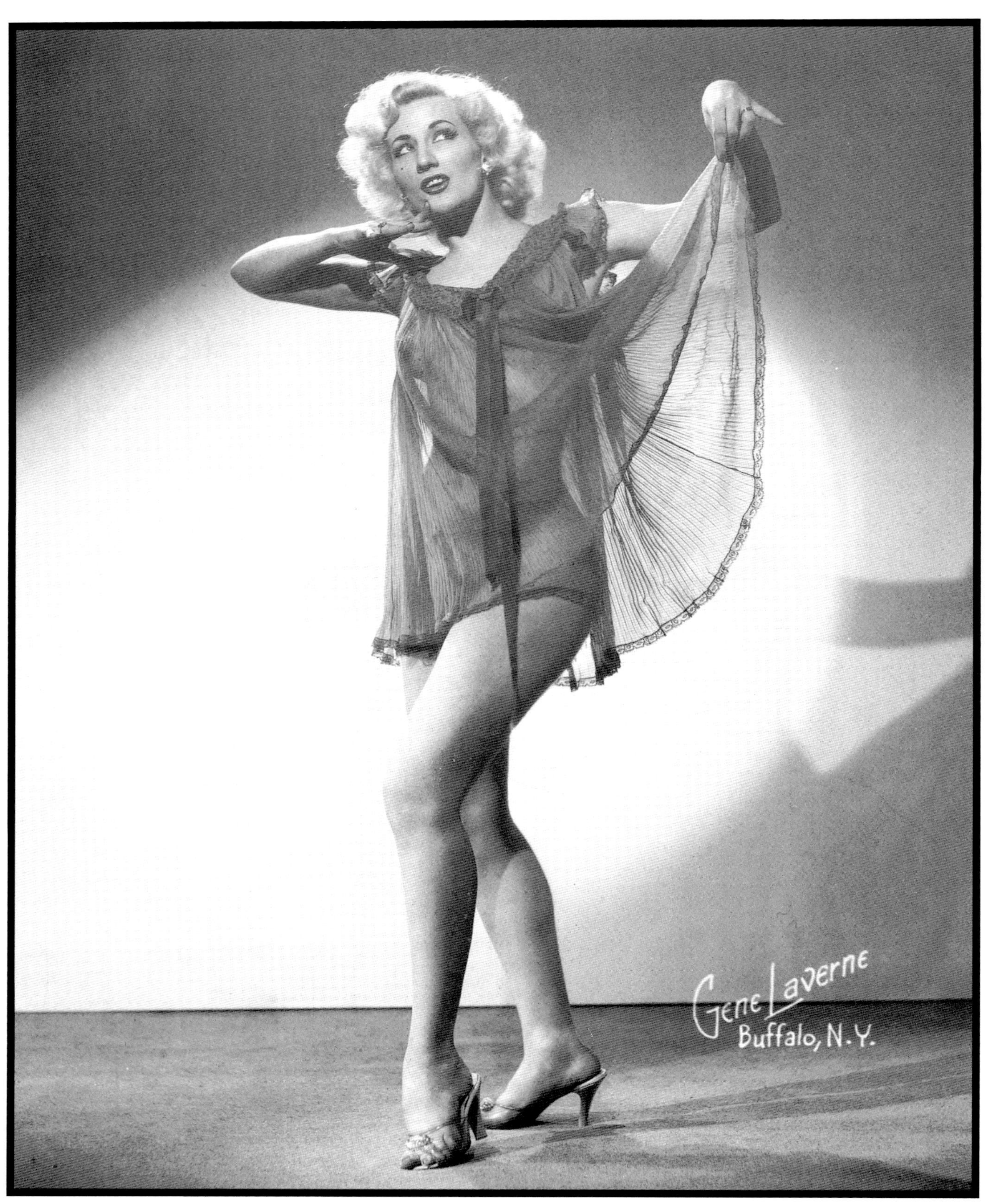

Sunny Dare

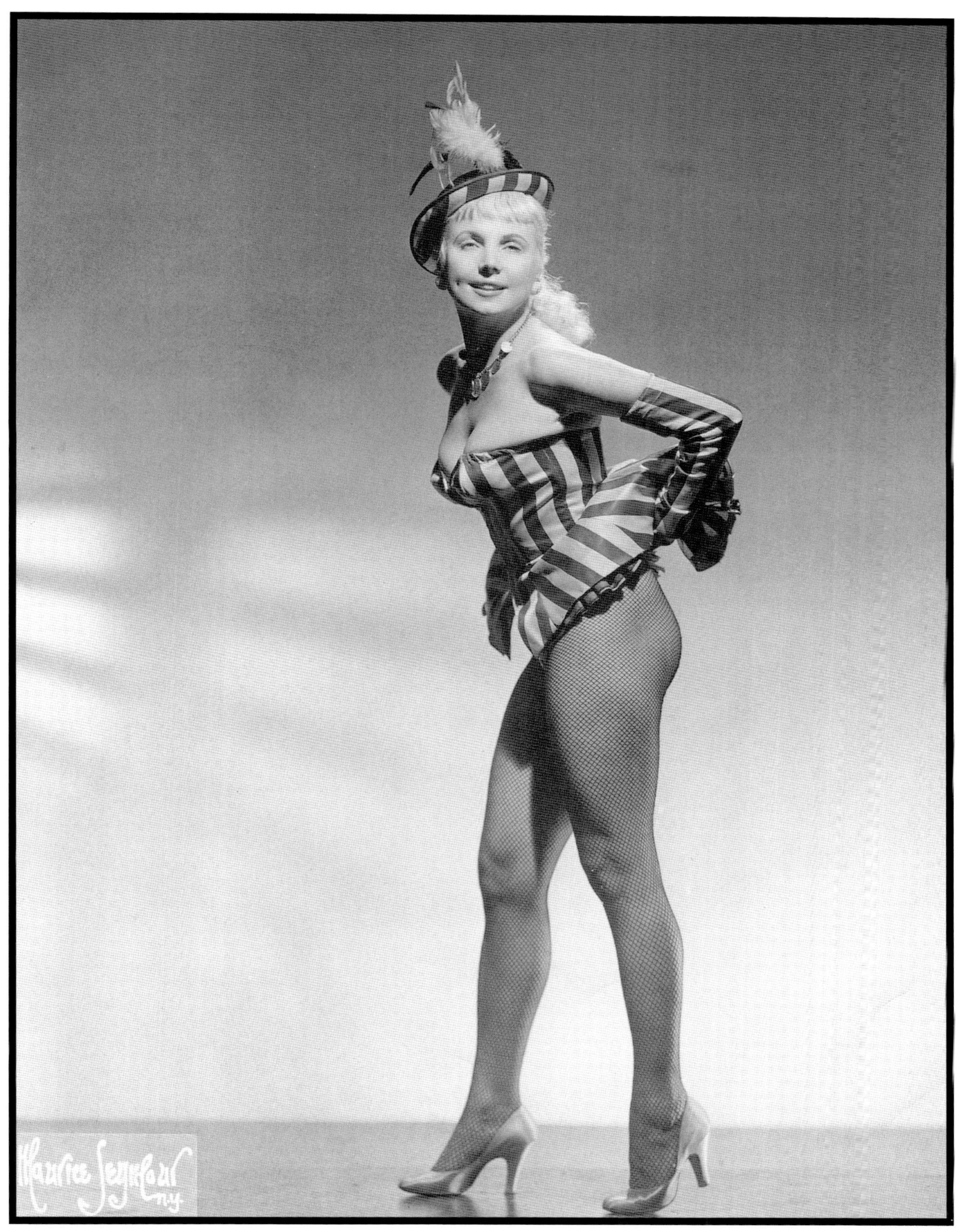

Bubbles Darlene

America's Most Exciting Body

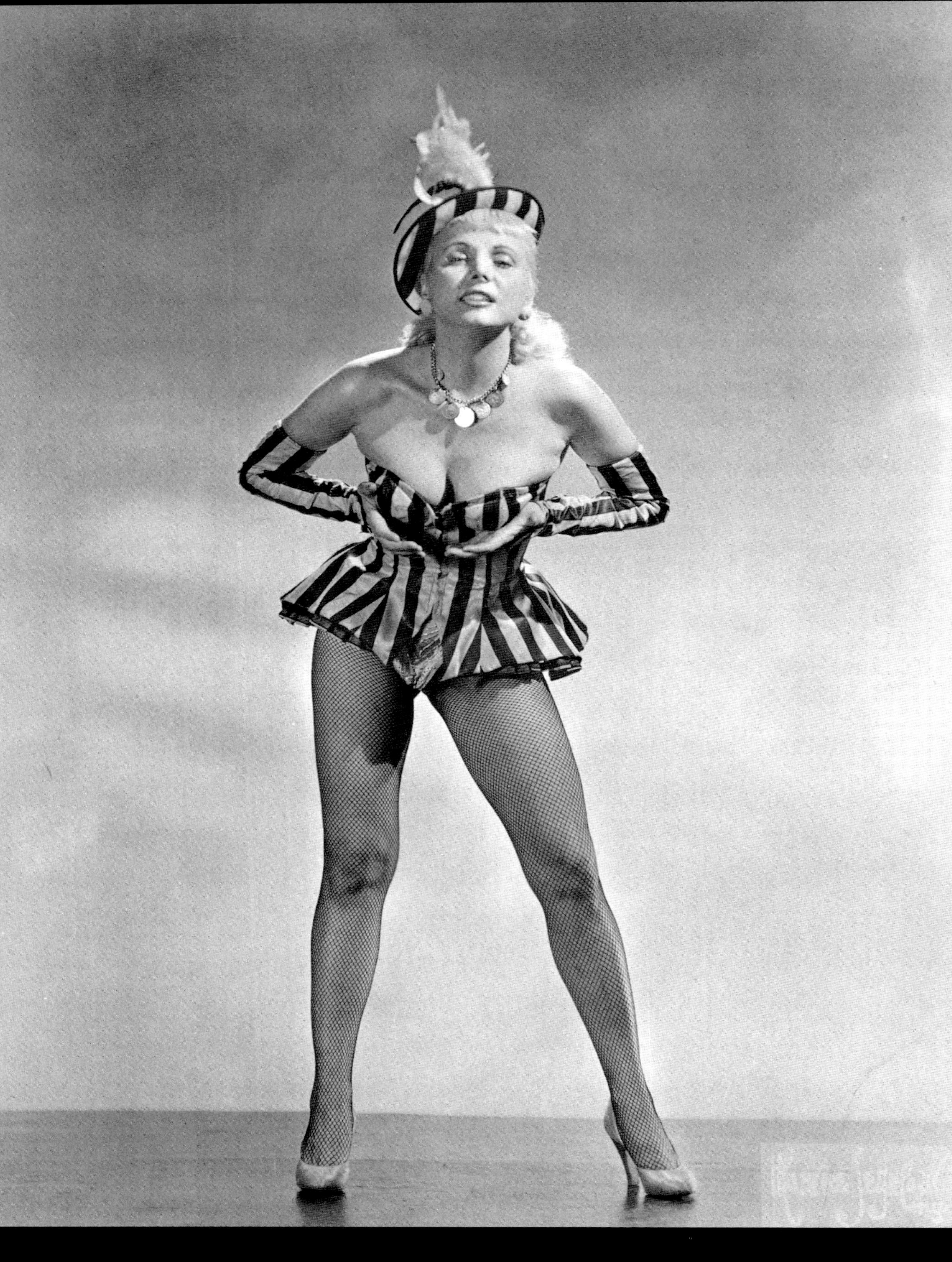

Bubbles Darlene

America's Most Exciting Body

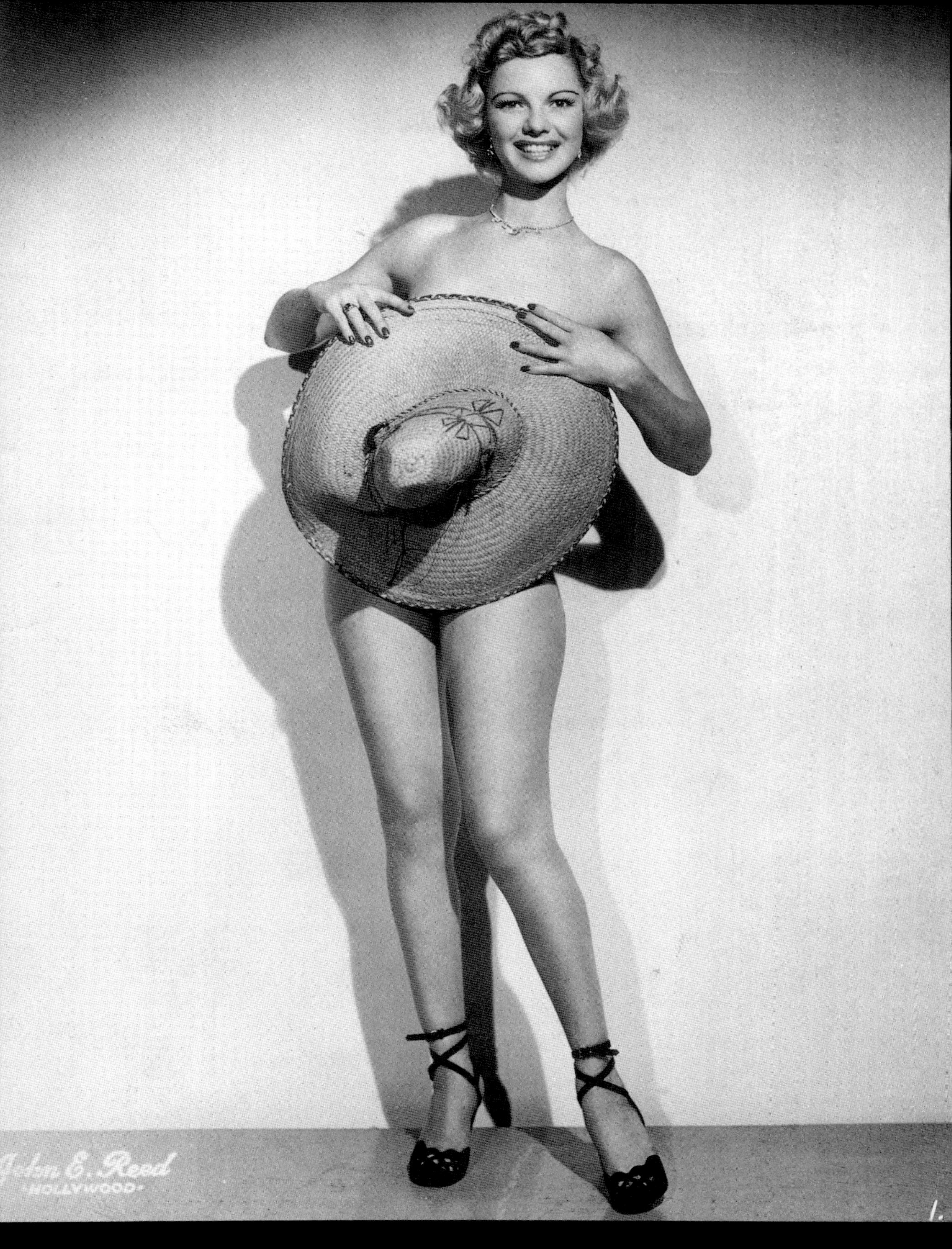

Gay Dawn

Tall! Tantalizing! Terrific!

...the Minsky brothers, decided, "If the people want it, we'll give it to them." And thus was born the "burleycue," "leg show," "bawdy show," also known as "burlesque."

Direct From Paree
Mitzi Doeree

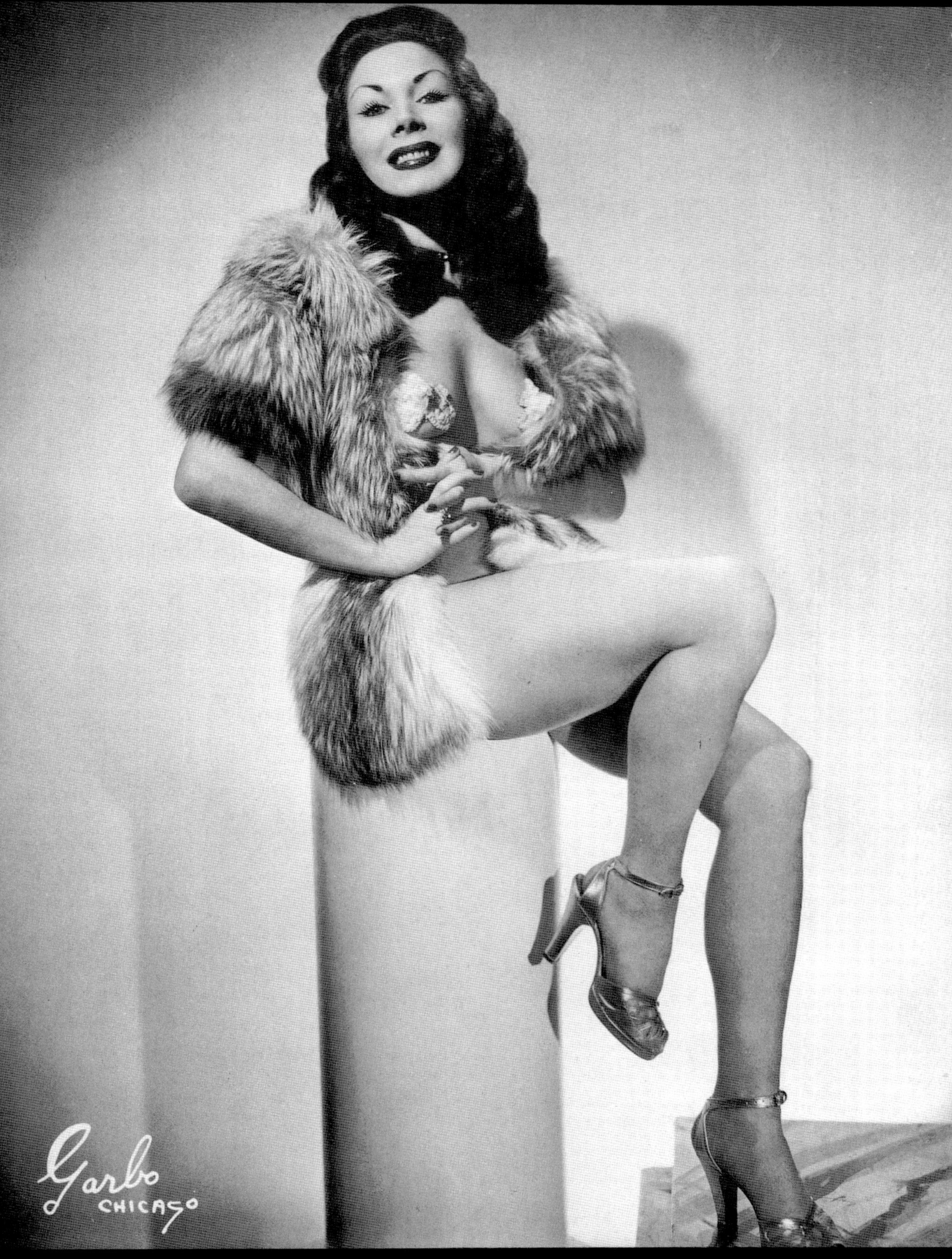

Princess Do May

Cherokee Half Breed

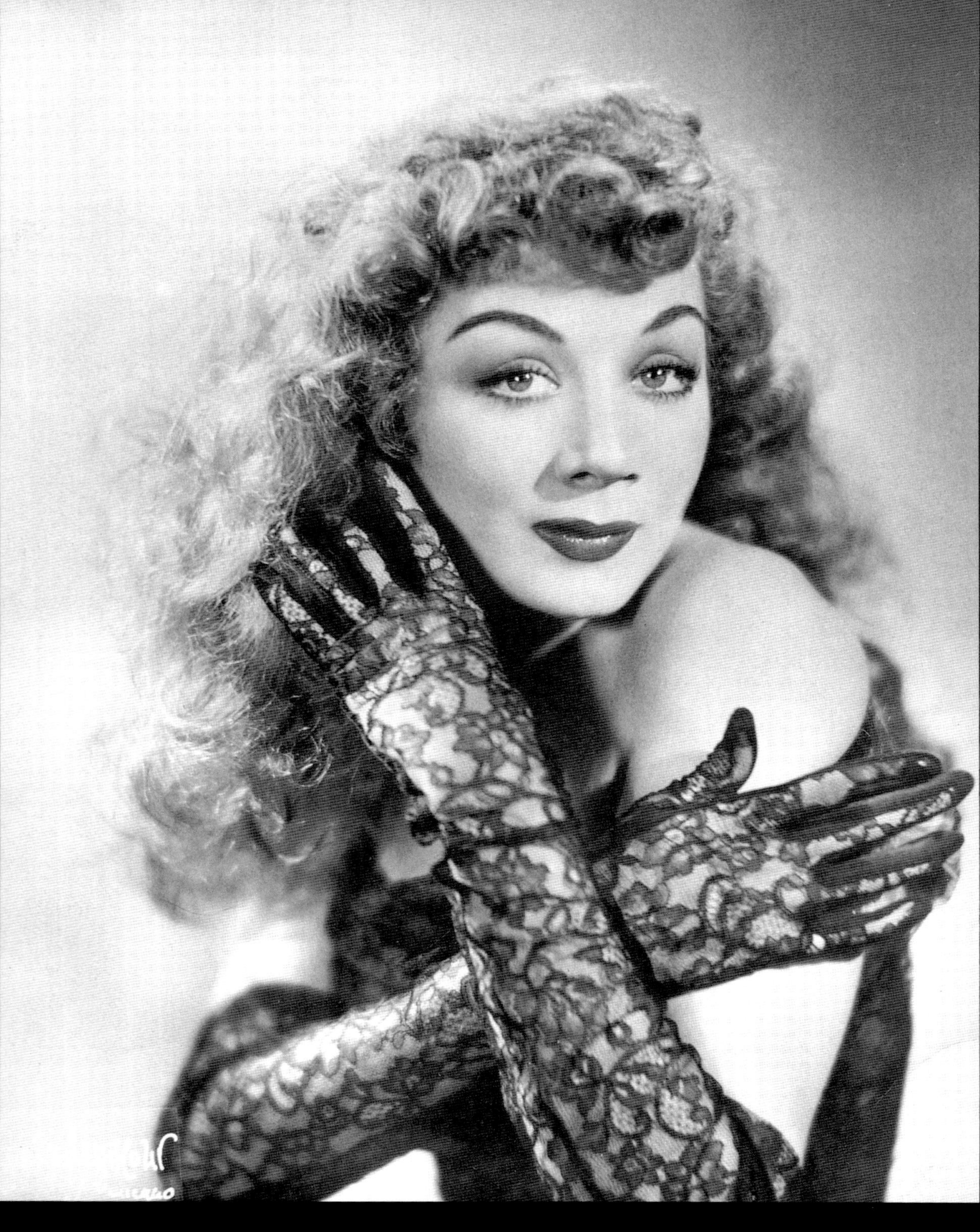

Lotus DuBois

The Parisian Un-Cover Girl

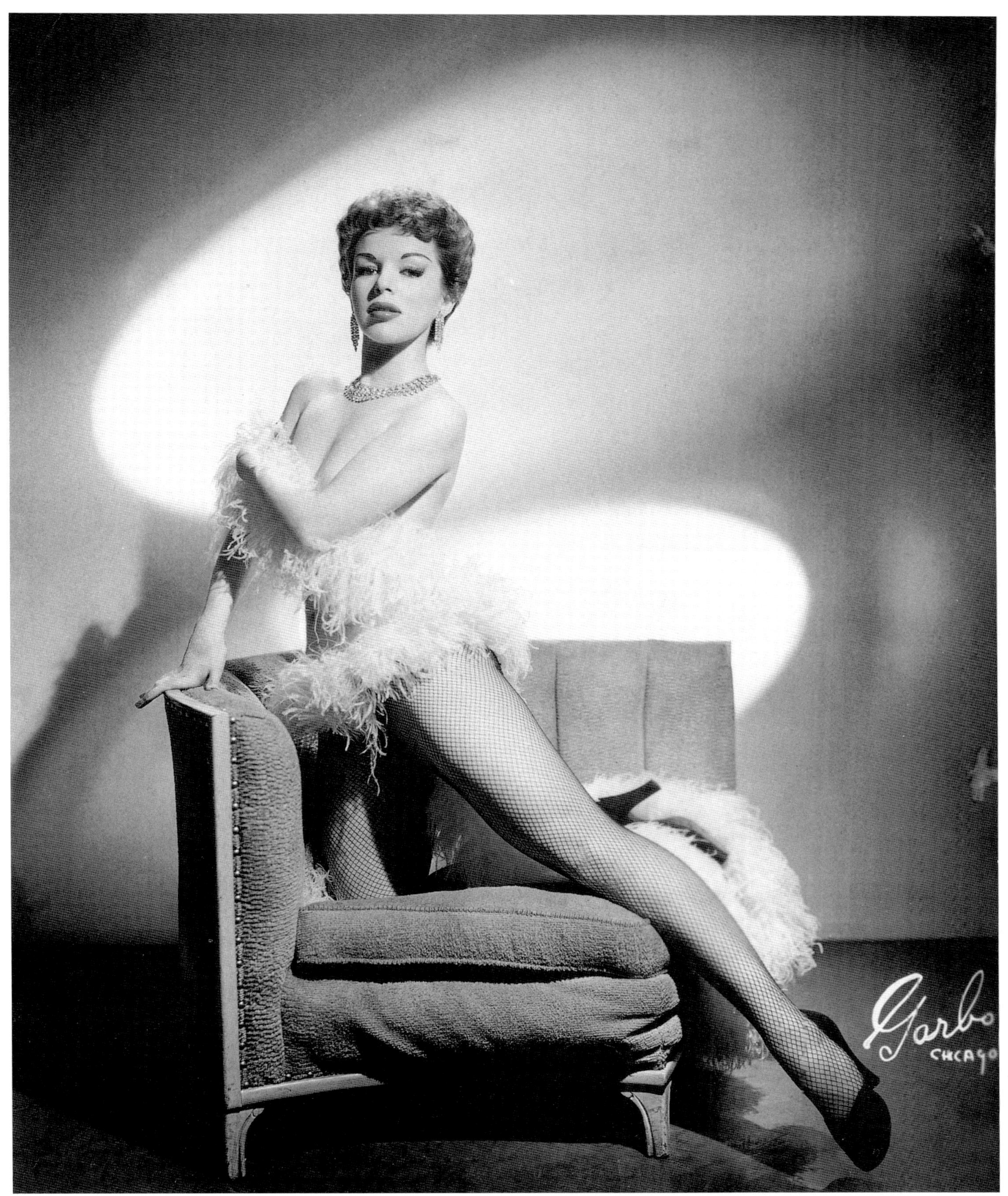

Marcia Edgington

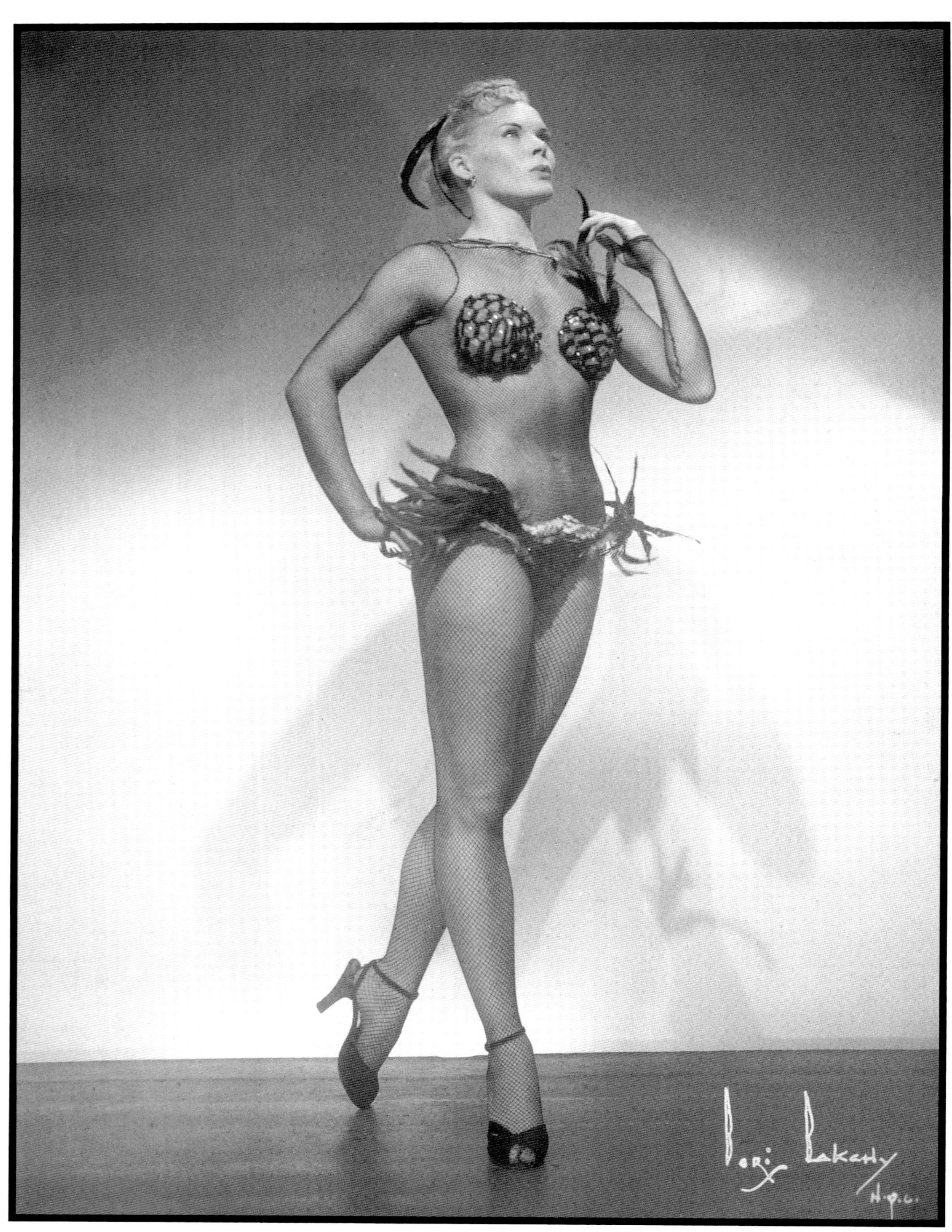

Oolan Farley

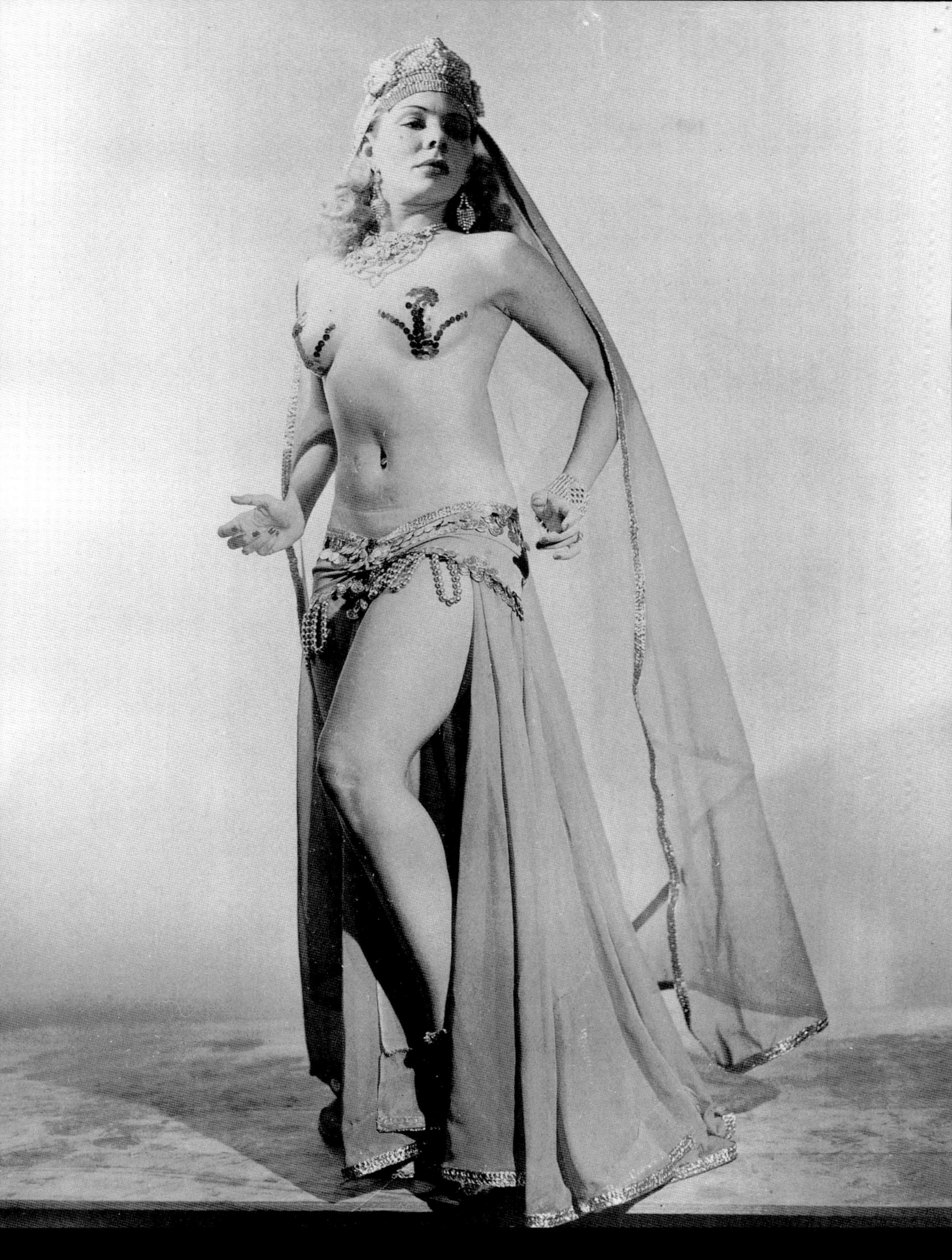

Laline Francis

Burlesque became a popular form of entertainment with gals, gags and music performed in a language so broad and slapstick it was easily understood,...

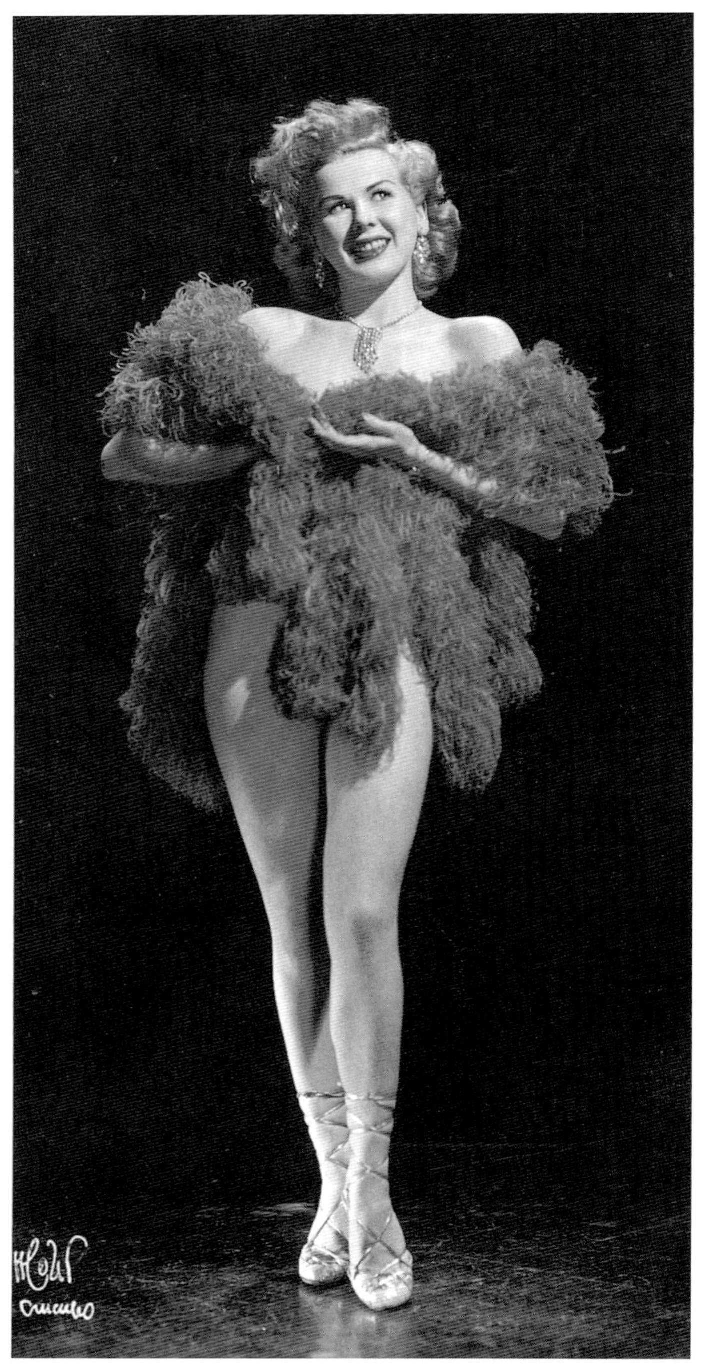

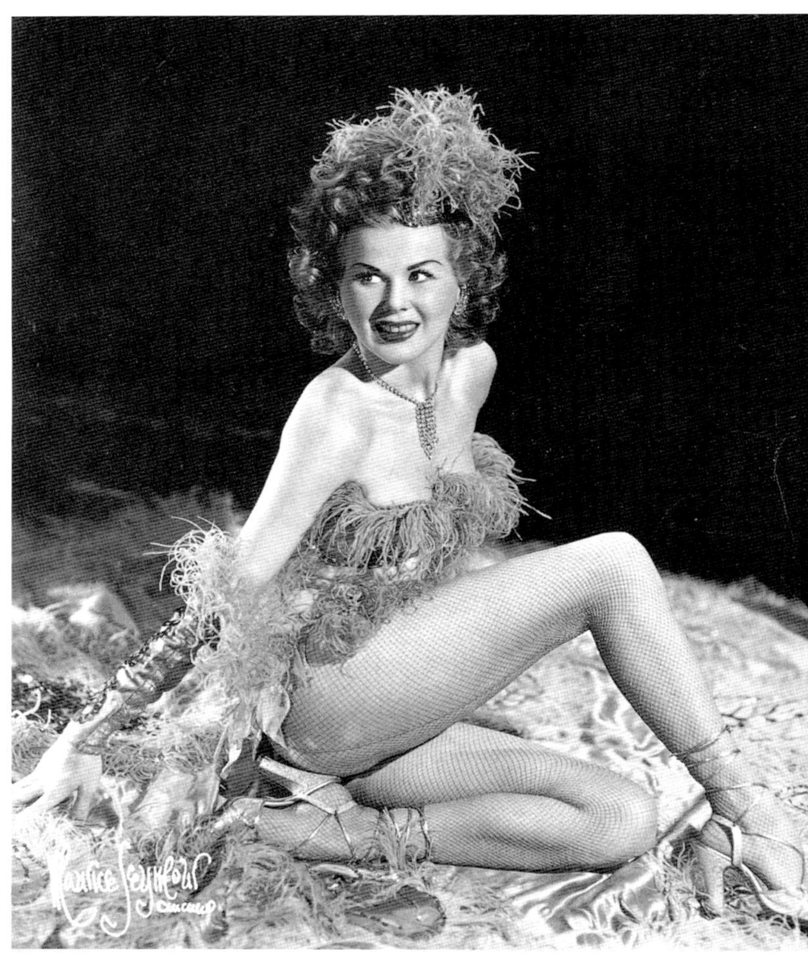

Helena Gardner
The Bewitching Beauty

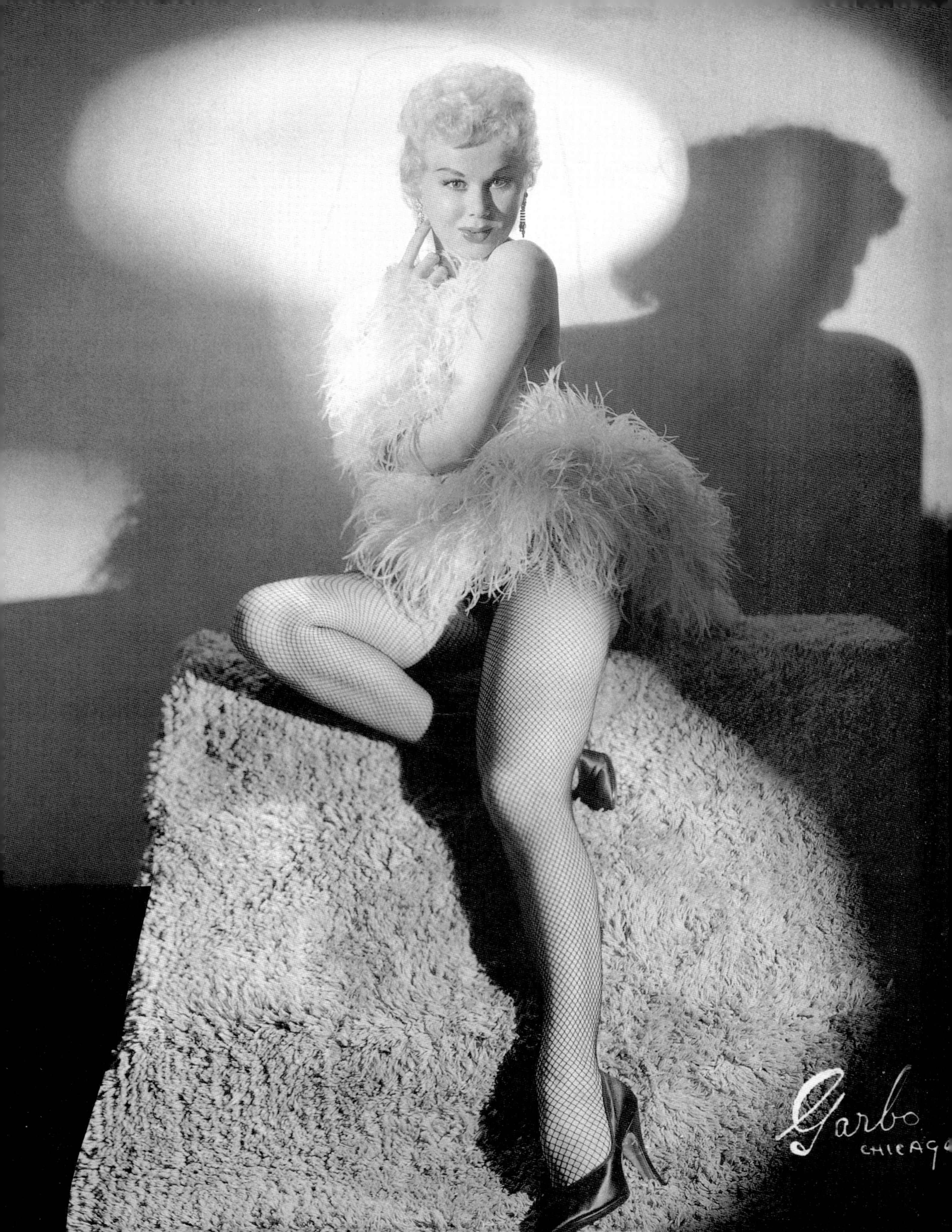
Garbo
CHICAGO

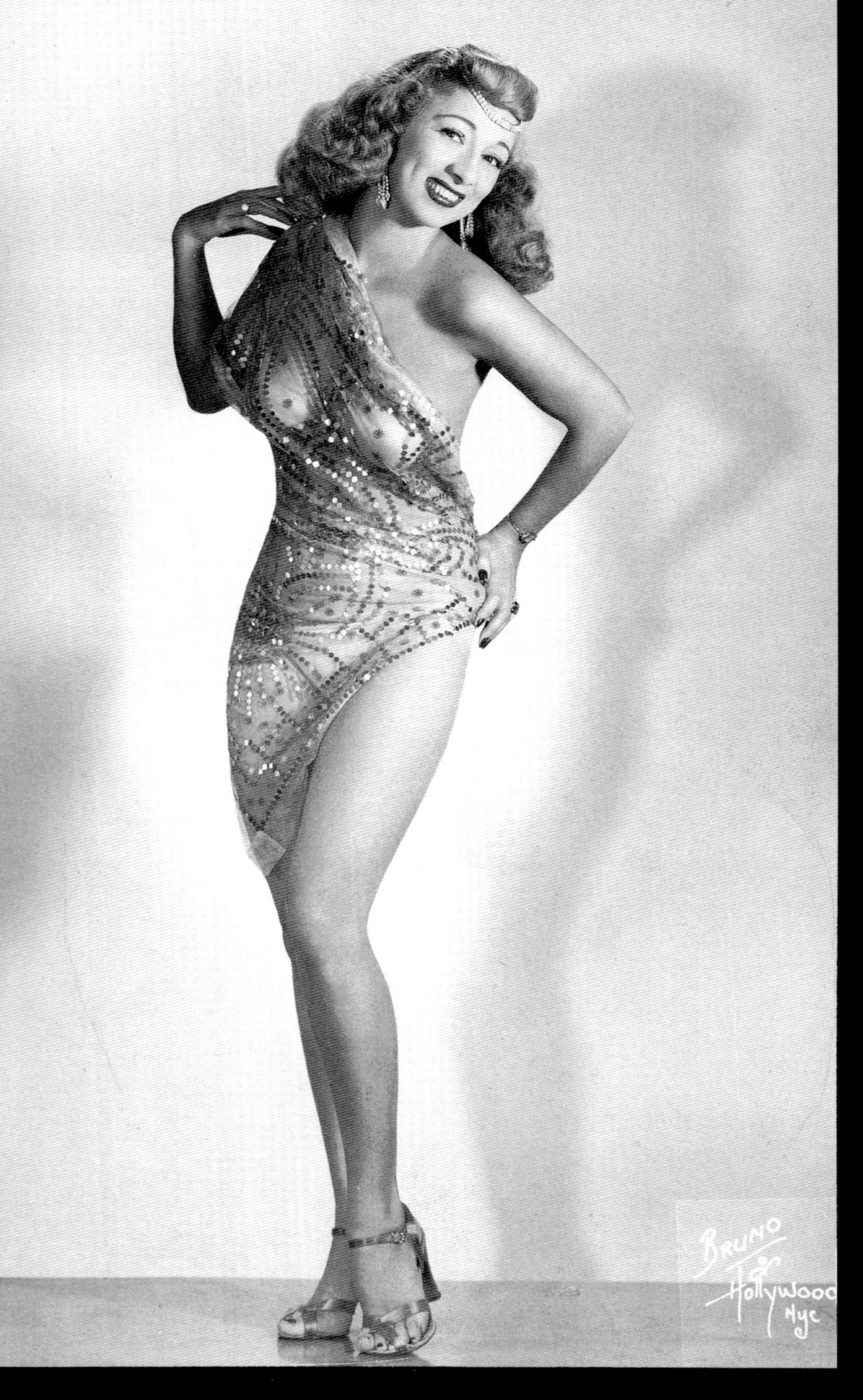

Winnie Garrett
The Flaming Redhead

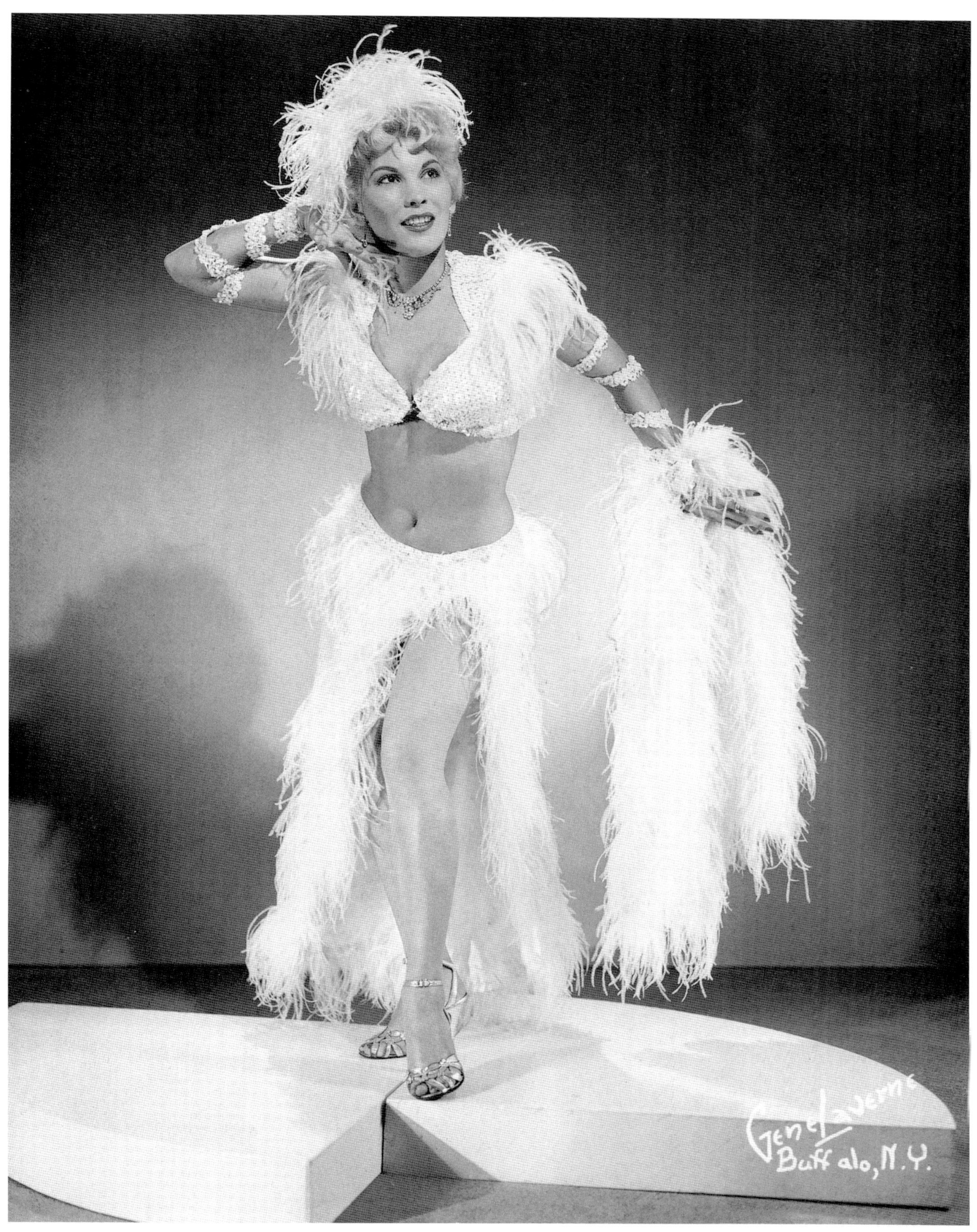

Windee Gayle

Minsky's was a place where "hoity-toity, uptown bluenoses" rarely ventured.

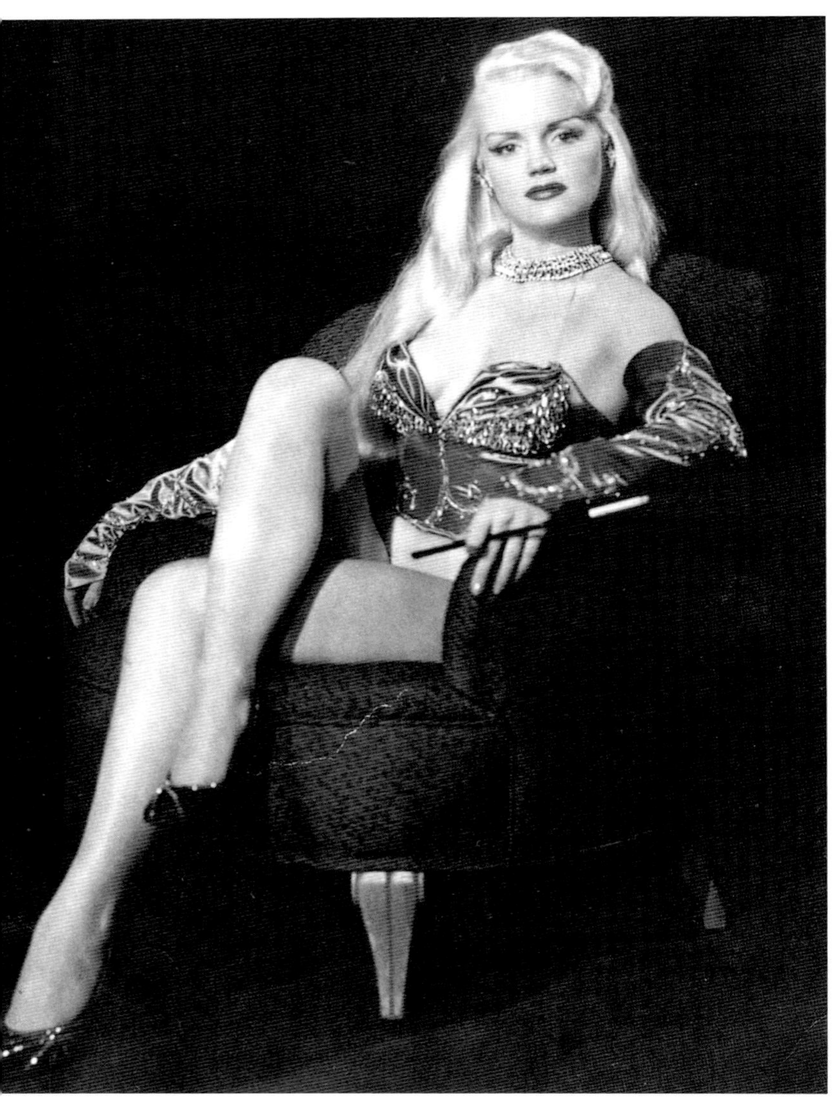

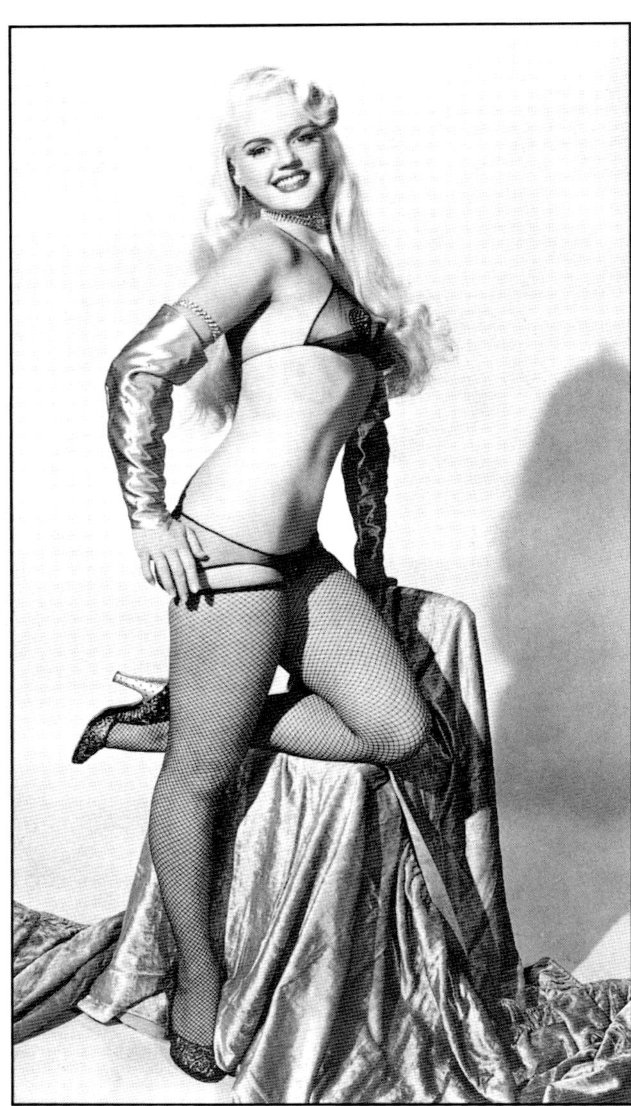

Gilda
Hollywood's Golden Goddess

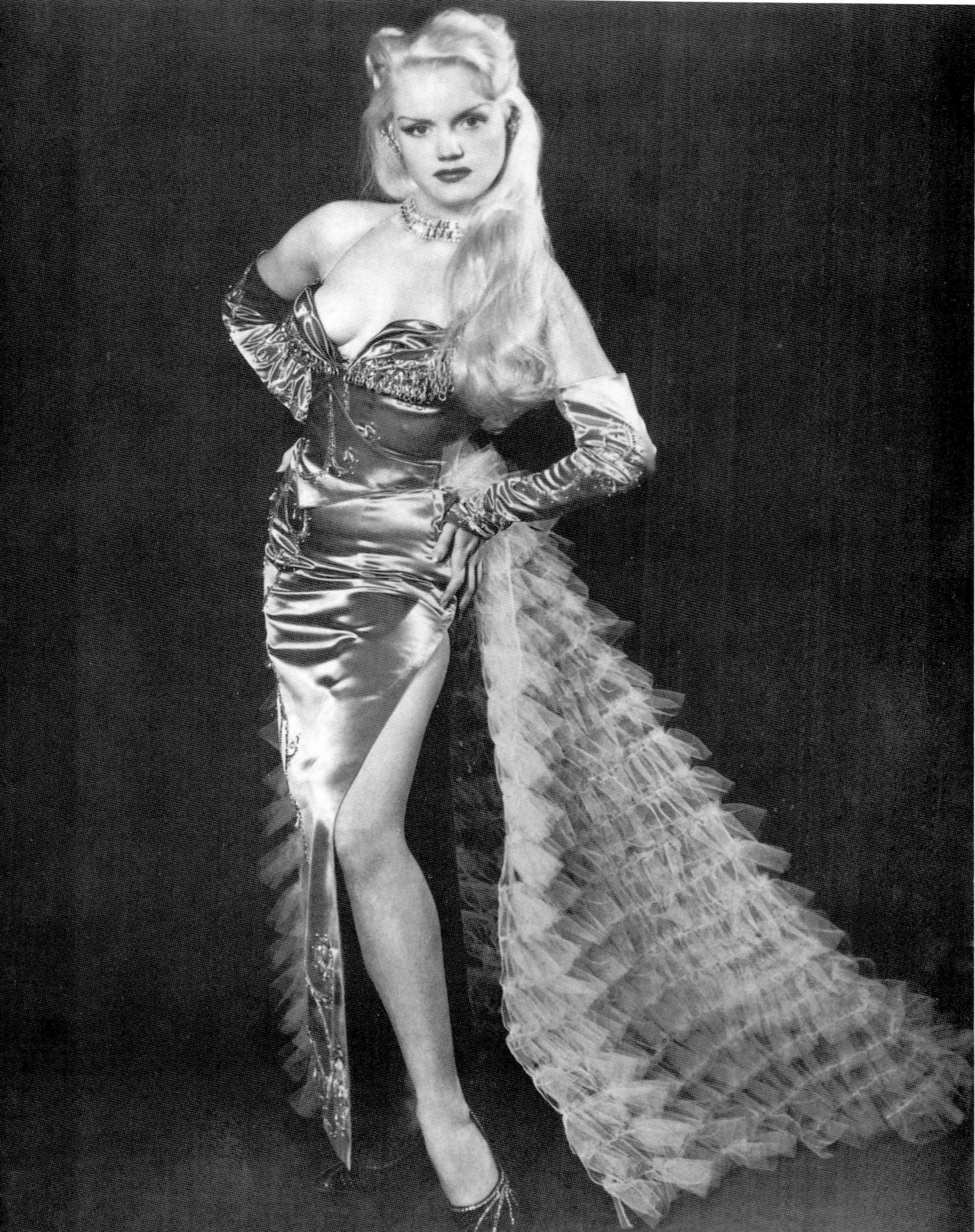

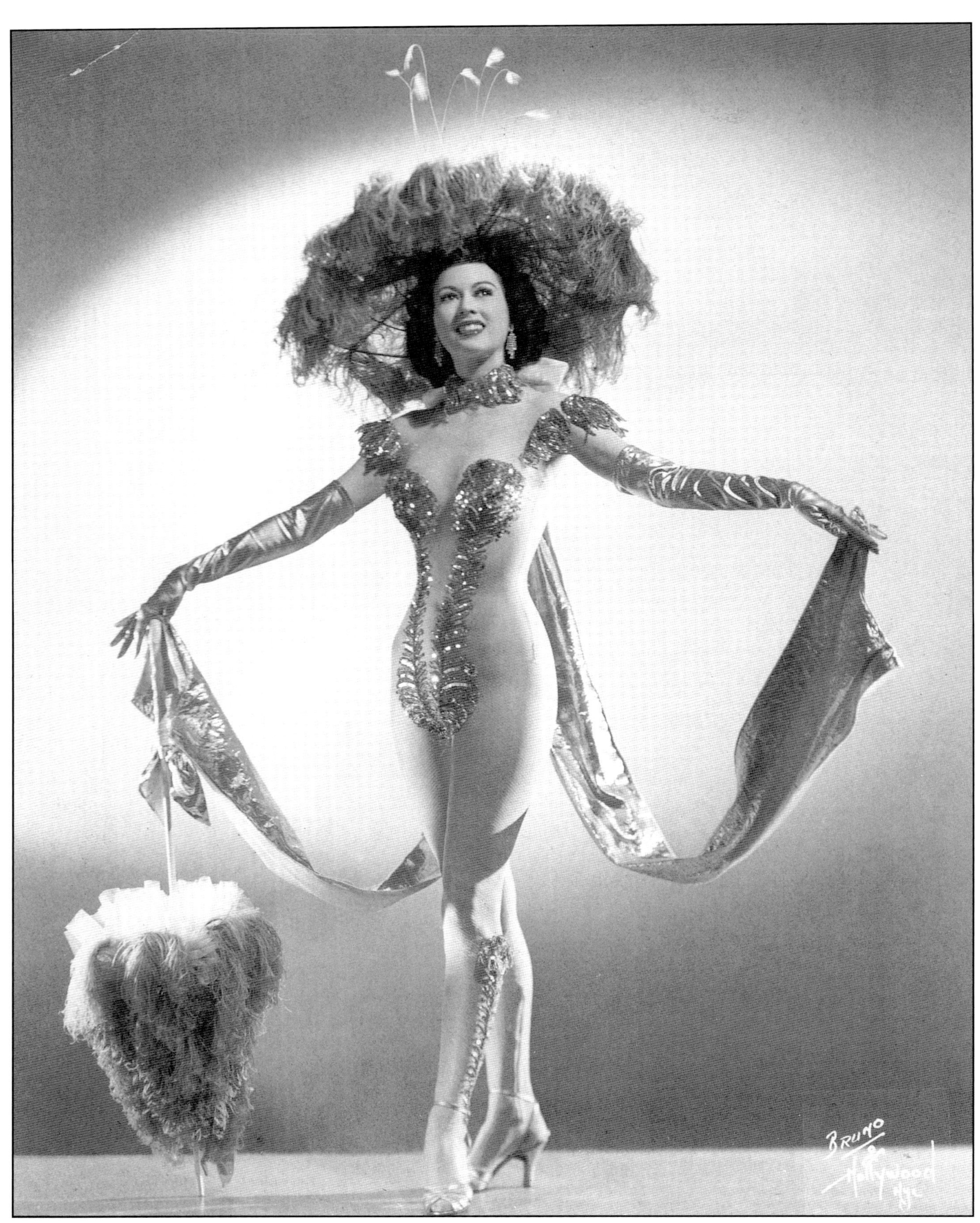

Glen Grayson

The Chorus Line

Before we get too involved with the queens of Burlesque, we will determine the bare truth about the "ponies" (young women dancers), many in their late teens or early twenties, who formed the chorus line. These girls very seldom, if ever, went out with "stage-door Johnnys." If one is to believe the noted comedienne Fanny Brice, who personally knew many of the girls, having often performed with them, "out of eighteen girls in the chorus, sixteen were virgins. They worked hard, always taking care of their families and saving their money. They didn't go to parties." *(David Dressler, Burlesque as a Social Phenomenon)*

Perhaps a chorus from one of the songs they sang in the 1930s provides insight to their lifestyle, both on and off stage.

If you love us, please don't mind
If now and then we bump and grind!
We will shimmy and we will shake
But please don't think we're on the make!

The girls worked an average of twelve to fourteen hours a day, six days a week, 42 weeks a year. As for their working hard, chorus girls had little time for anything but work. They reported for work at noon, did two shows in the afternoon, were off from 5 to 7 p.m., and did two more shows, the last ending after 11 p.m. Saturdays they also did a midnight show. After finishing on Thursday, they had a dress rehearsal which usually lasted until 3 or 4 in the morning, learning the next week's dance routines. Their only time for socializing was Friday, after the last show. Sunday was their only day off.

When they were not rehearsing or practicing new routines between shows, the dancers were mending their costumes or creating new ones, gossiping, listening to the radio, reading, or playing poker with the comics, musicians, electricians, carpenters, ushers, and ticket takers who were also locked into the same schedule. Burlesque was their family.

When the dancers wanted to eat, the doorman was sent out for food, which the dancers paid for. They paid as well for their costumes, makeup, and shoes and earned between $35 and $40 a week. Some of the chorus dancers made extra money by catching articles of clothing tossed into the wings by the strippers, who tipped them for retrieving what they had peeled off.

Chorus dancers usually rented a cheap hotel room near the theater in which to sleep. They would watch out for one another, lend one another money during hard times, and console one another about romantic problems. Cleanliness was important to them, as dancing under hot lights was hard, sweaty work. Backstage was hot and crowded with only primitive toilet and bathing facilities; understandably, they had little tolerance for slobs who were quickly fired. There was never a shortage of pretty young girls who wanted a "glamorous" career on the stage.

Very few of the chorus dancers went on to become featured performers. Occasionally, a particularly well-endowed girl would become a "talking woman", a performer who gave straight lines to the comedians. There were almost no cases of a romance between a dancer and an audience member; they primarily dated the men who worked in the theater and with whom they spent most of their time. On the average, dancers worked for ten to twelve years before leaving variety shows. By then, most were approaching their early thirties and they went on to raise a family or take a job in another field.

H.M. Alexander, the author of the book *Striptease*, once asked a chorus girl, "Does the audience ever embarrass you?" Her answer reveals the deep pride felt by many. "Them? I should say not! I make more money, twice as much as any of them, I'm better than they are. And that goes for the actresses in legit too. Most of them could never make the grade as strippers. They have bum bodies, bow legs and incisions." The girls of the chorus line considered themselves artists, and the fact that matinees attracted so many women, who appeared to enjoy the show as much as the men, was affirmation of their acceptance as legitimate performing artists.

A paradox developed as downtown chorus girls objected to working in the "classy" uptown nightclubs, where they primarily would be required to mix with the patrons and encourage them to drink sometimes illegal alcoholic beverages. Downtown, they had to have dancing ability and the show had to have good production value.

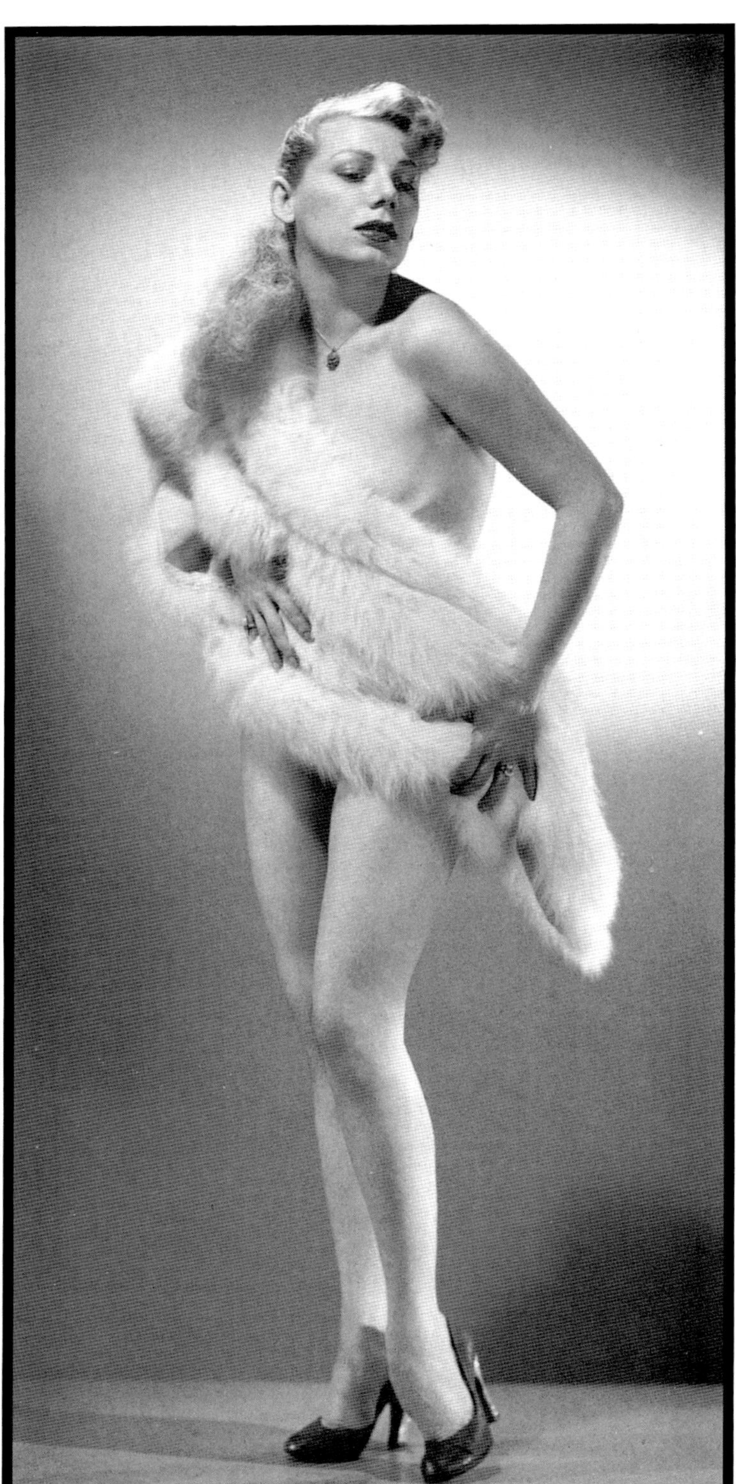

Nannette Hall
The Parisian Pippin

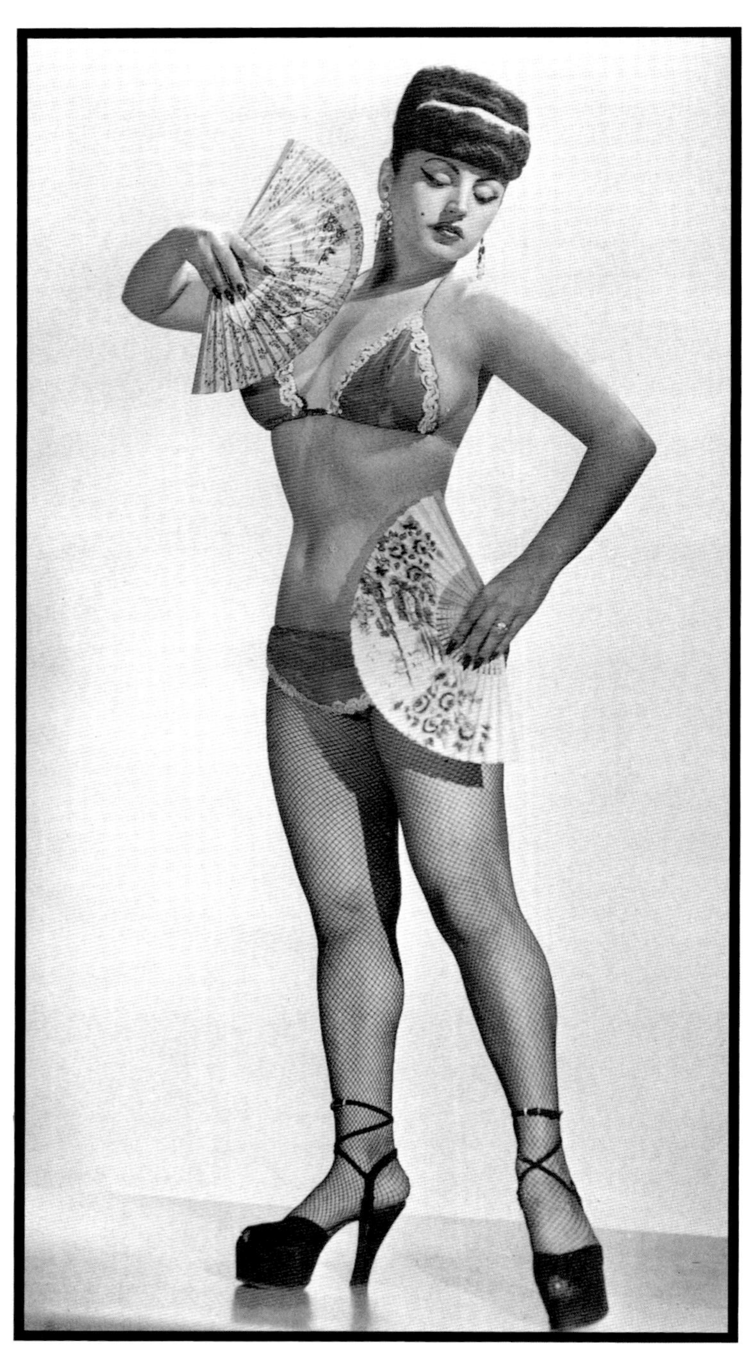

Gung Hai
The Erotic Eurasian

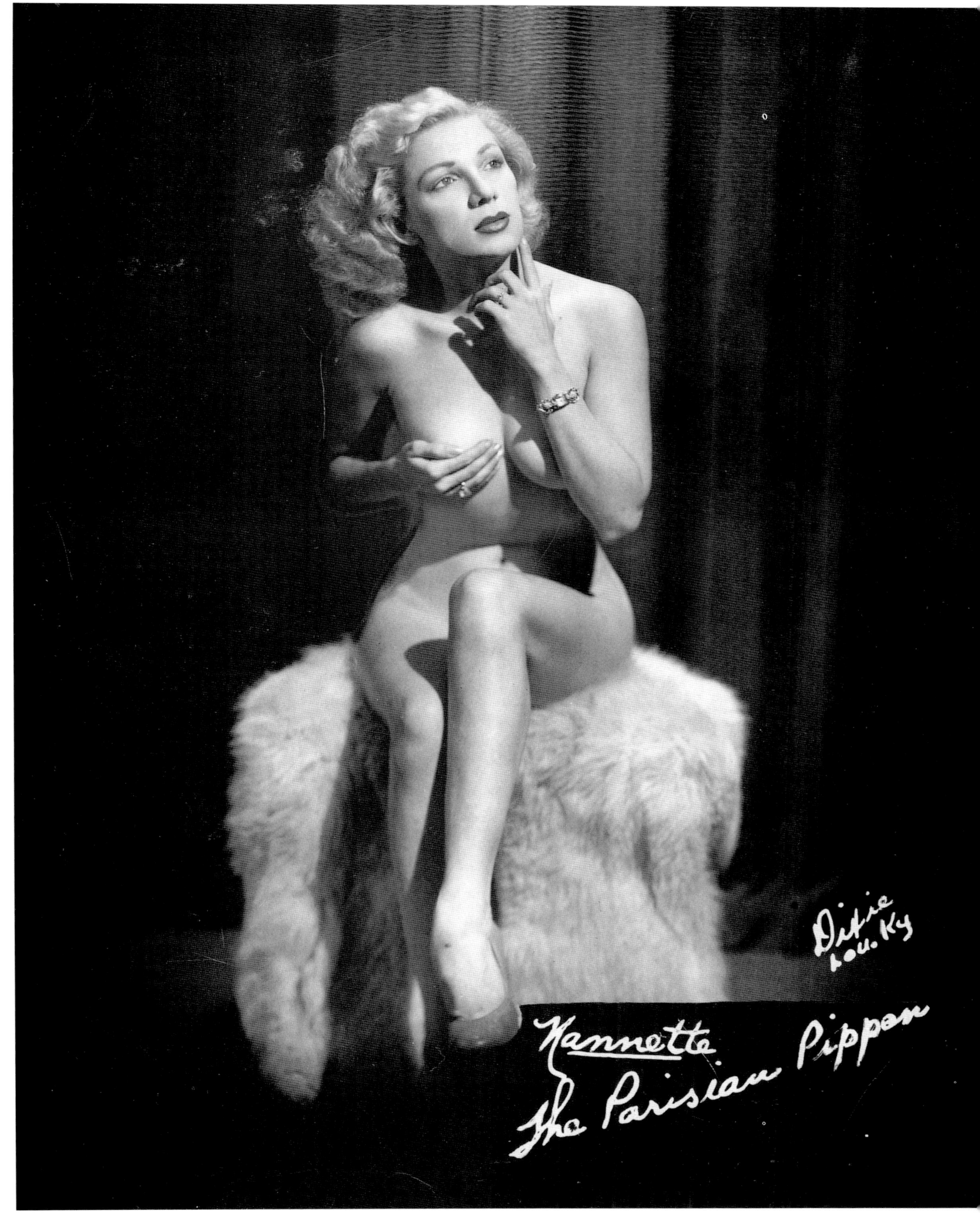

Dixie
Lou. Ky

Nannette
The Parisian Pippen

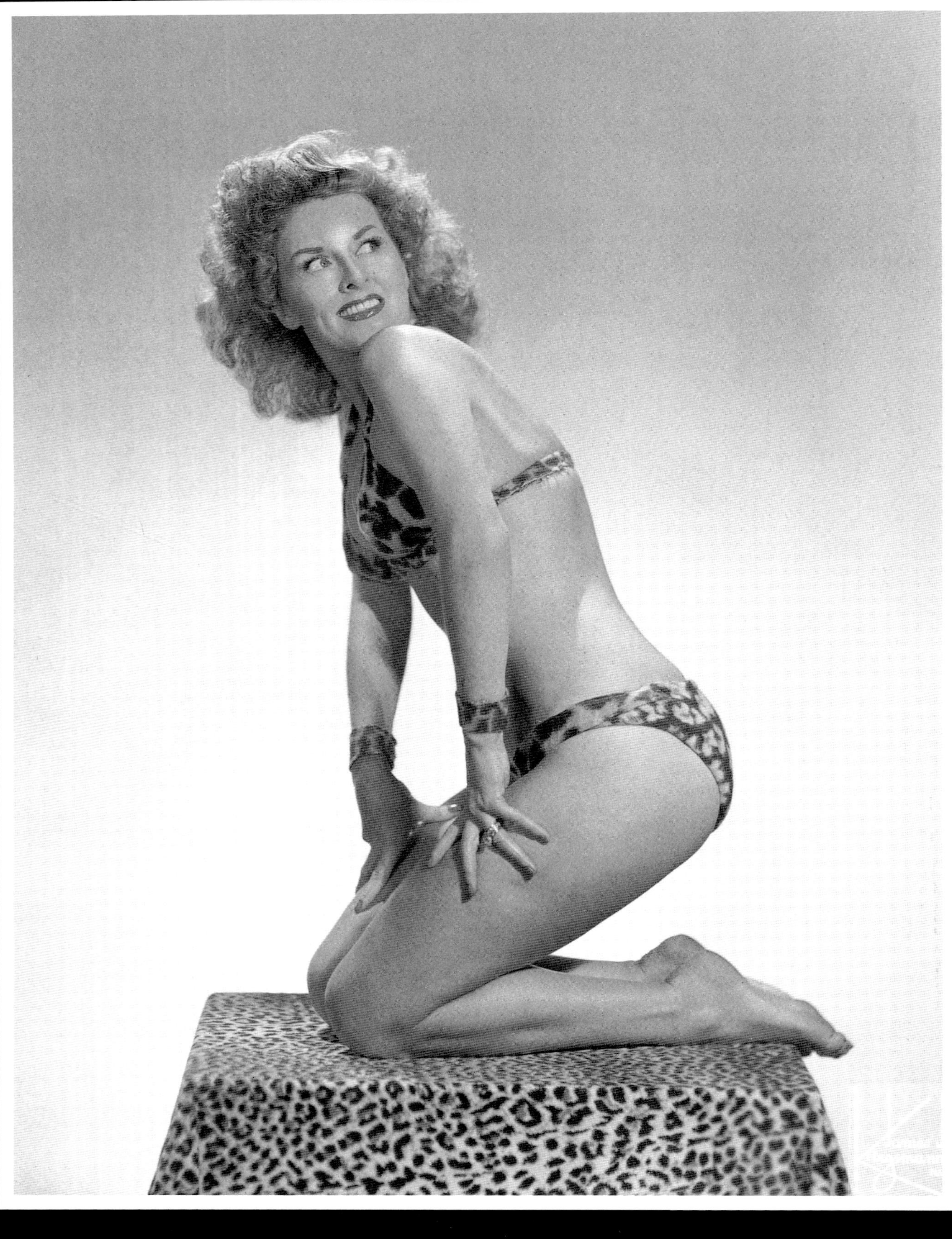

Par "Amber" Halladay

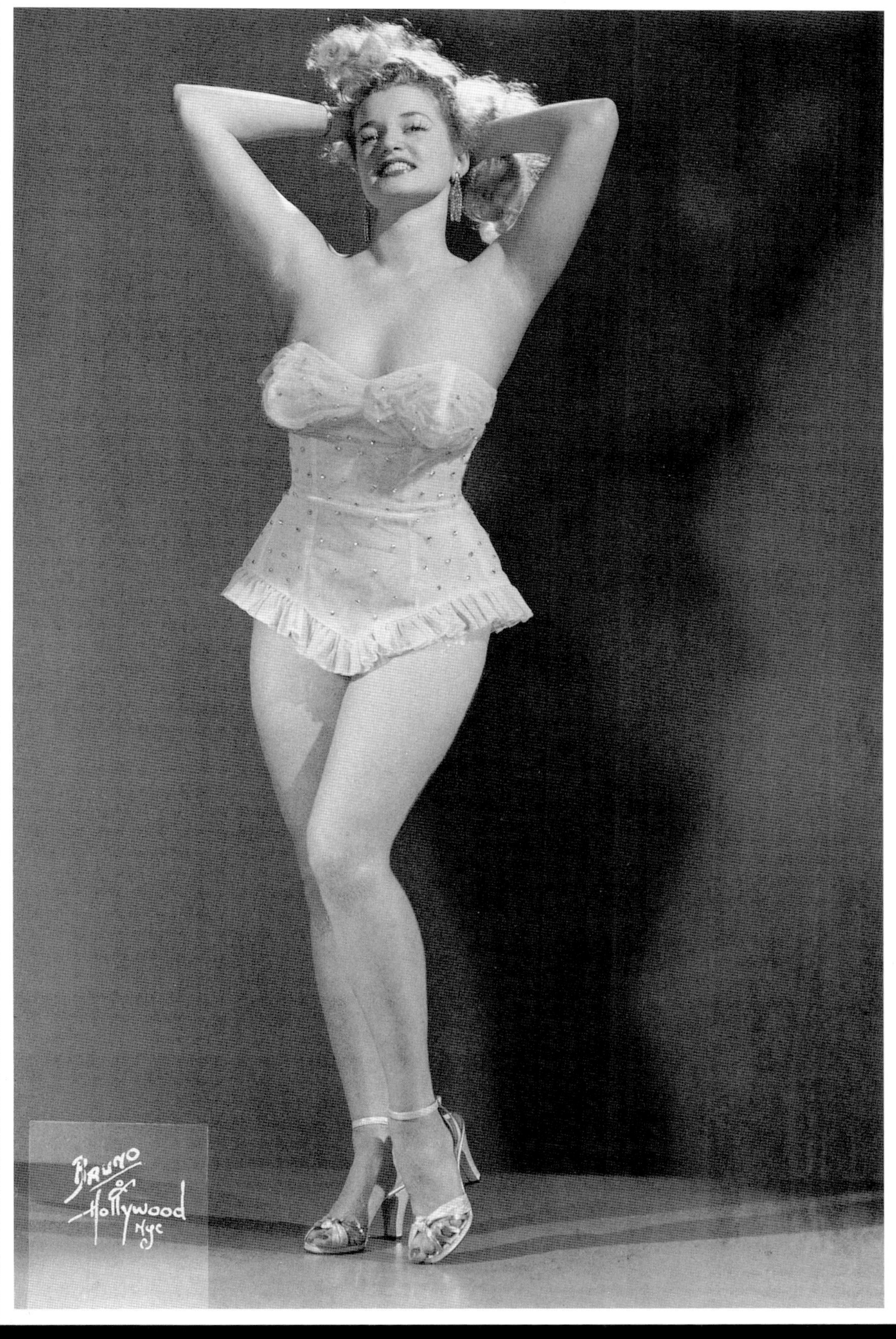

Betty Howard

The Girl Who Has Everything

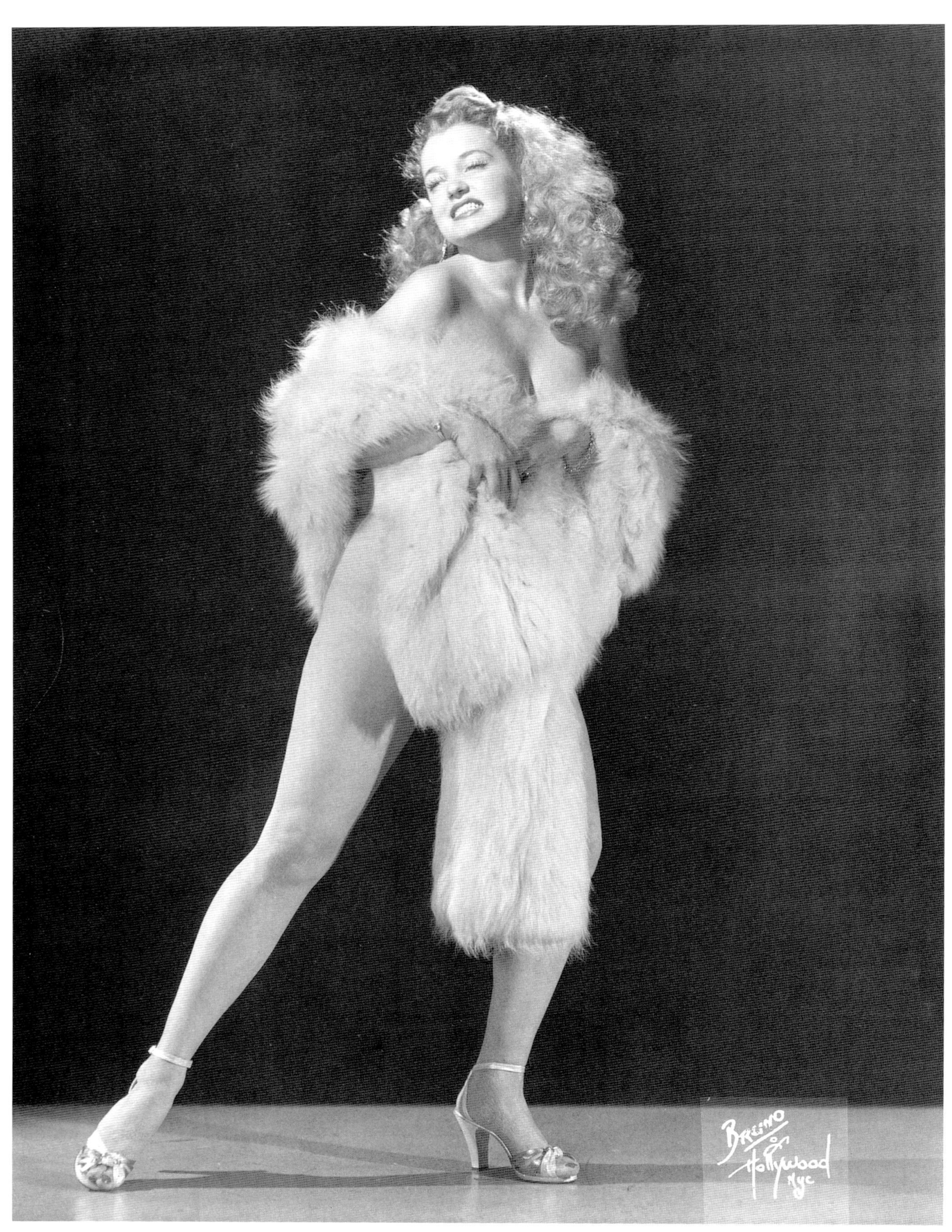

Betty Howard

The Girl With the Big Beautiful Blue Eyes

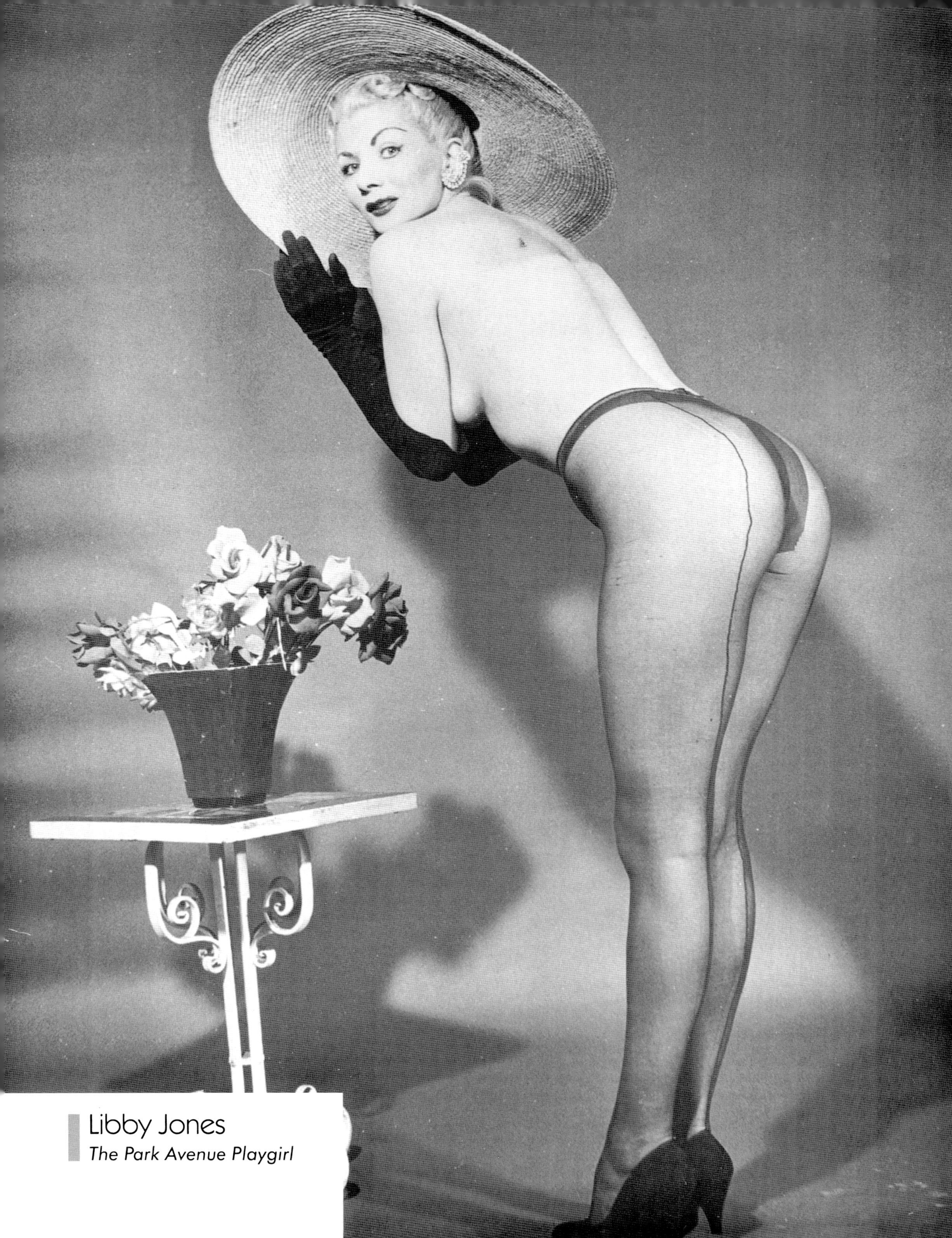

Libby Jones
The Park Avenue Playgirl

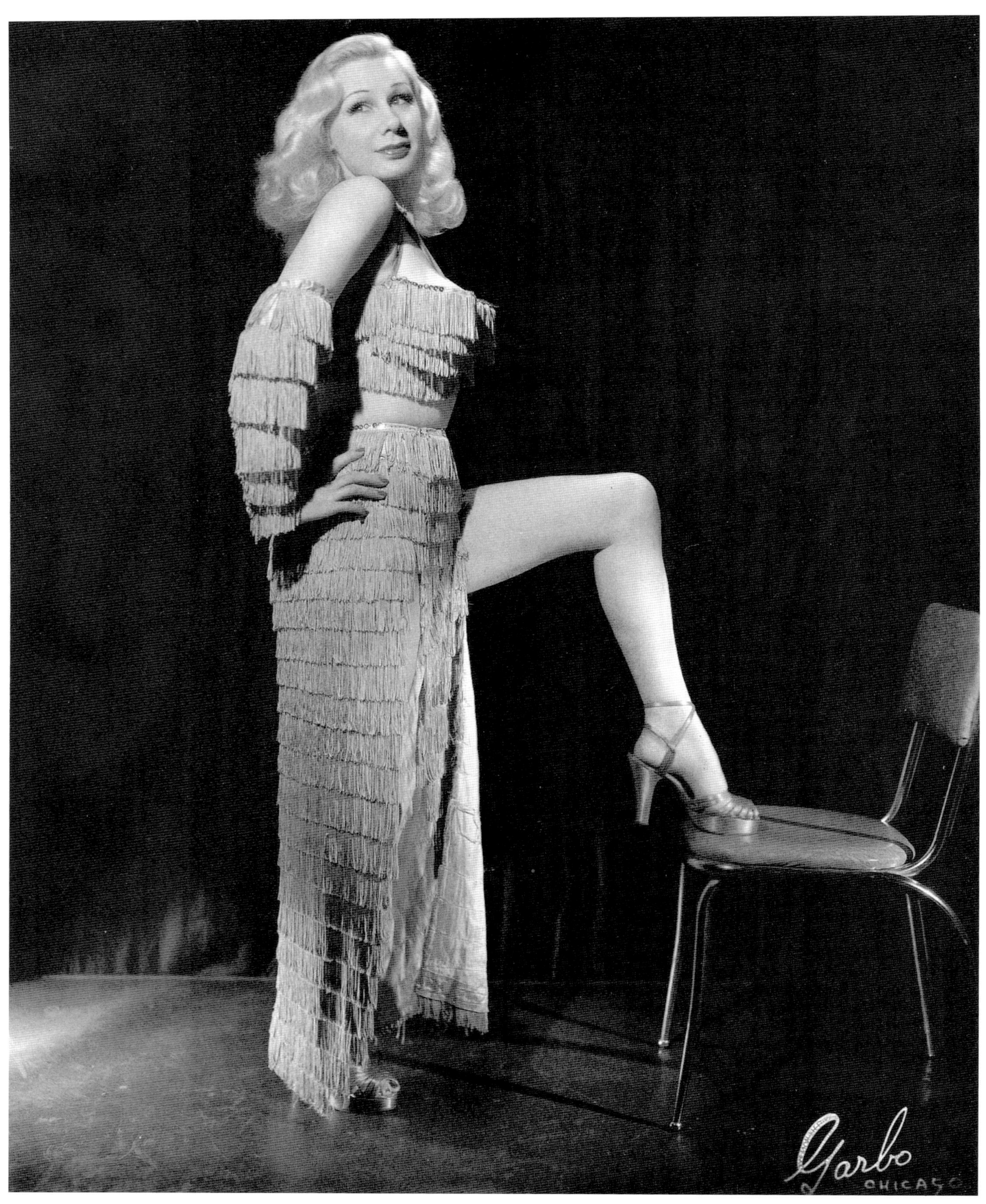

Mickey Jones

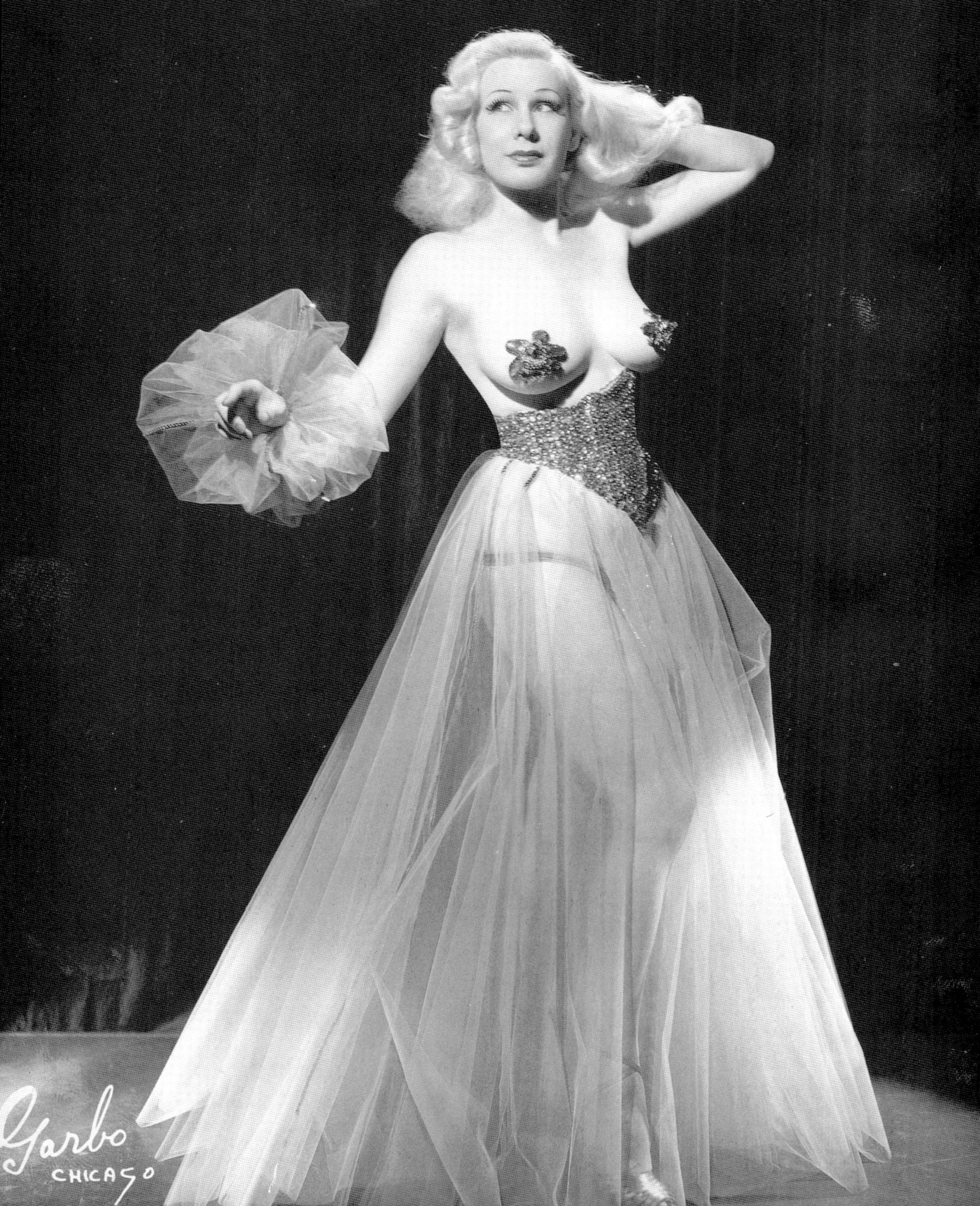
Garbo
CHICAGO

When they were not rehearsing or practicing new routines between shows, the dancers were mending their costumes or creating new ones, gossiping, listening to the radio, reading, or playing poker with the comics, musicians, electricians, carpenters, ushers, and ticket takers who were also locked into the same schedule.

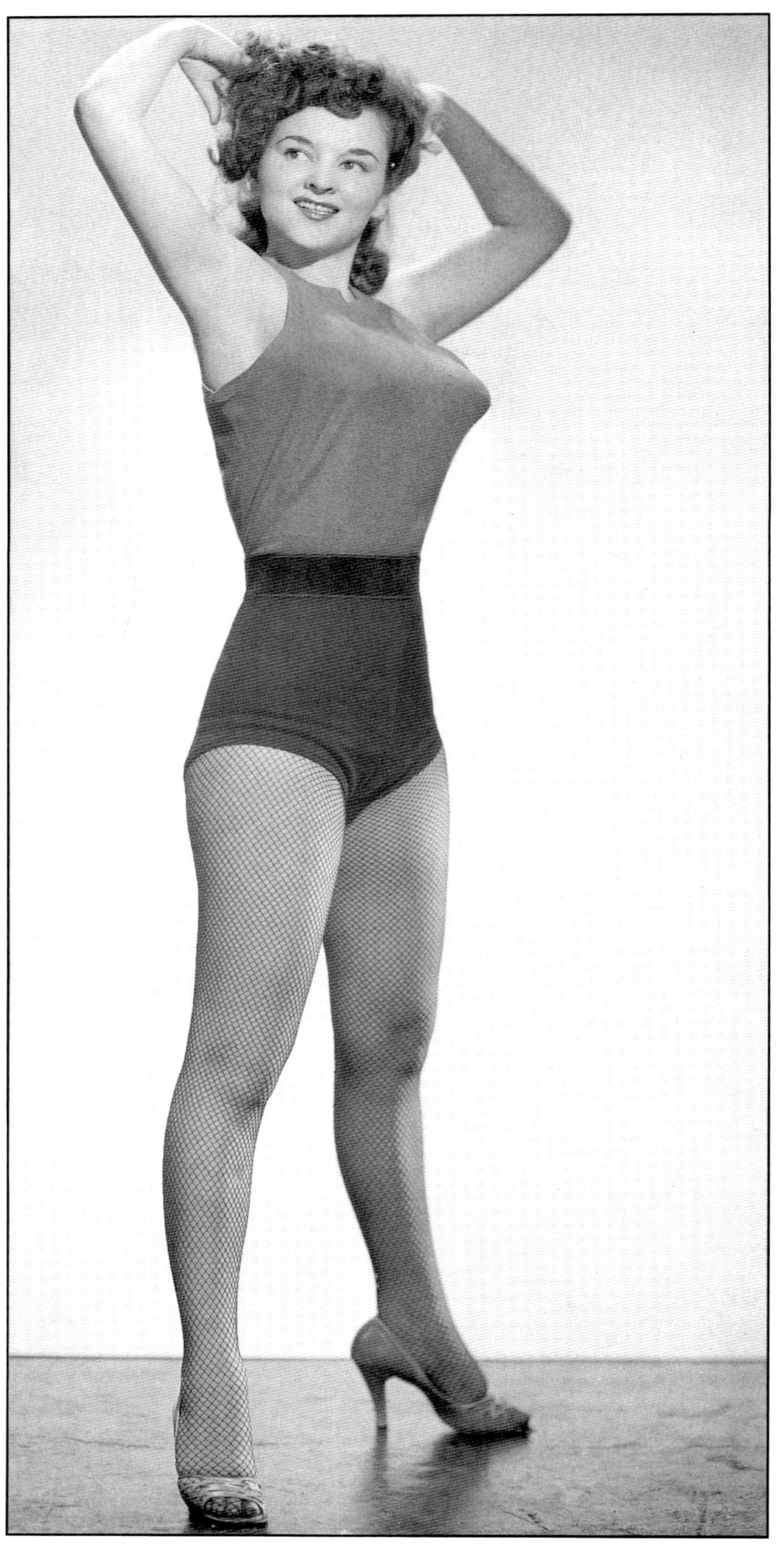

LiLi La Mont
The Academy Award Winner

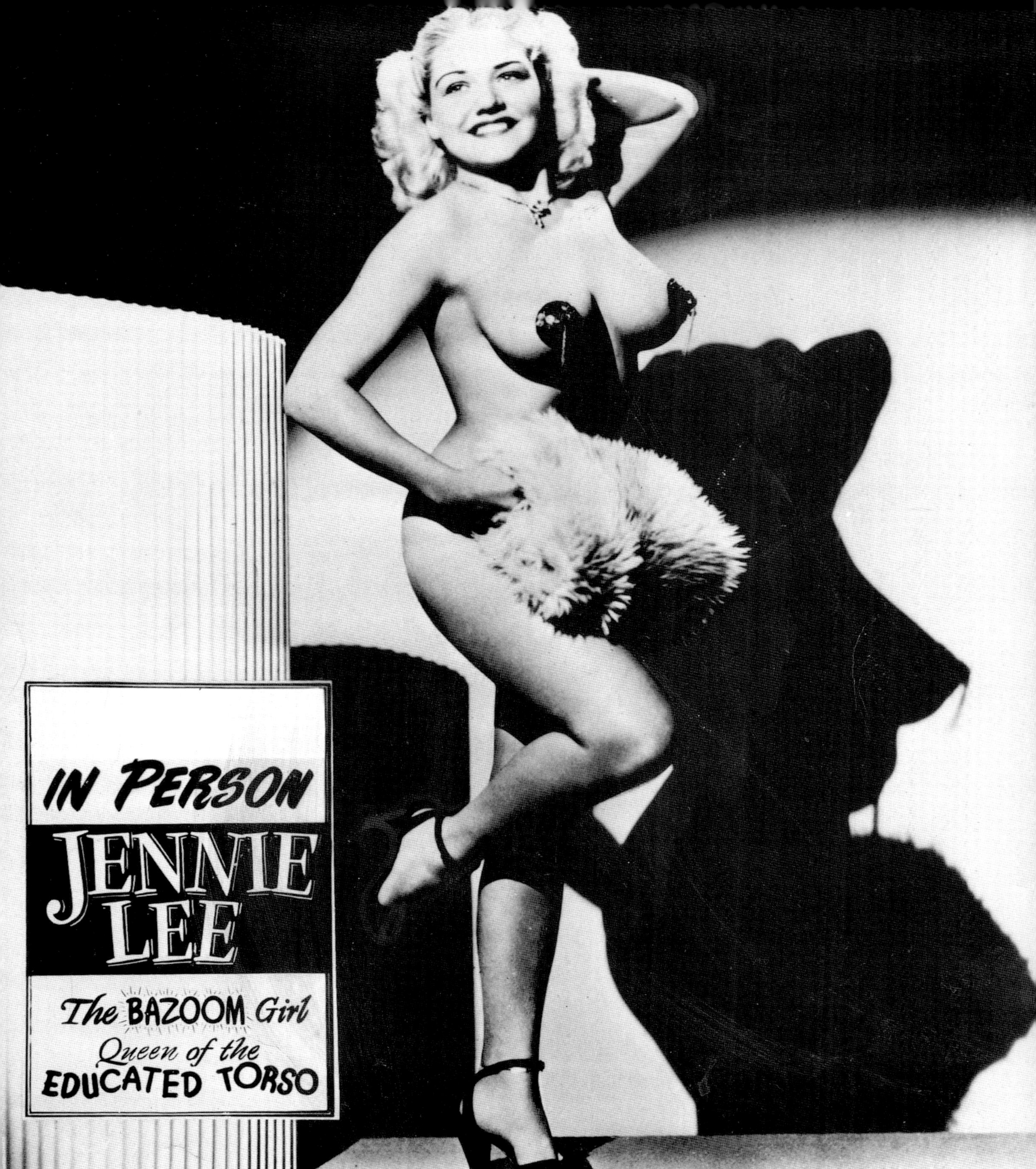

Jennie Lee
The Sexiest Girl in Burlesque

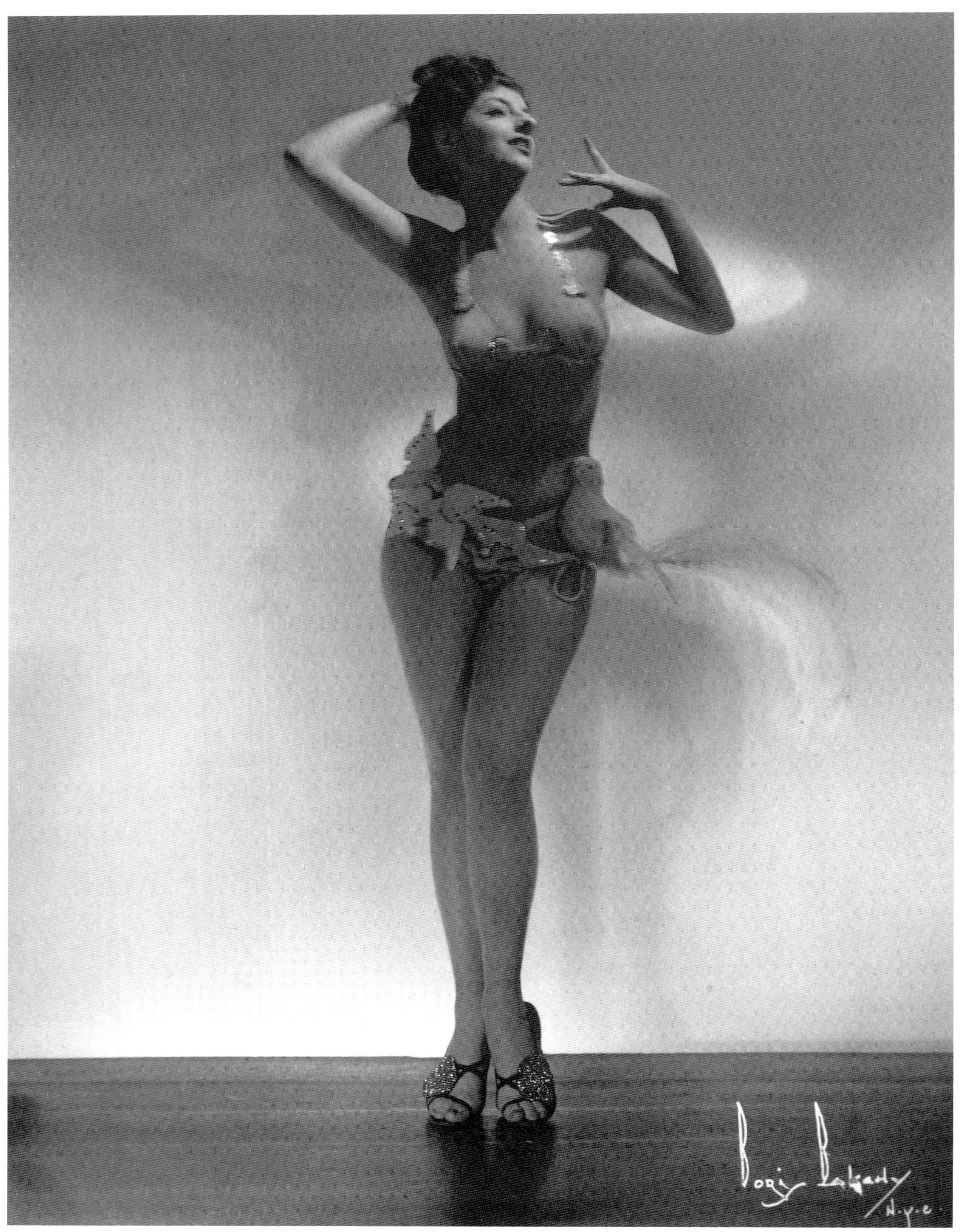

Lela

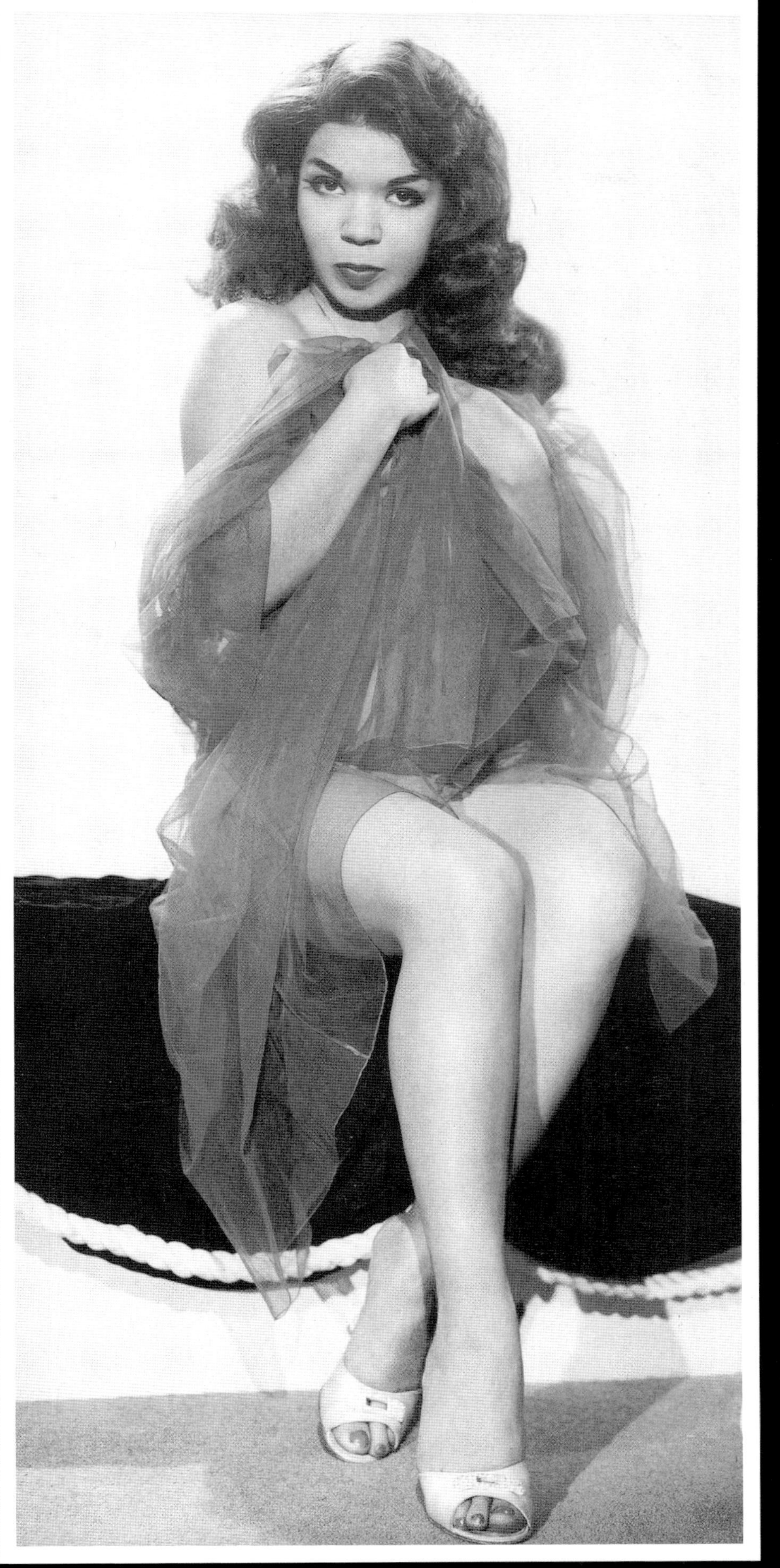

Blanche
Loman

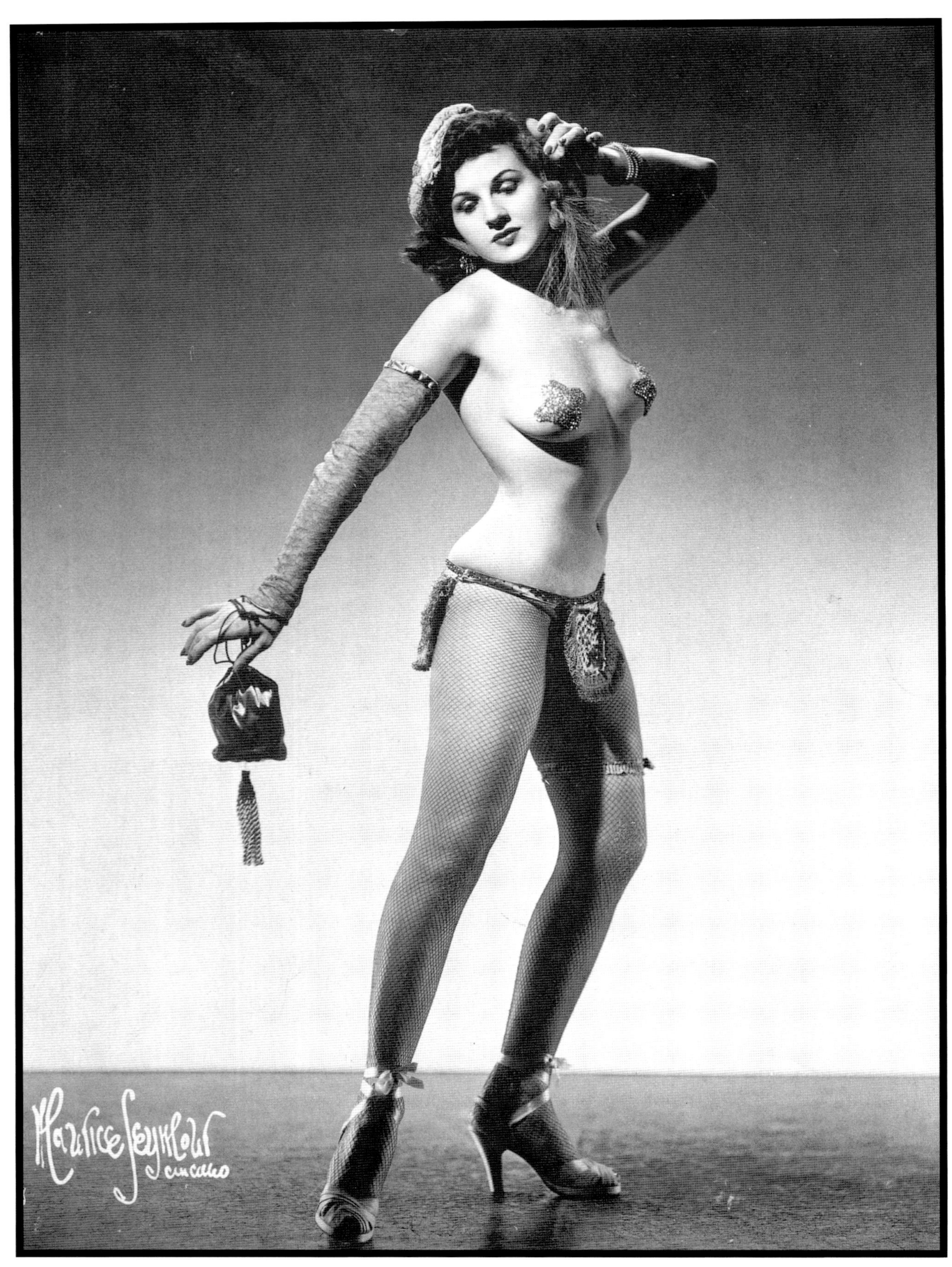

Lori Long

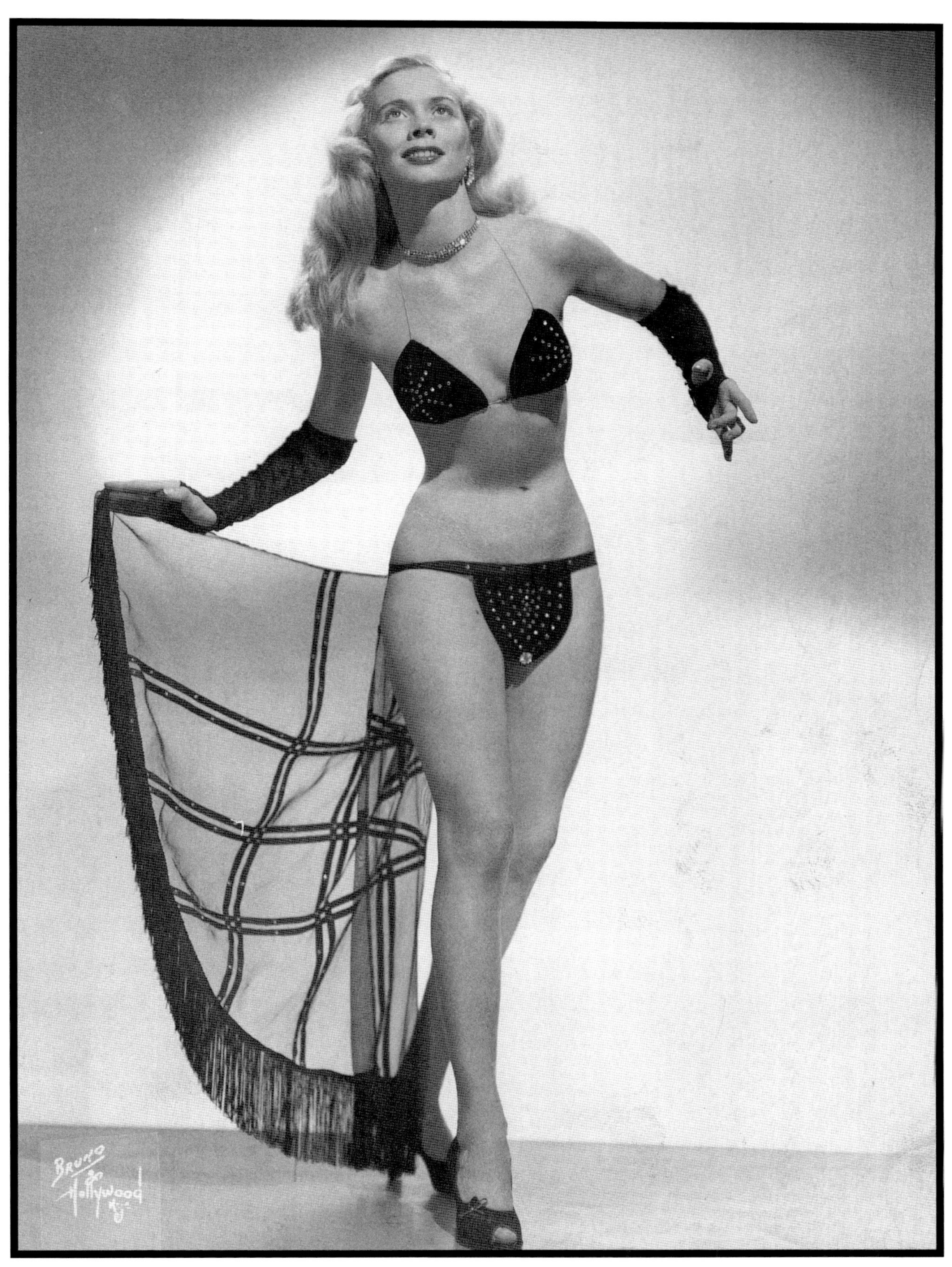

Patricia Lord

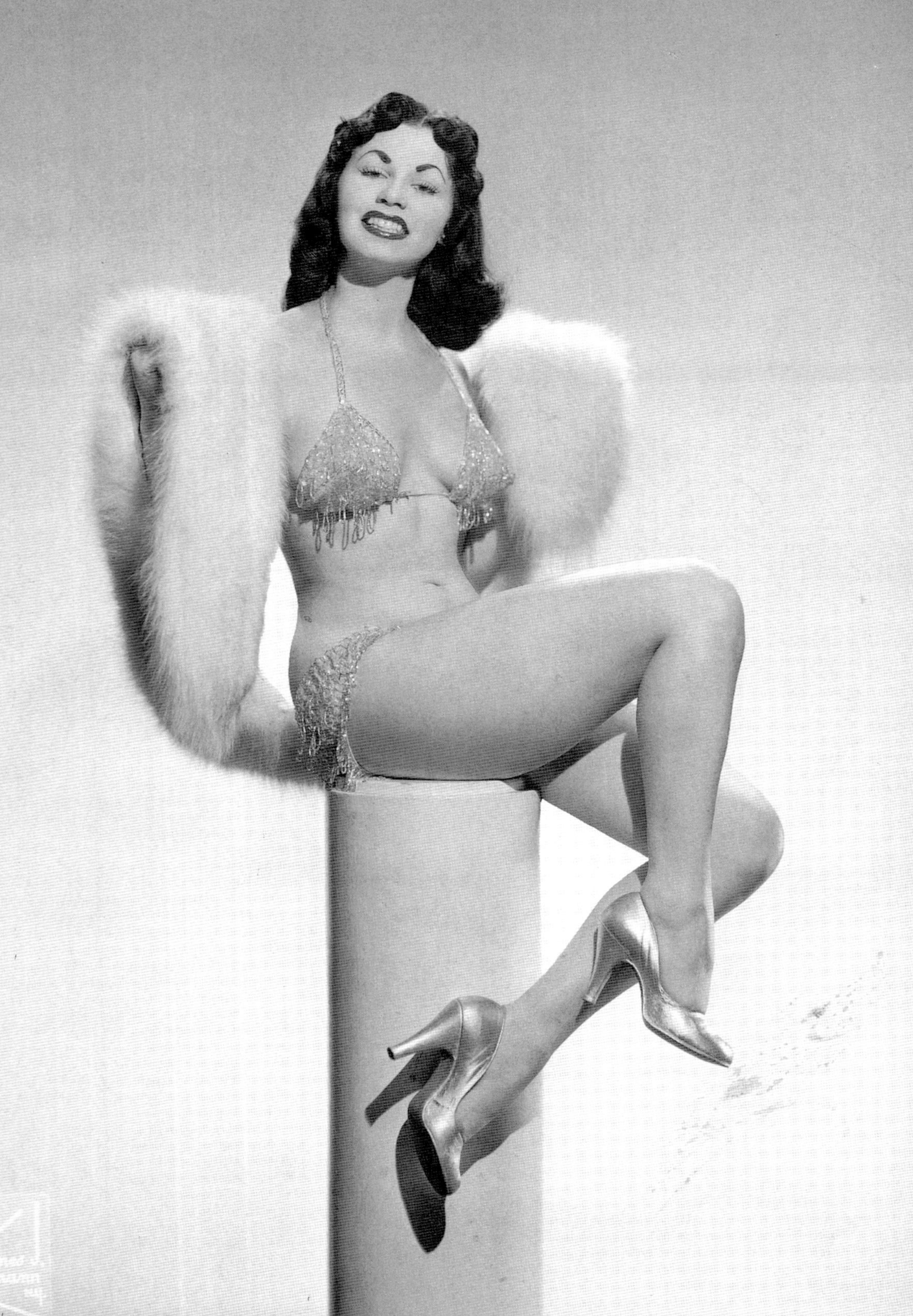

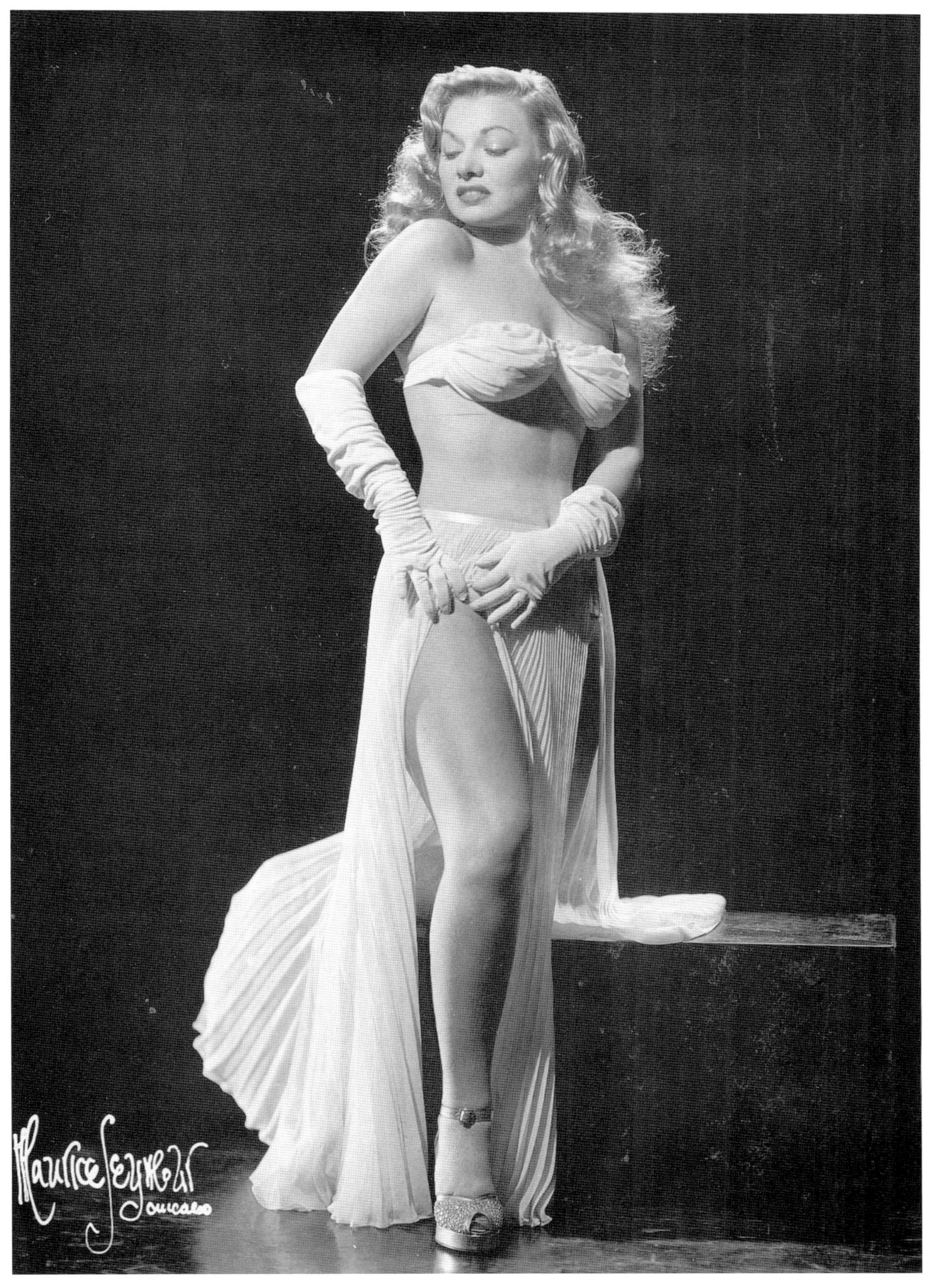

Lilli Marlyne

Comics

The allure of sex, made by advertising Burlesque dancers on the theater's marquee, was used only to pull the audience into the theater, the comics were what most people loved once they were there. Comics were classified by their various types. They included the **Technician** who figured out each and every move of his routines; the **Natural**, a goofy, unpredictable comic with inspired humor; and the **Rube**, a country comic who was chased through the audience, climbed up the scenery, had his pants pulled down and his fanny hit, and who oogled bosoms, etc. Also popular were the **Tramp**, a dialectician with a number of accents, and the **Silent**, who could leer, register pain, and look around pretending to be innocent, shrug his shoulders and make gestures and facial expressions so broad that the audience completely understood and thought him hilarious (judging by their howls of laughter). The **Sad** comic usually wore drooping baggy pants, putty noses, and ludicrous wigs as he was the butt of the situation. He was the one who got hit in the face with a pie, had seltzer water squirted down his pants, was seduced by the pretty girl, and then couldn't perform because he got hit over the head with a bladder etc. The **Dancer** comic also played the **Straight Man**, dapper in his striped suit, vest and straw hat, he was constantly out-sharped, swindled and conned but could break into a crowd-pleasing comic dance routine with grace and style.

Comedy bits were so familiar to the drummer, every time a pretty show girl wiggled across the stage as part of the bit, he blew his wolf-whistle and banged the bass drum, to the delight of the audience who was anticipating it. Timing was the key element of success for the comic; he had to know when to deliver a punch line, how to wait for the laughs, how not to step on his own line when the laughter was building, and how to do a double-take that left you breathless with anxiety awaiting the punch line that was sure to follow.

Comics were the glue that held Burlesque together. They could be counted on to fill any time period (stretch) when a crisis or unexpected event occurred backstage. Comics were familiar with more than two hundred different routines and could pick up on any one of them without advance warning from a member of the comic team. Surprisingly, the audience knew almost all the routines, too, and looked forward to seeing familiar material. One thing the audience would not tolerate, especially from comics, was tampering with burlesque "bits." Tampering made the audience feel very uncomfortable and they let the performers know it with rude shouts, loud booing, the Bronx cheer, and other sounds associated with displeasure. Until burlesque comedians developed their craft, the American public was never quite comfortable in the presence of comedy, but burlesque comics changed that!

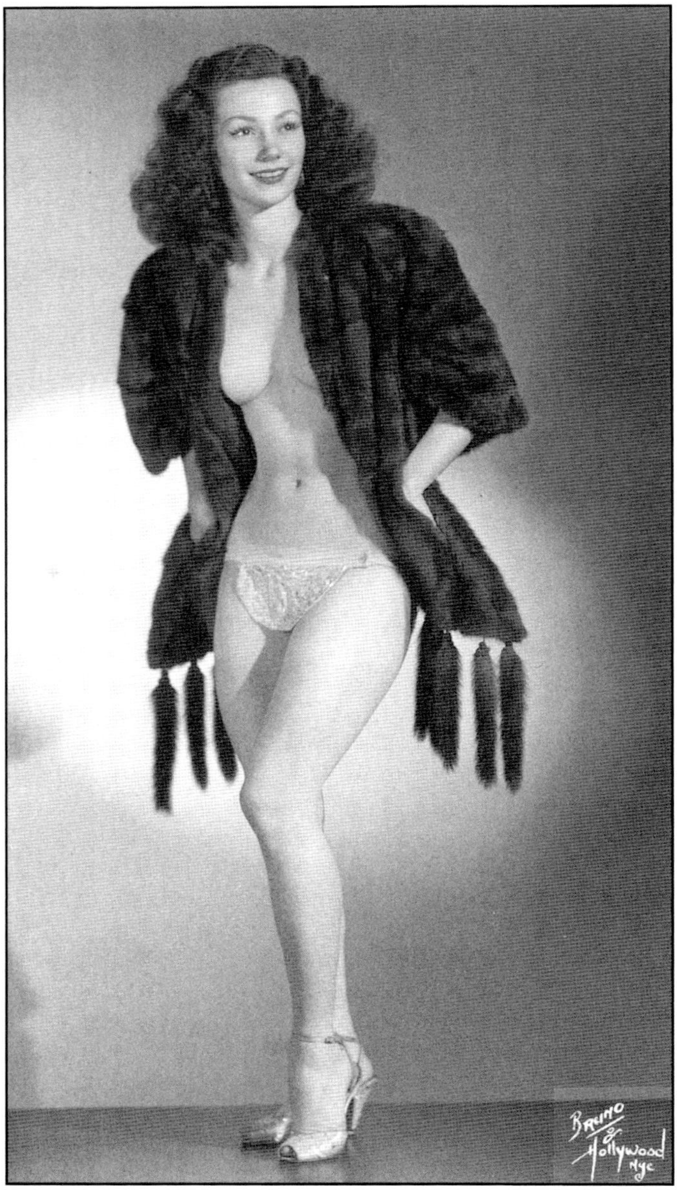

Bruno of Hollywood NYC

Maureen Marsh

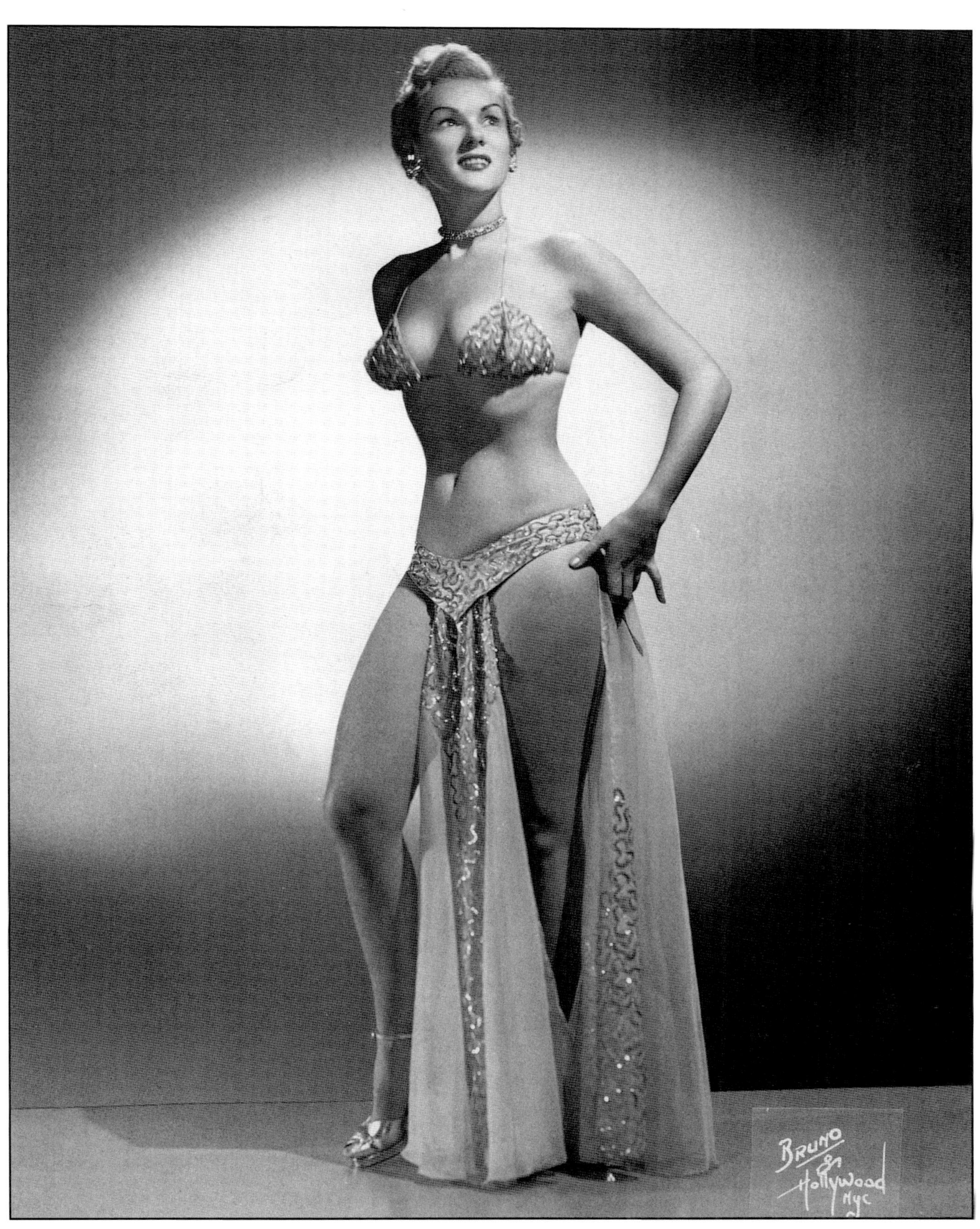

Brandy Martin

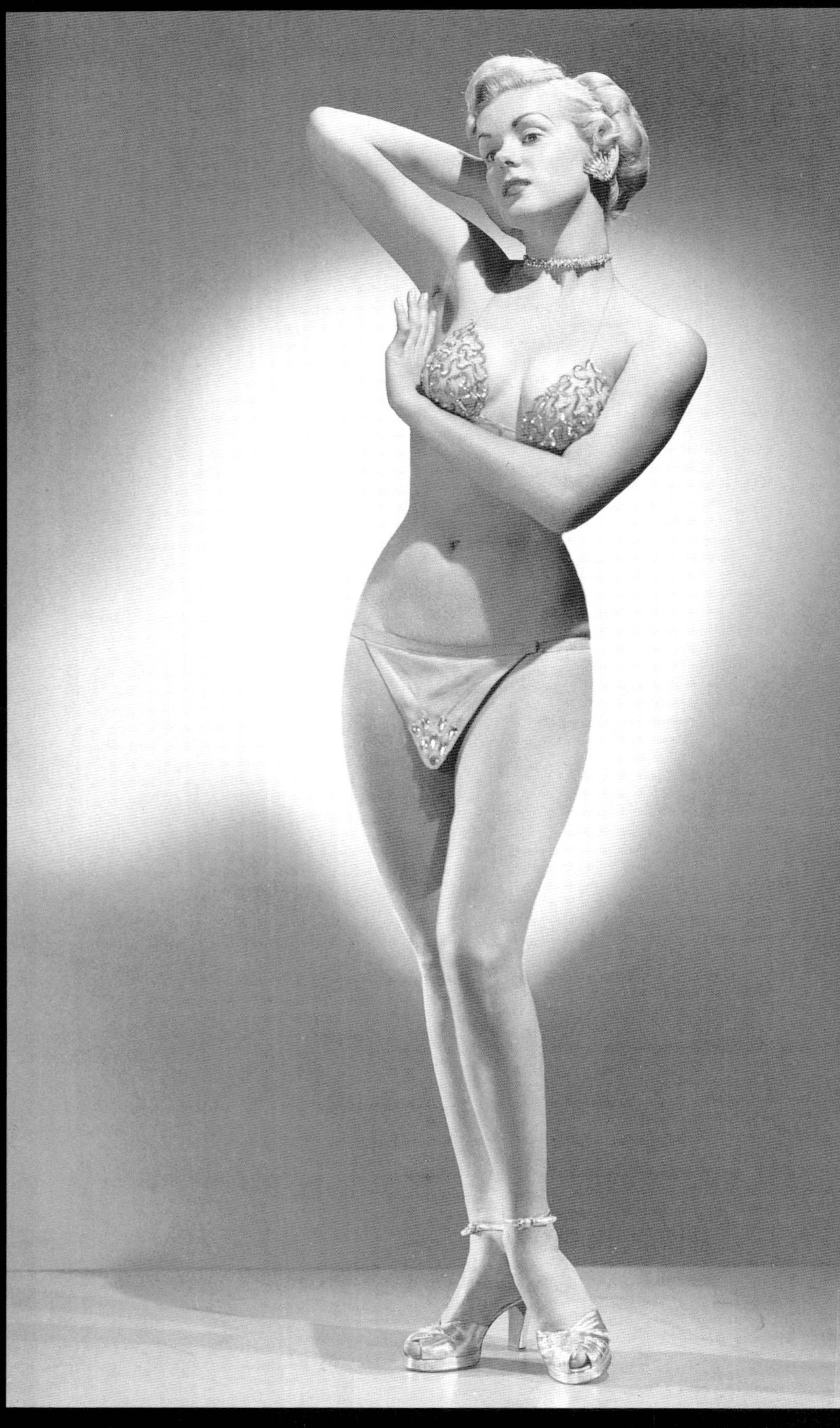

Brandy Martin

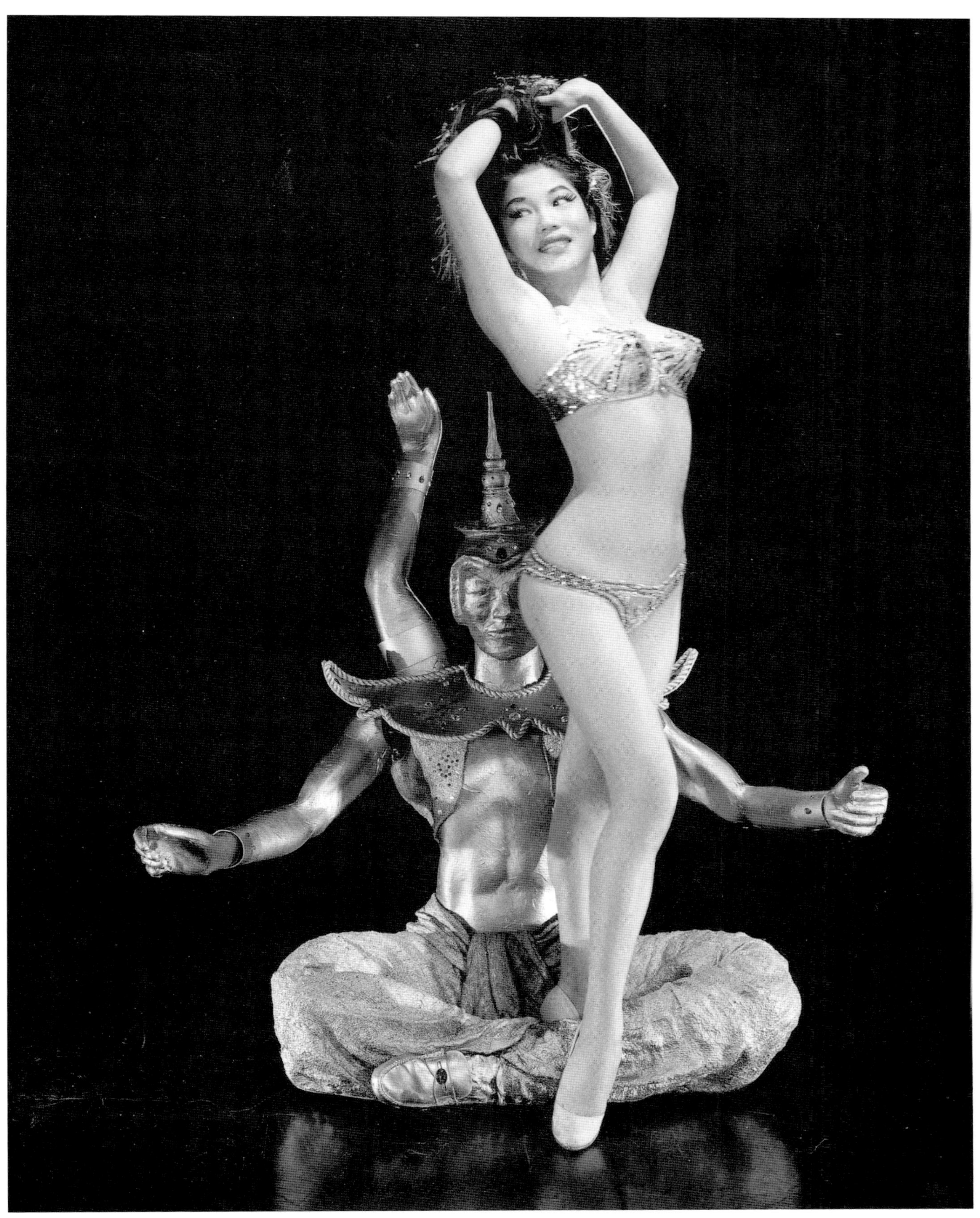

Gia Mo

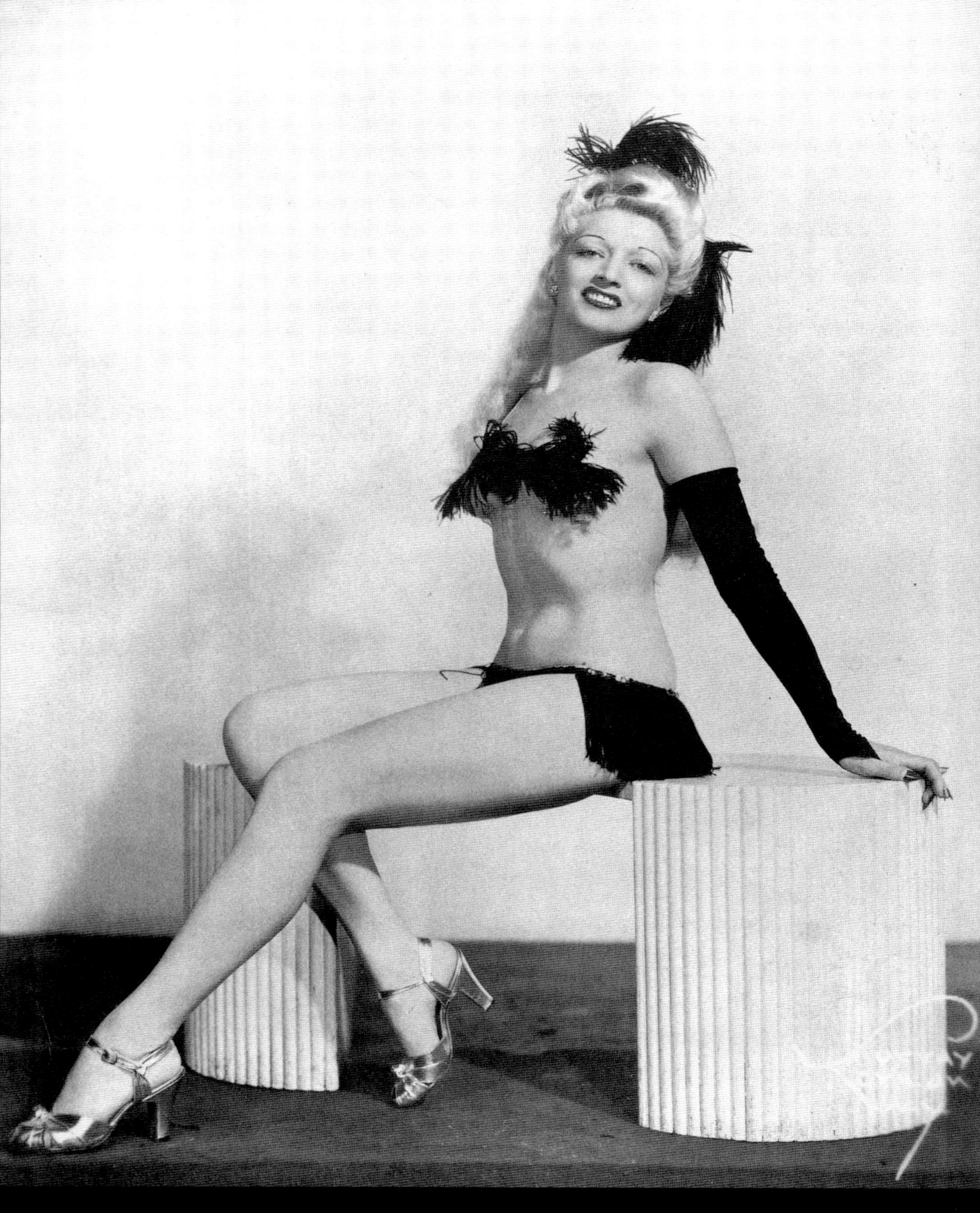

Nadine

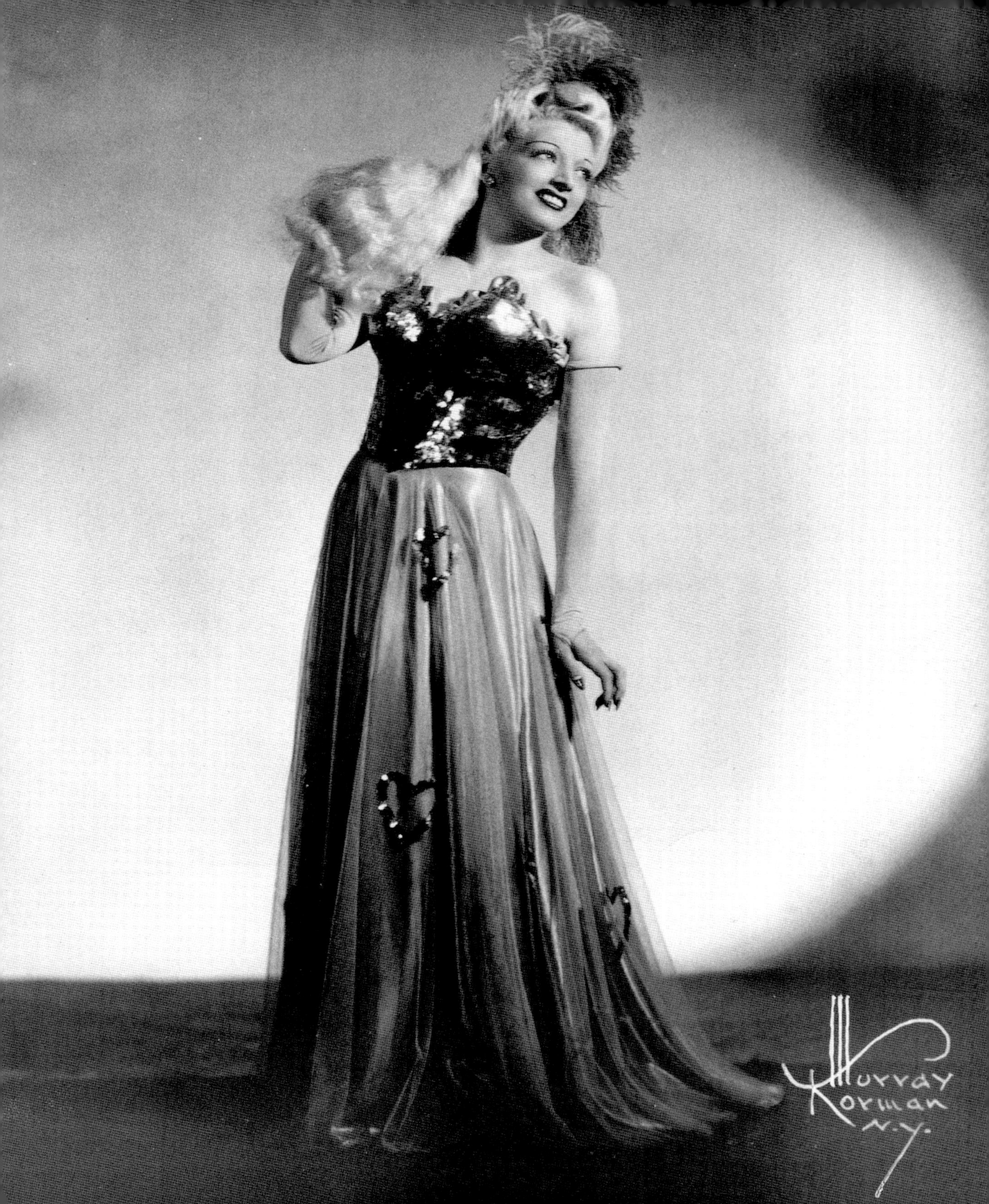
Murray
Korman
N.Y.

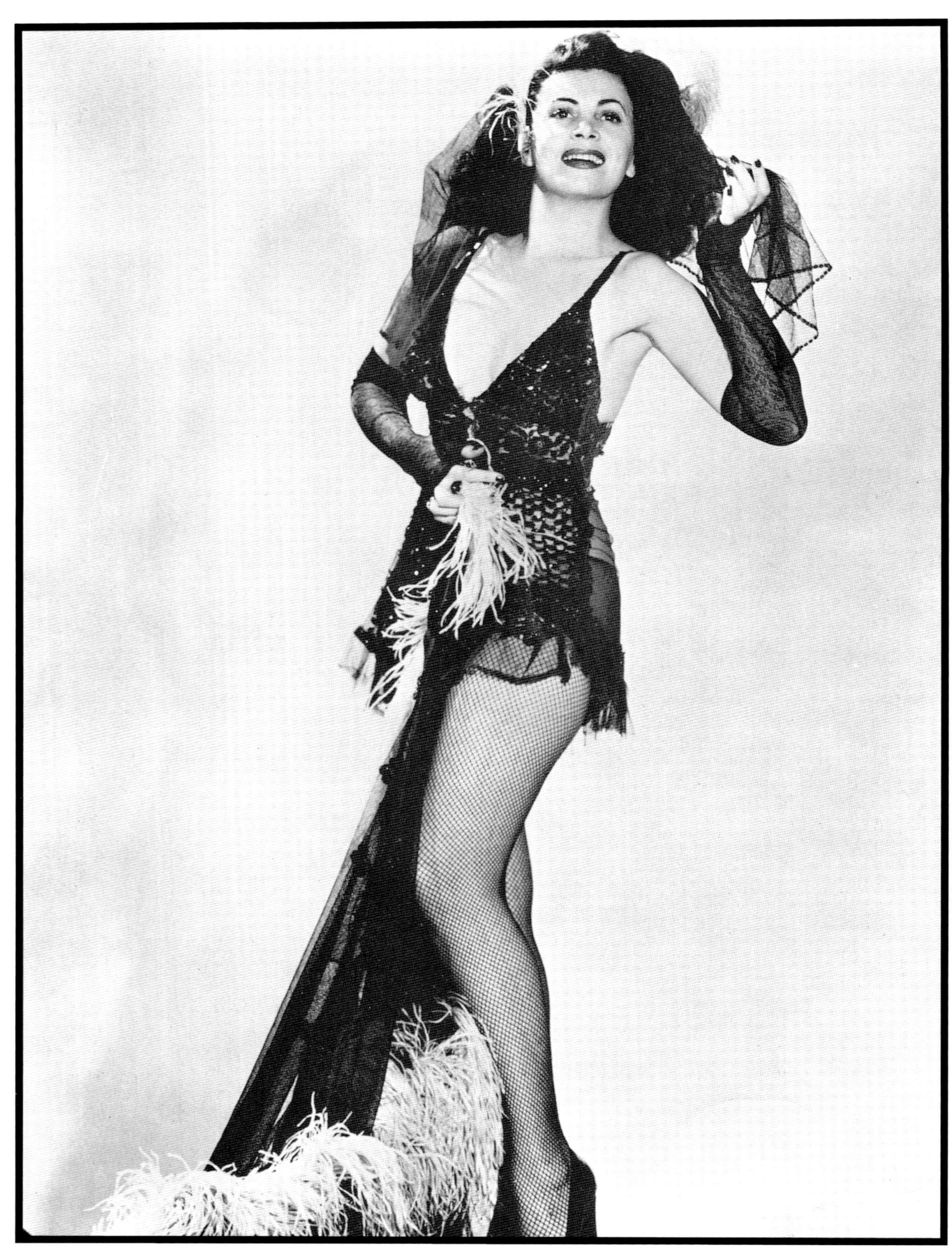

Naomi

Comics were the glue that held Burlesques together. They could be counted on to fill any time period (stretch) when a crisis or unexpected event occurred backstage.

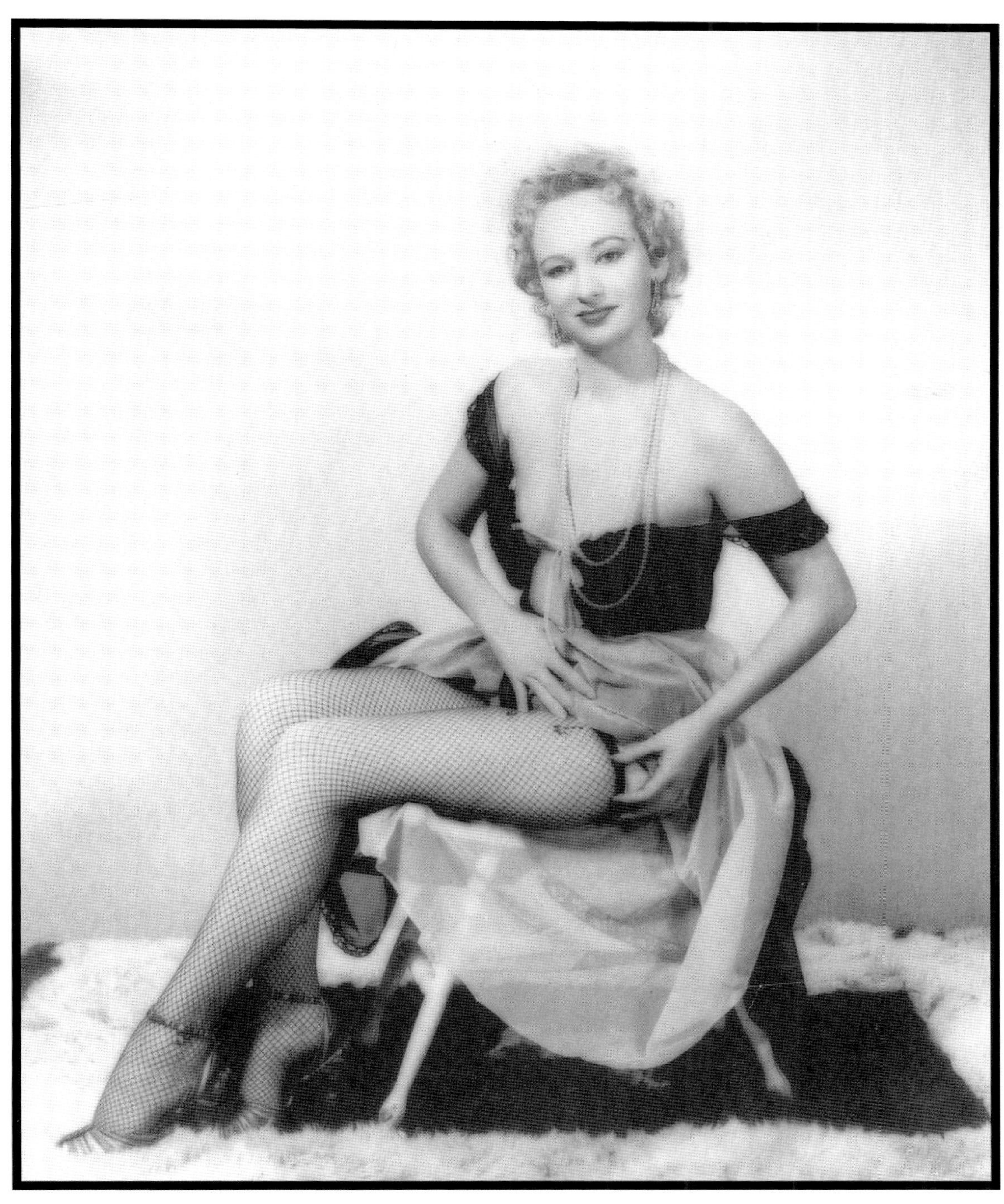

Nudema

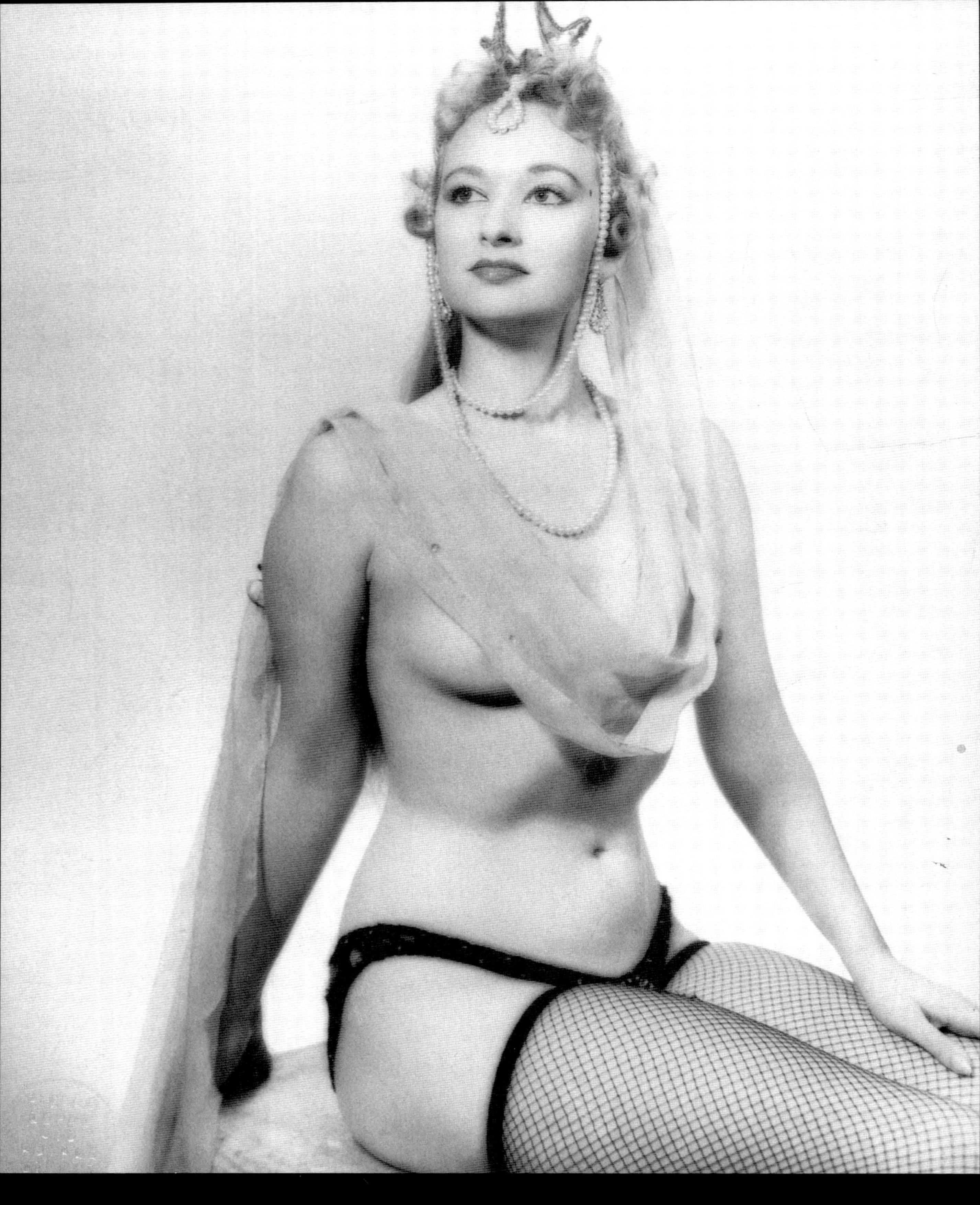

Nudema

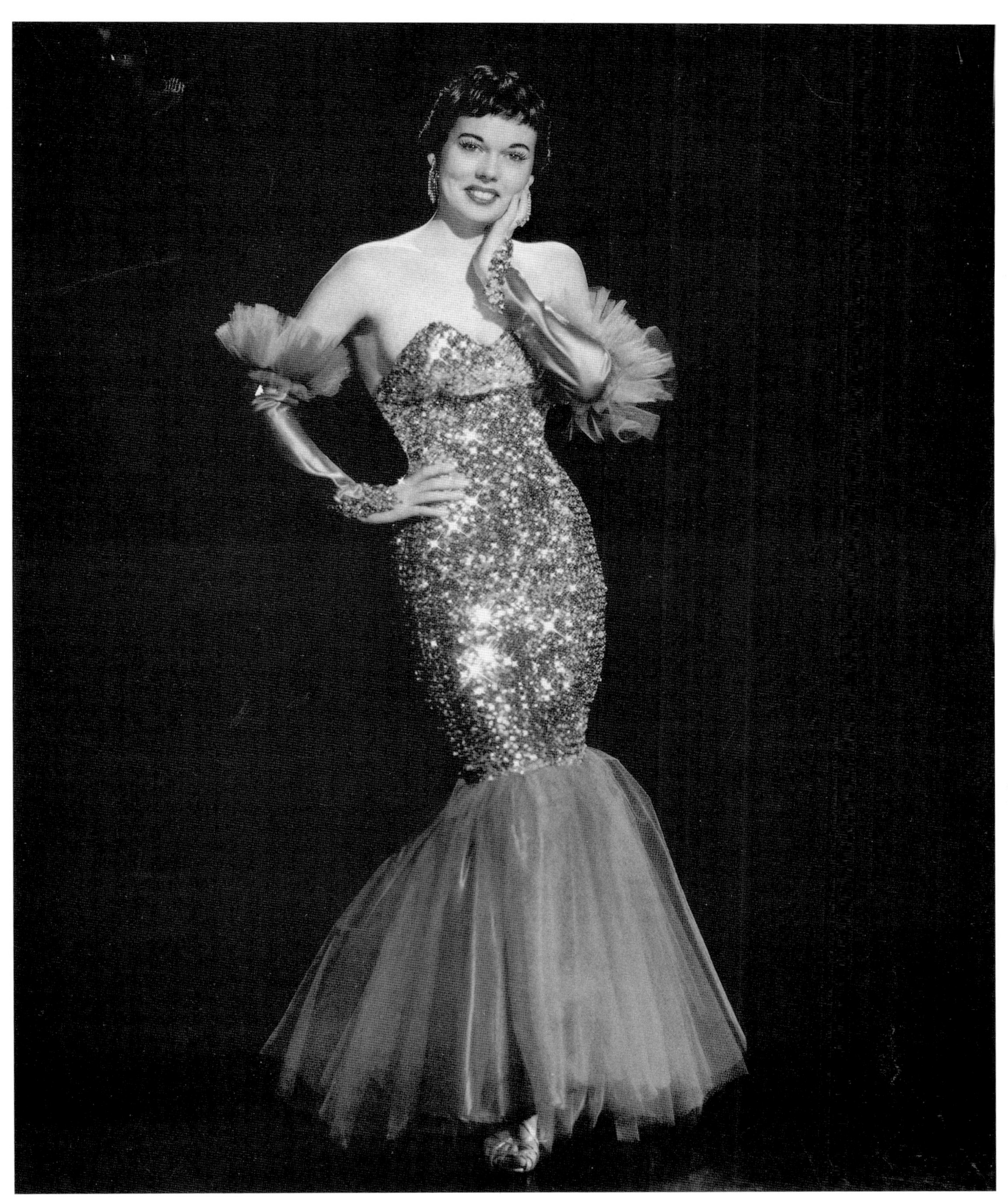

Scarlett O'Hara
The Exciting Lassie with the Classy Chassis

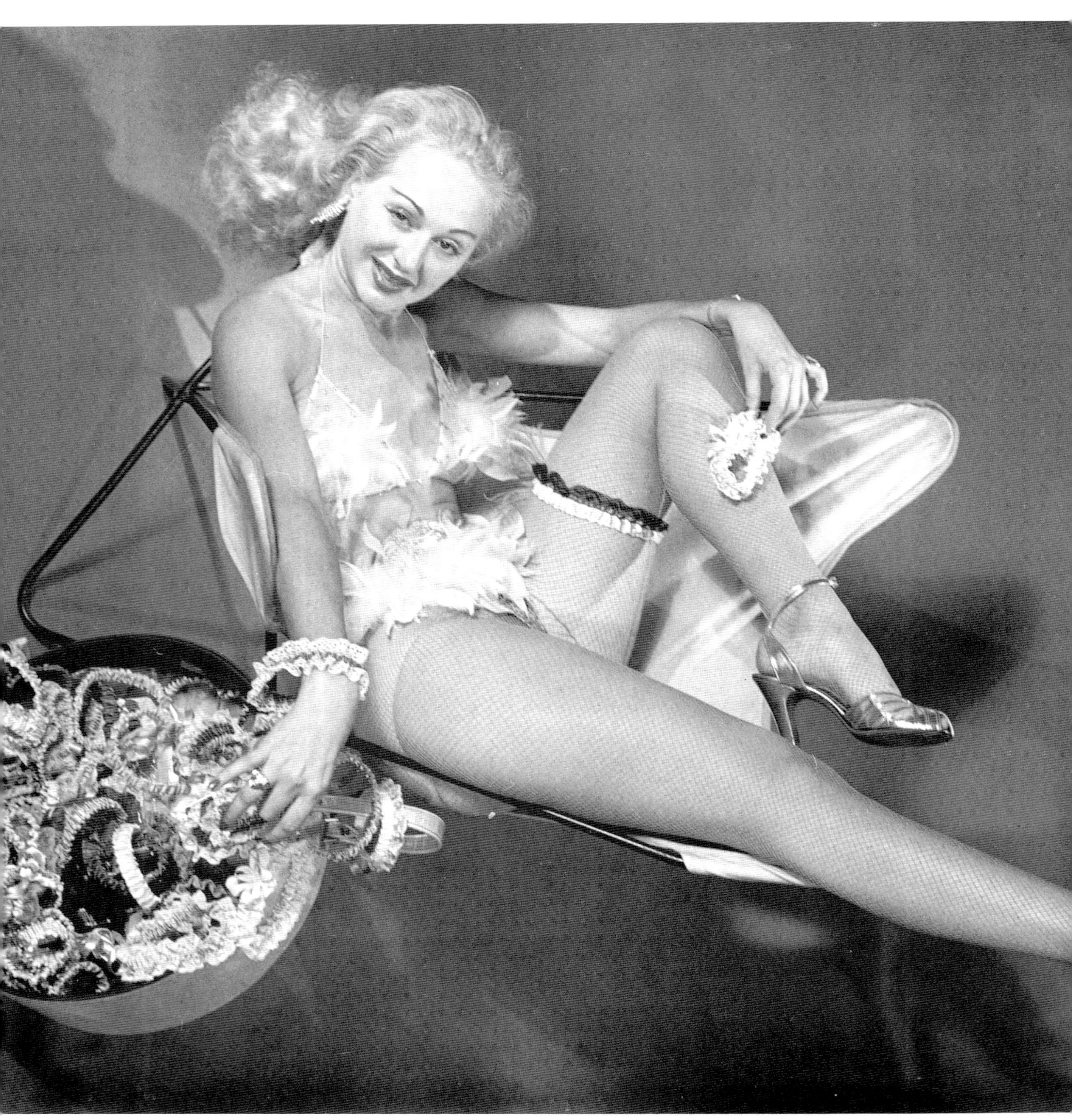

Lynn O'Neil
The Original Garter Girl

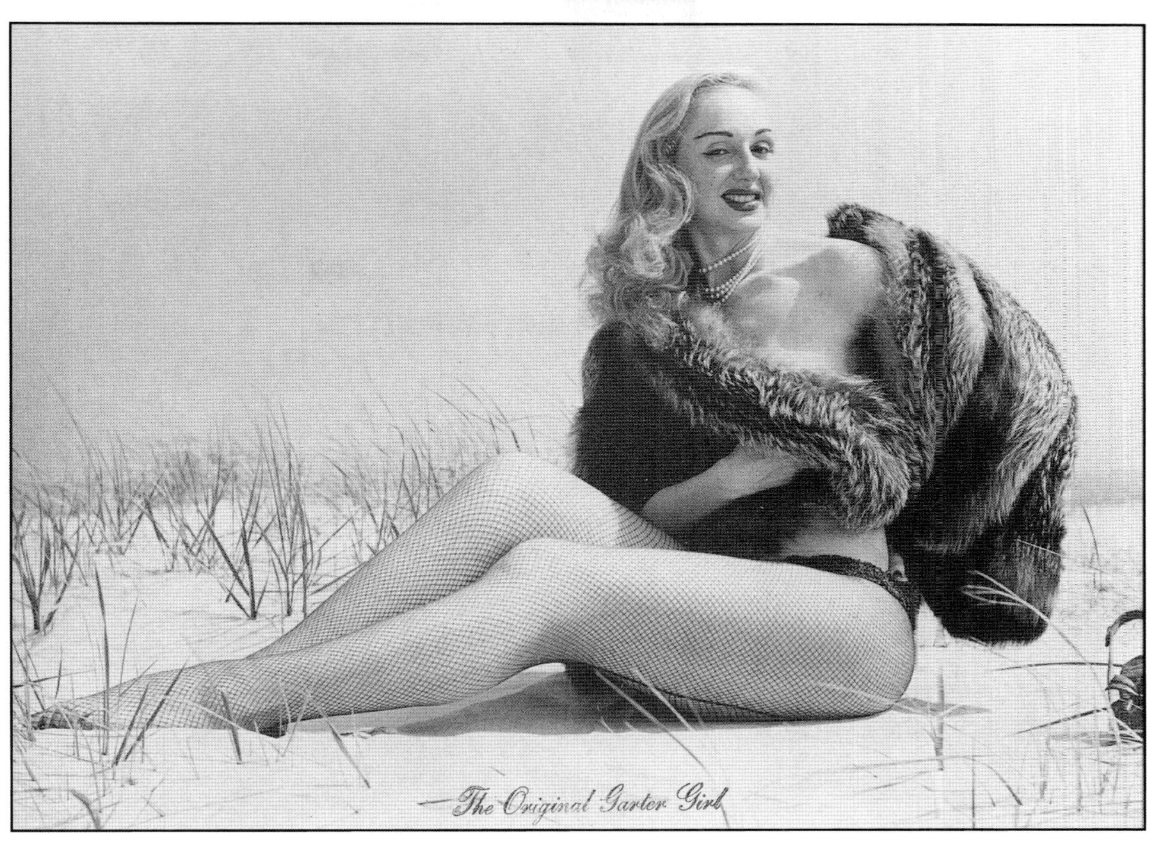

The Original Garter Girl

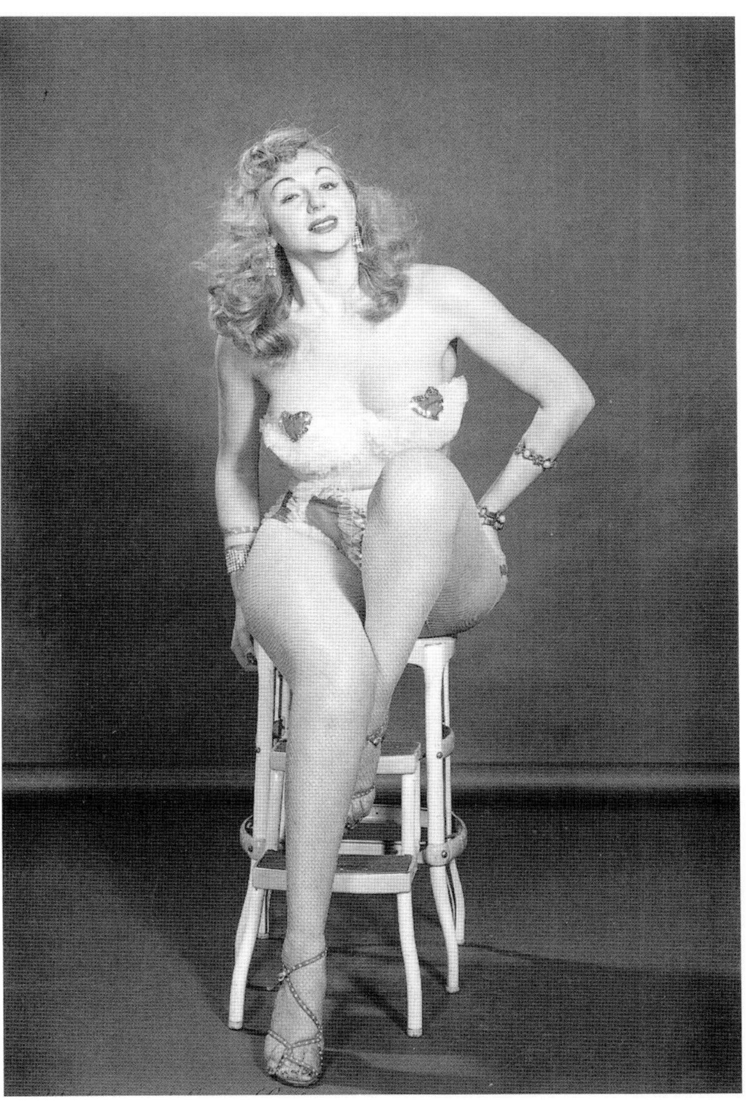

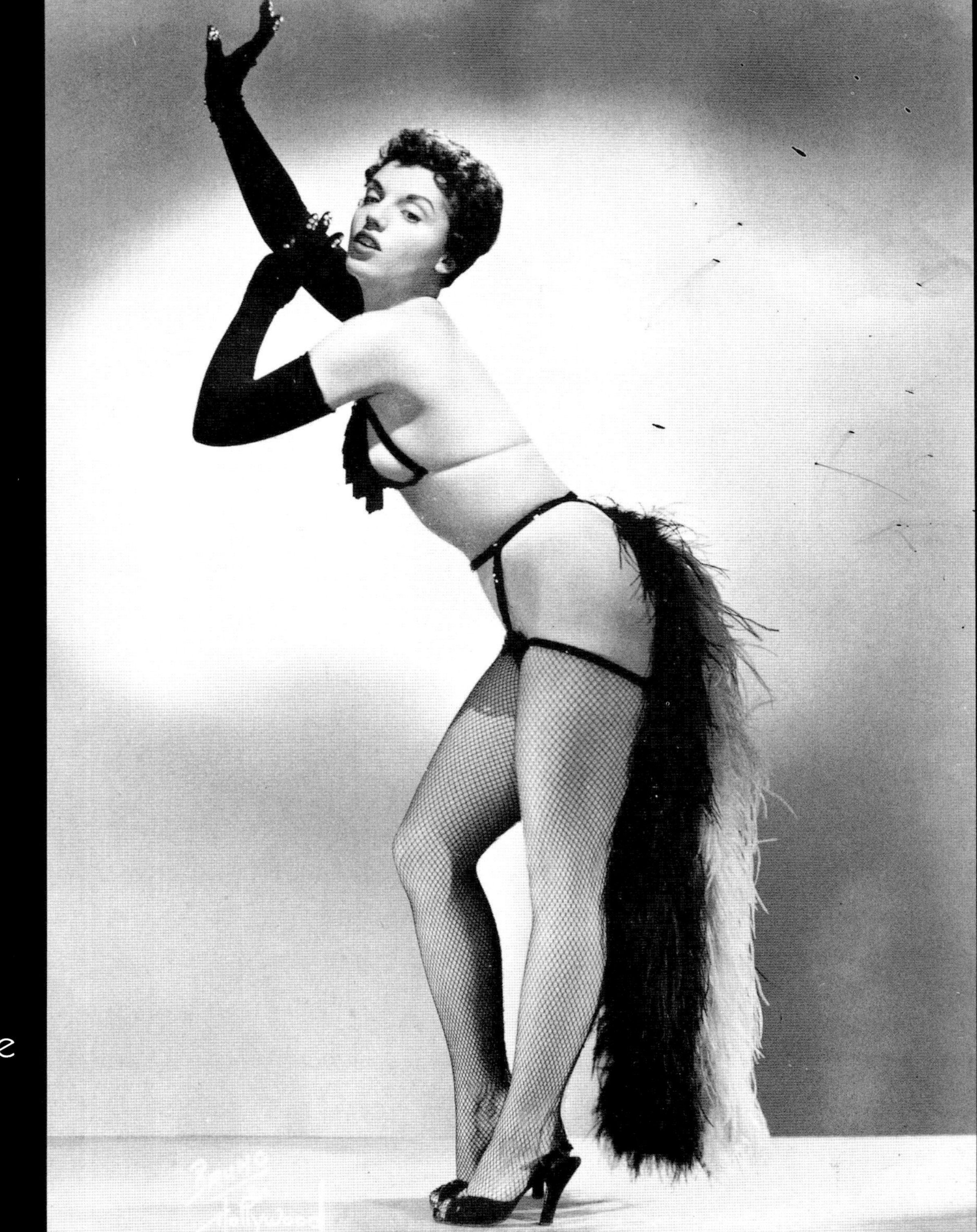

Penny Page

The S-E-X Girl

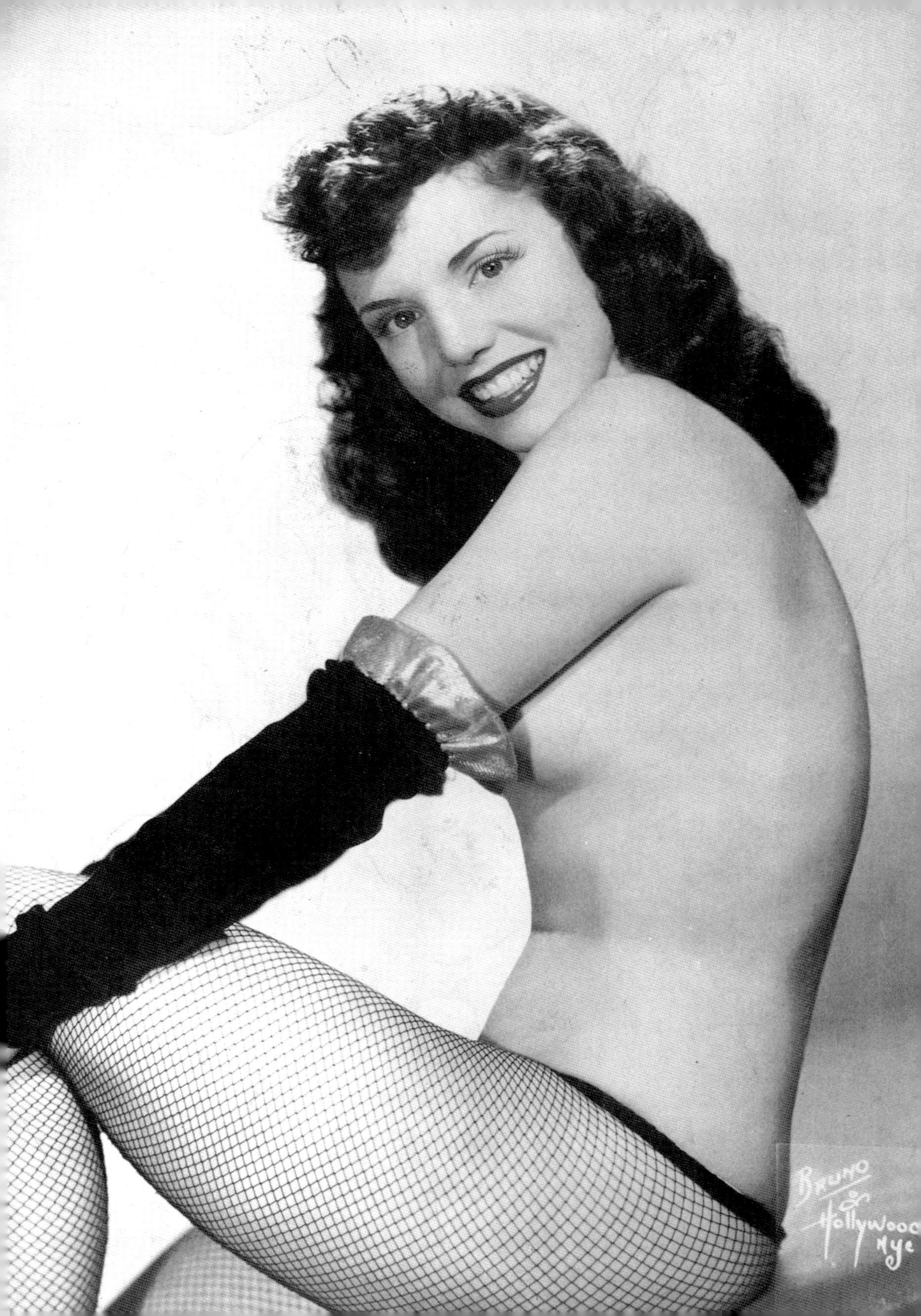
Bruno
of
Hollywood
Nyc

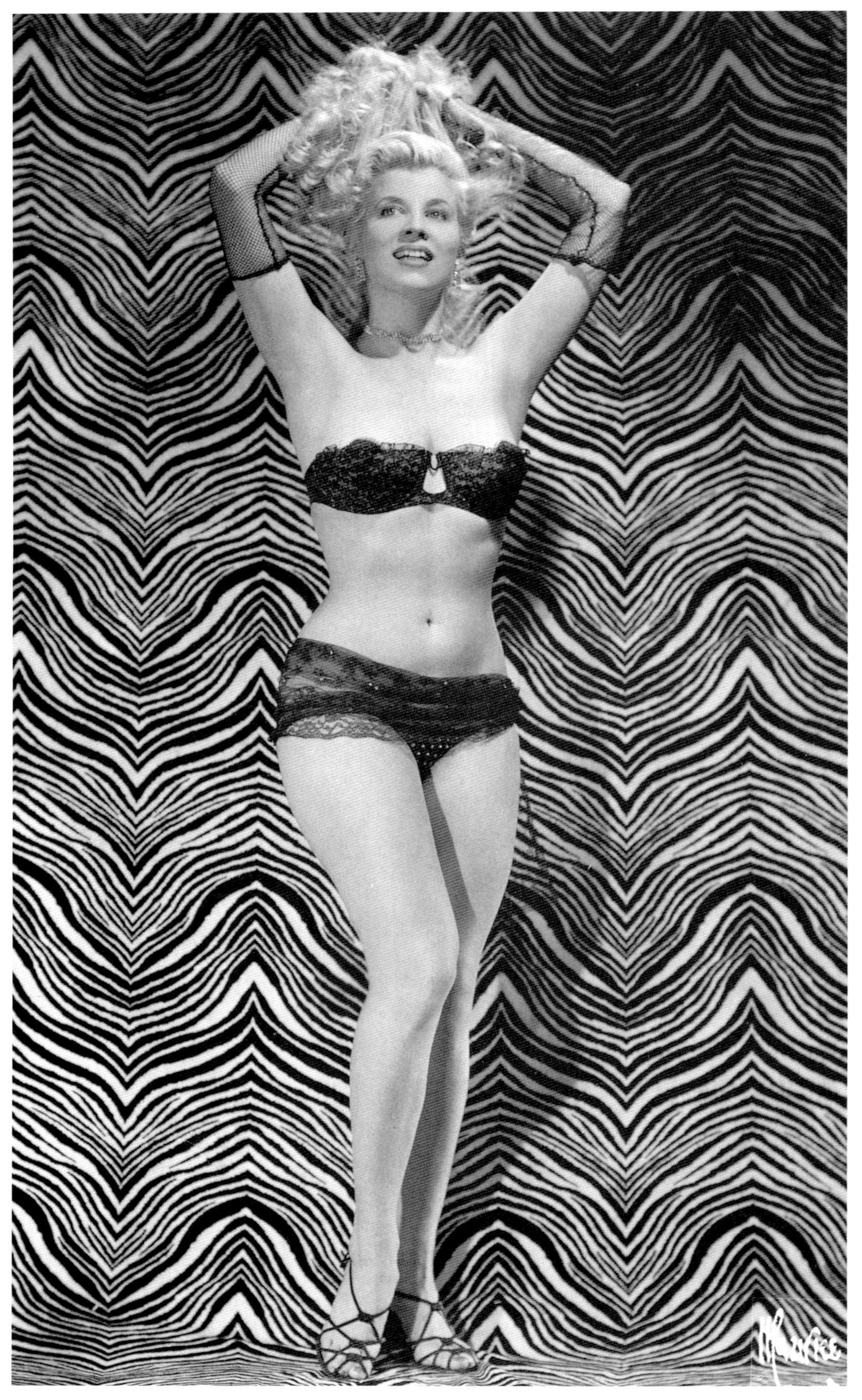

Patti Paget

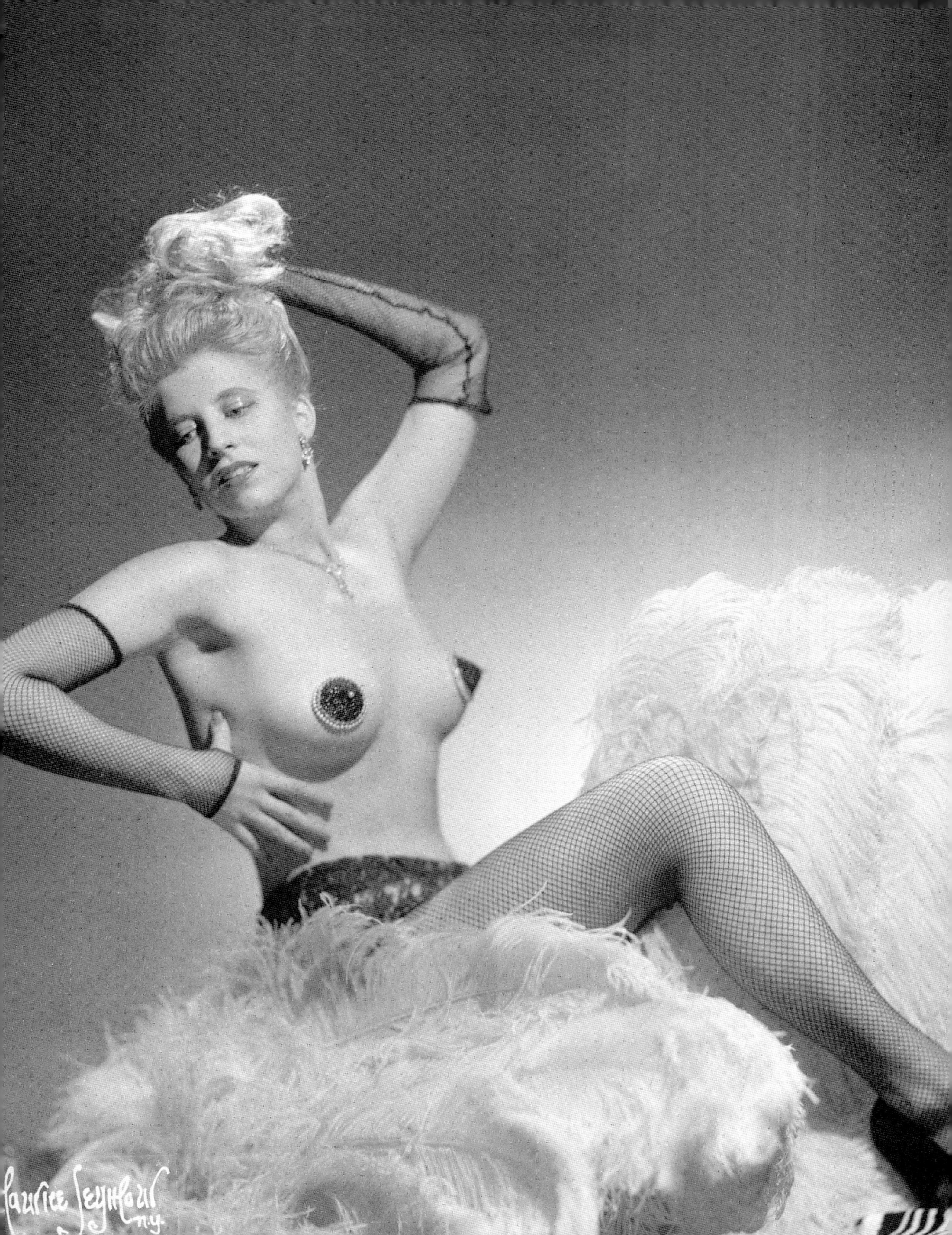
Maurice Seymour N.Y.

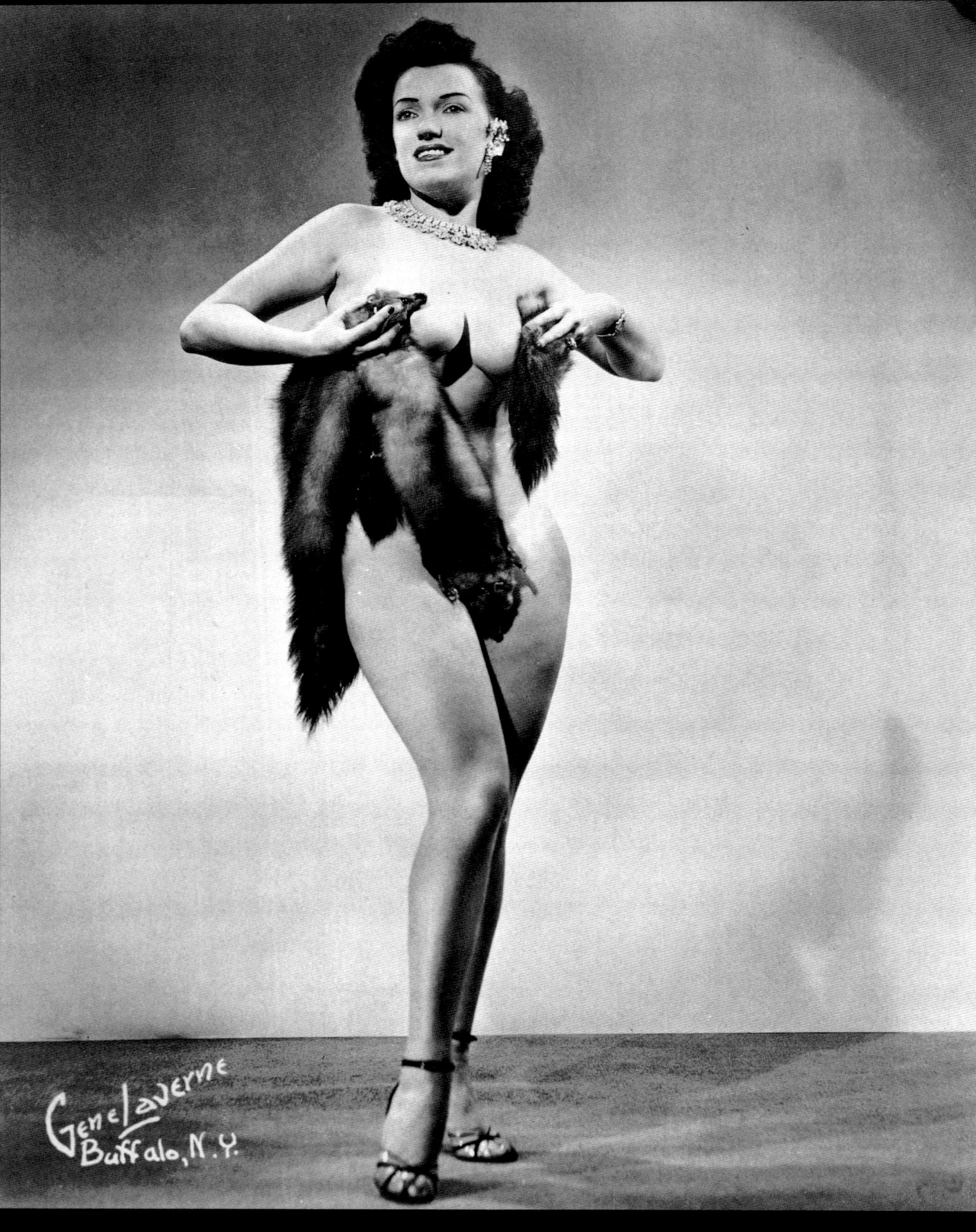

Ann Perri
The Parisian Jane Russell

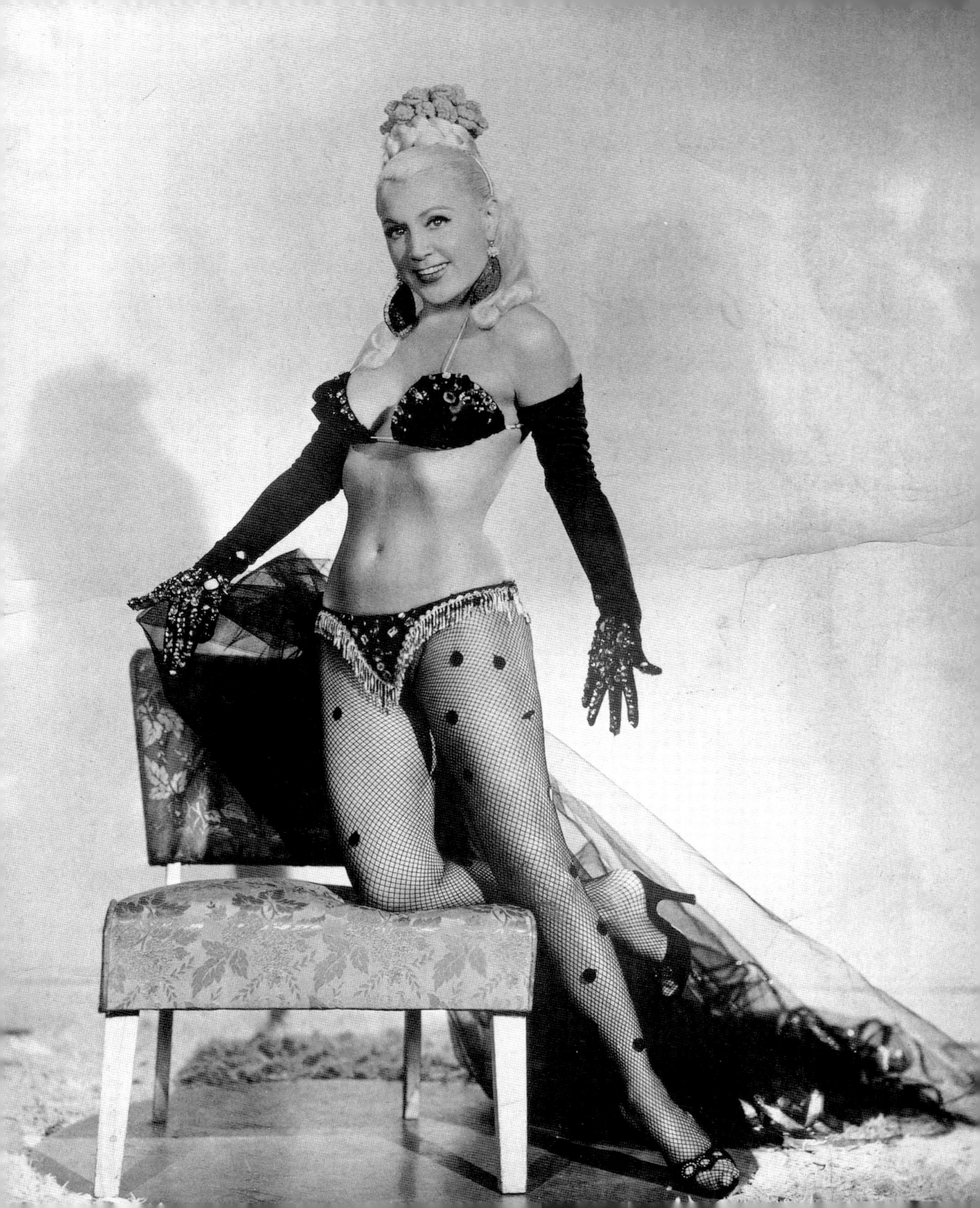

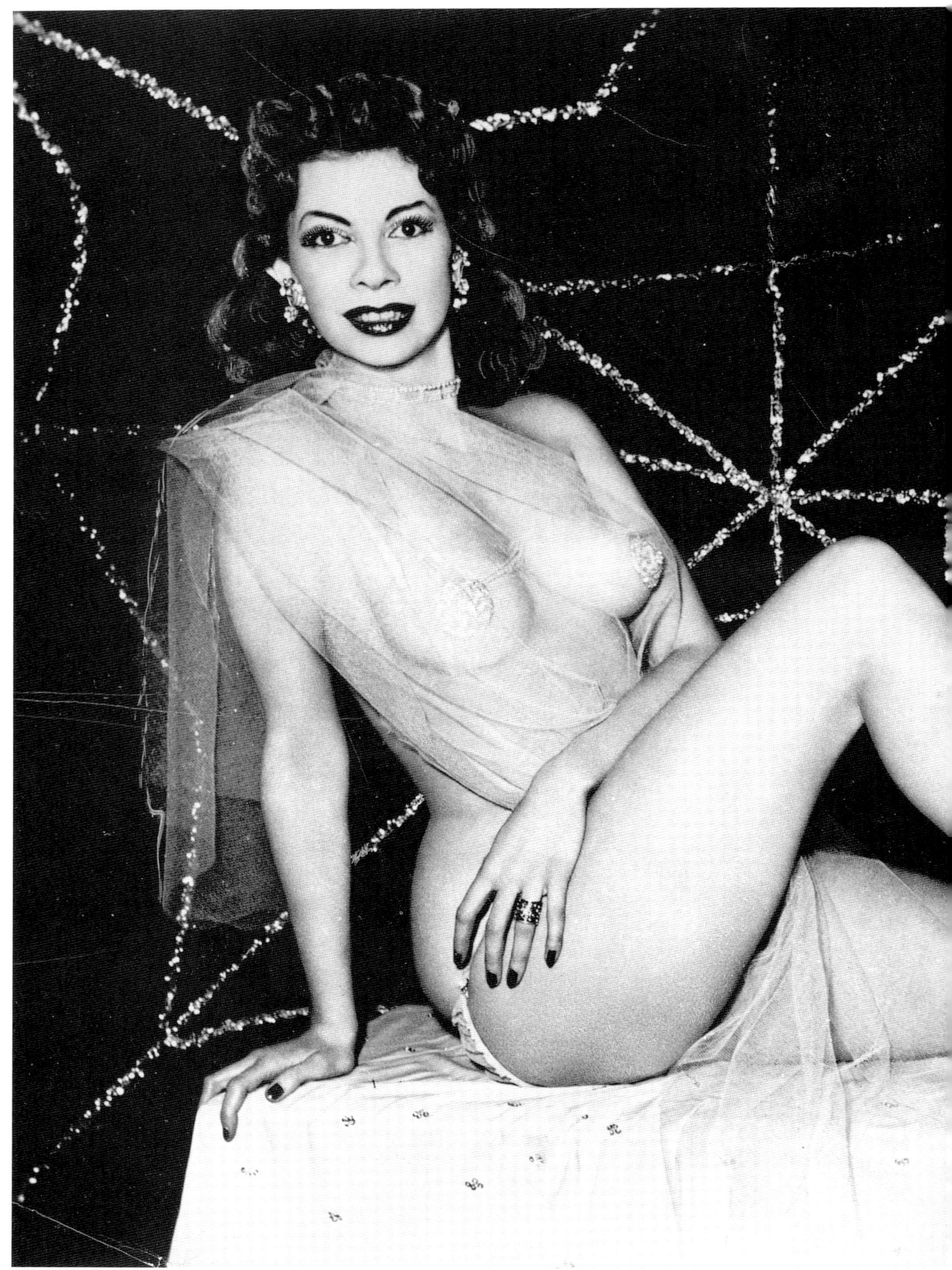

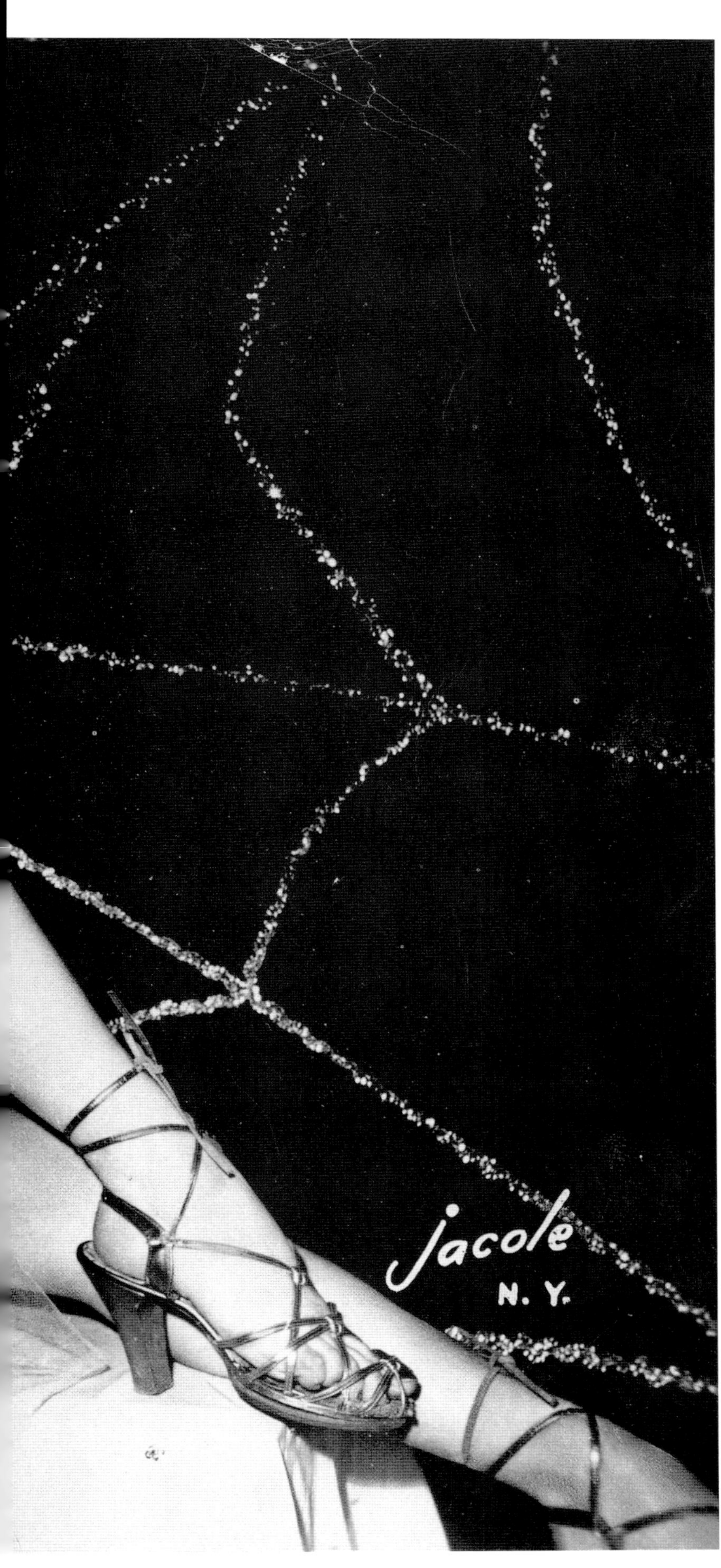

Pepper Powell
Miss T-N-T Herself
The Torrid, Titian Haired, Tantalizer

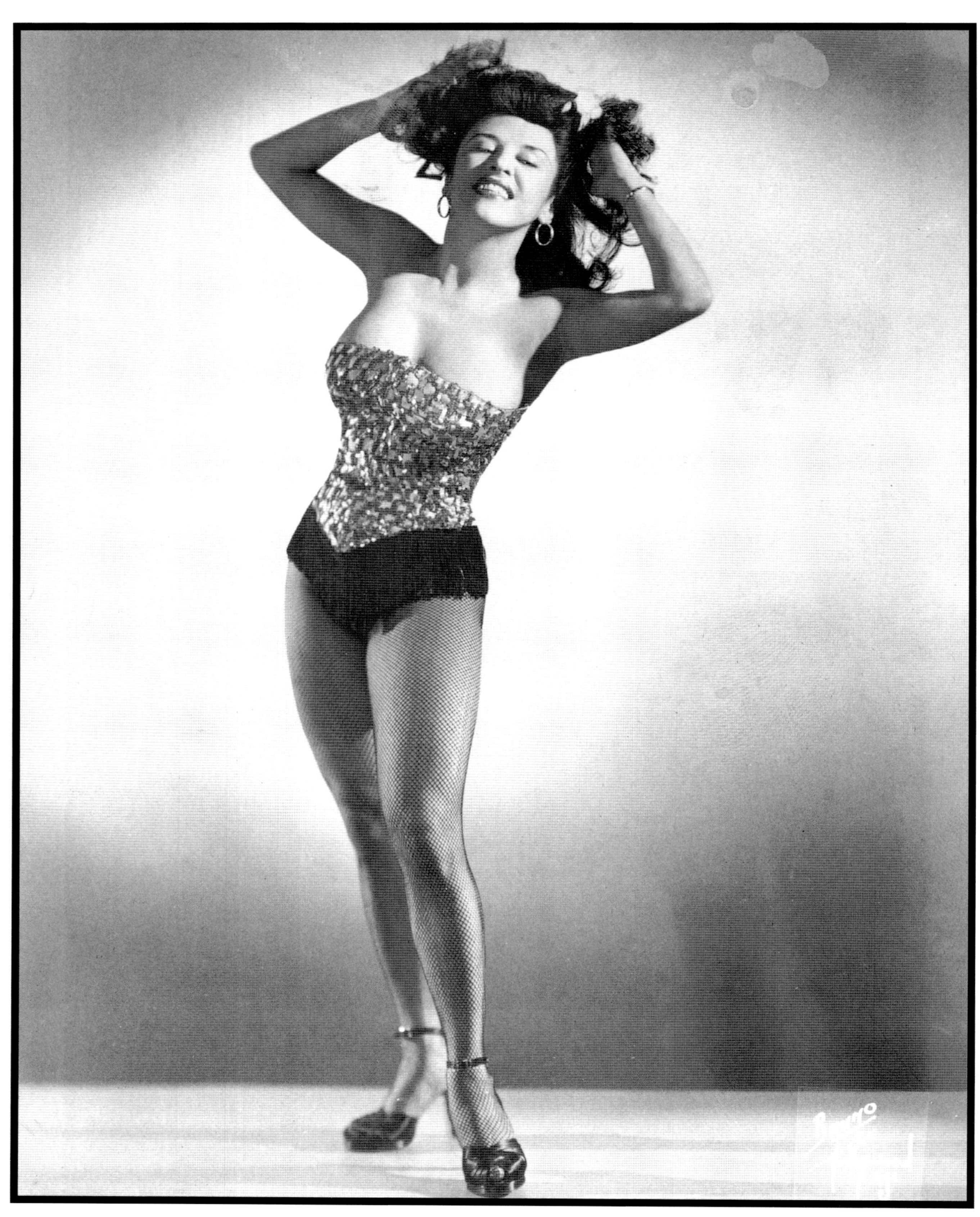

Rita Ravell
The Latin Temptress

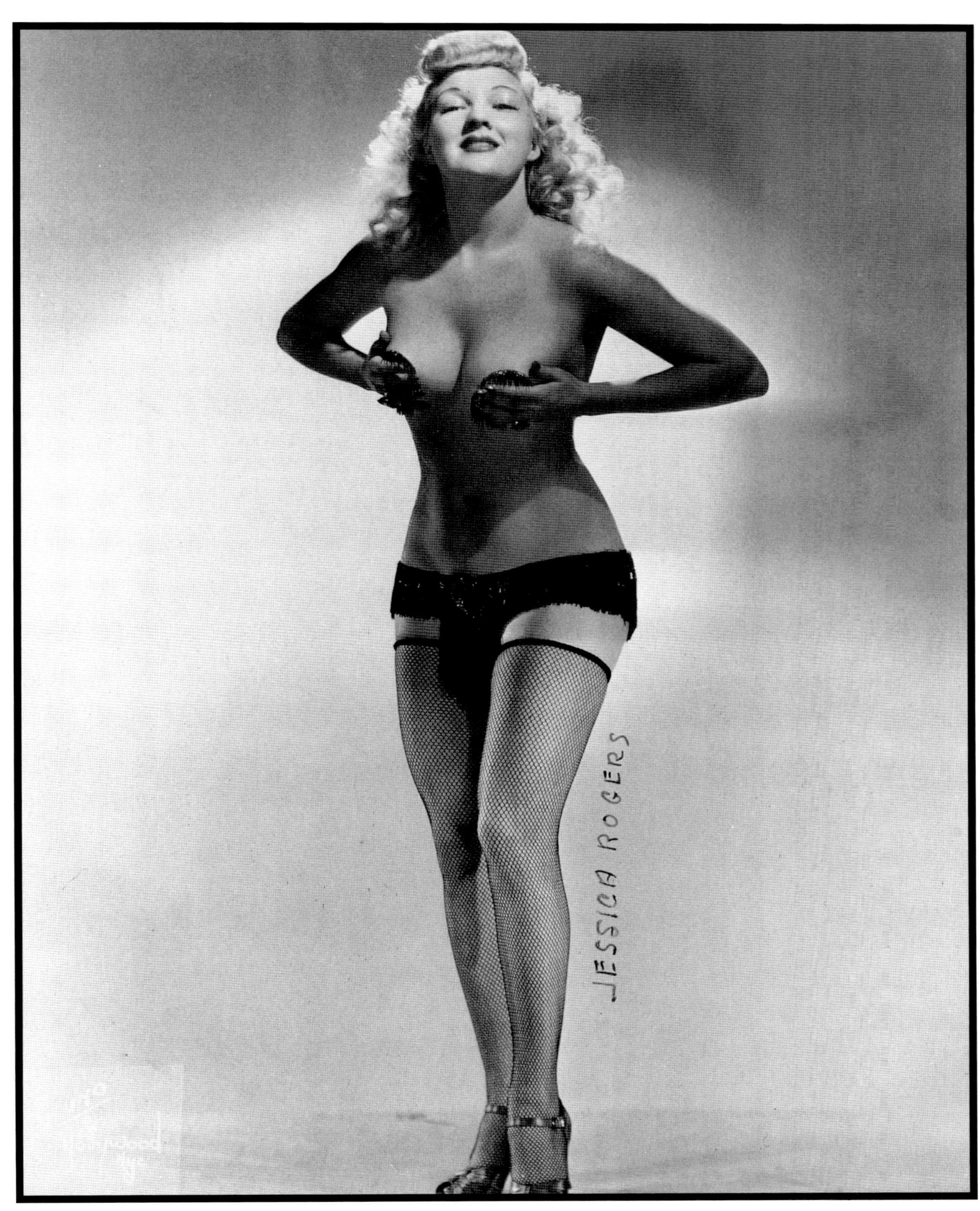

Jessica Rogers
The Wow Girl

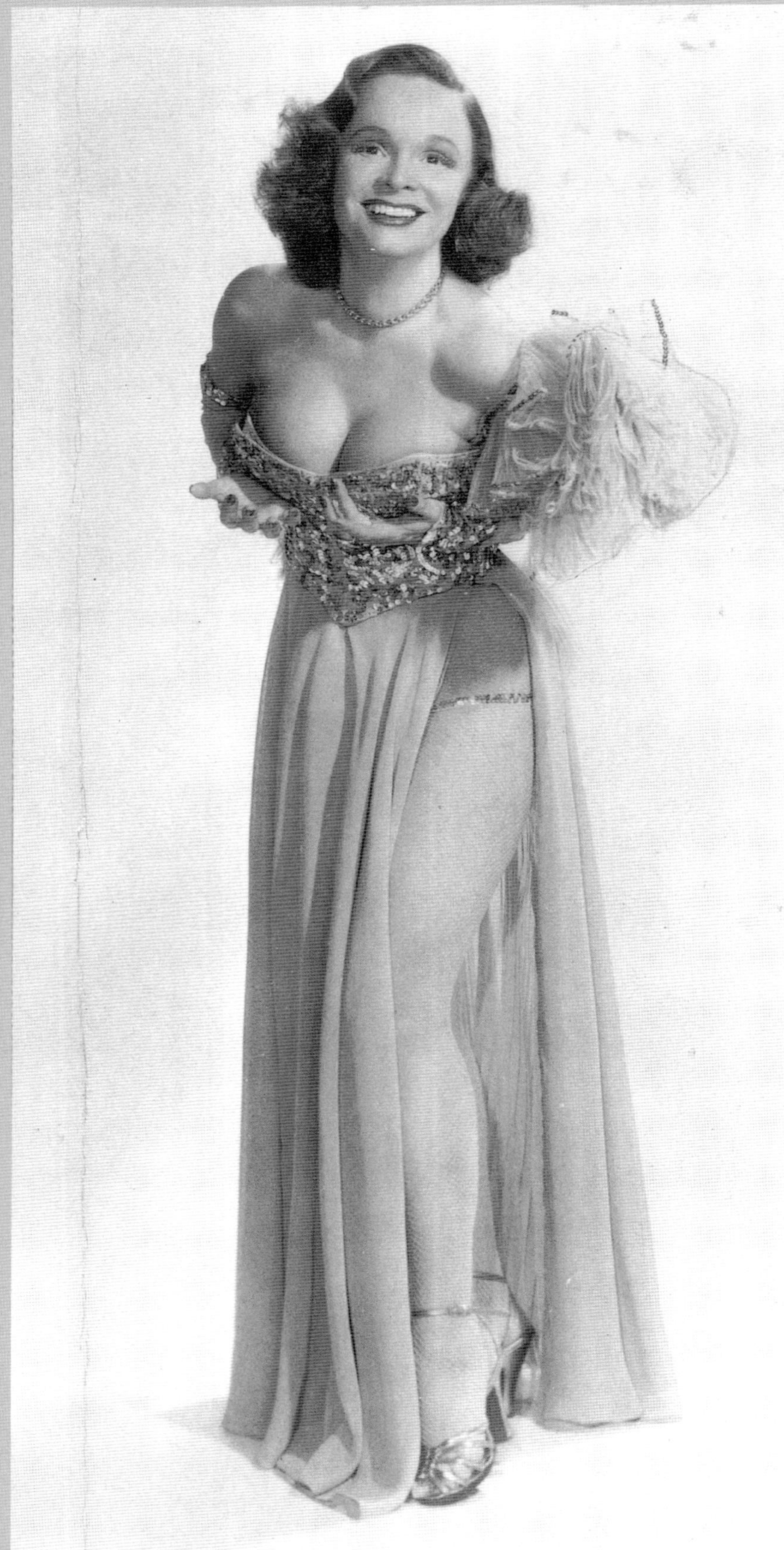

Betty Rowland

The Stars

The Bare Truth about burlesque, involving the star performers, is yet another story. Burlesque was a great training ground for many famous stars of musical comedy, revue, motion pictures, radio and television. Among burlesque's alumni were: Al Joelson, Eddie Cantor, Bert Lahr, W.C. Fields, Phil Silvers, Jackie Gleason, Red Buttons, Danny Thomas, Ed Wynn, Joe E. Brown, Abbott and Costello, Will Rogers, Sophie Tucker, Fannie Brice, Pinky Lee, Rags Ragland, Jack Pearl, Bobby Clark, Joey Faye, Robert Alda, Dan Dailey, Jack Albertson, and James Barton.

The Striptease

Striptease dancing first entered the dancers' routines about 1916 when Minsky's constructed the first runway in a theater, allowing strippers and chorus girls to walk into the audience on the raised platform close to, but not quite close enough to be touched by grasping hands from below. This made a normally exciting experience even more so, and gave his theater an advantage over all others.

Morton Minsky tells his version of how the striptease first began in his book *Minsky's Burlesque* written with Milt Machlin. Mae Dix, a talented, red-haired gal with a figure to die for, had a great way of putting over a comic song. While performing in one of Minsky's theaters where the heat was oppressive, she wore a black, short-skirted dress with a detachable white collar and cuffs. In her hurry to exit the hot stage, and in a probable attempt to avoid laundering the white articles every day, she pulled off the collar and tossed it off the stage, not knowing the audience had seen her. A member of the audience began applauding for an encore, which caught on and grew. In response, she reappeared without the collar and was greeted with a loud outburst of enthusiastic applause, whereupon she bowed, pulled off her cuffs and left the stage for what she thought was the last time. However, the audience, now in a frenzy, refused to let her go and clapped until she reappeared. Not having anything prepared, she asked the orchestra for a short chorus, did a brief dance, and possibly in a moment of panic as to what to do next, unbuttoned her bodice as she again left the stage. Thus was born the striptease, according to Minsky. There are numerous other versions.

The striptease, however, did not become a recognized art form until 1933 when the "A Century of Progress" exhibit opened at the Chicago World's Fair. While Little Egypt's belly dance may have begun a new trend in burlesque at the 1893 Chicago Exposition, it was Sally Rand and her fan dance who fittingly revolutionized burlesque in America at the Century of Progress. The "tease" in striptease had made its official debut, and tease them she did; suggestively and seductively undressing was never more artfully done, and all behind constantly moving fans through which the audience believed they could see something ordinarily forbidden. Such was the power of illusion.

A new art form had been created. The striptease artist had to first develop a walk which would establish the character she was creating for the audience. Either she could be a "*demure*" stripper; a "*hot*" stripper; or the "*ingenue*" type. She also had to develop a pace that could be maintained at a steady level, a tempo from when she first appeared until she exited. Timing was all important, as she had to know exactly when to take off what; how much to take off; how much to leave on and what to do for an encore. The way she held her hands was important, they had to be graceful, but not too much so. The thing was the tease. . . the seductive walk or strut. . . the graceful dip promising more to come. . . and then the slow grind (forming the letter "O" with the pelvis) followed by the suggestive bump. . . knowing just how much a quick flash of the breast or bare hip-bone to show, how to create the illusion of sex without violating the law. . it took months of hard practice, talent and imagination to pull the whole thing off.

They were truly in a class by themselves. They had to have personality, poise, and a sense of rhythm. . . for stripping was an art, one of the most difficult in burlesque. The number of "*headliners*" who could do it all, and do it in a way to stir one's imagination and blood in equal proportions, was extremely small. Among the best were Sally Rand and her fans, Gypsy Rose Lee, Georgia Sothern, Ann Corio, June Havoc, Margie Hart, Rose La Rose, Sherry Britton, 6'4" Lois De Fee, Zorita and her doves, and Dorothy Henry's milk bath. They all had "gimmicks" which received more curtain calls than an opera star did. The one thing no performer ever dared was to copy another performer's costume or routine

By the time burlesque became recognized as a legitimate entertainment, and the best whiskey was selling for between 15 and 25 cents a shot, headline striptease artists were paid up to $2,000 a week and were escorted by the most wealthy and prominent men in all fields of endeavor. Among the regular Minsky clientle were publishers Conde Nast and Frank Croninsheild, writers John Erskine and John Dos Passos, columnists Walter Winchell and Mark Hellinger, and commentators Robert Benchley, Irwin S. Cobb and George Jean Nathan. They not only came to see the stars, but for the shows so full of parody and satire, in addition to the ridiculous and sublime comedy.

Names for the second-line strippers were often made up for their comic value. These were usually the *soubrettes* (the youngest featured stripteasers) who willingly agreed to adopt such names as Countess Schmaltz from Capon, Ada Onion from Bermuda, or Carrie de Booze from Canada.

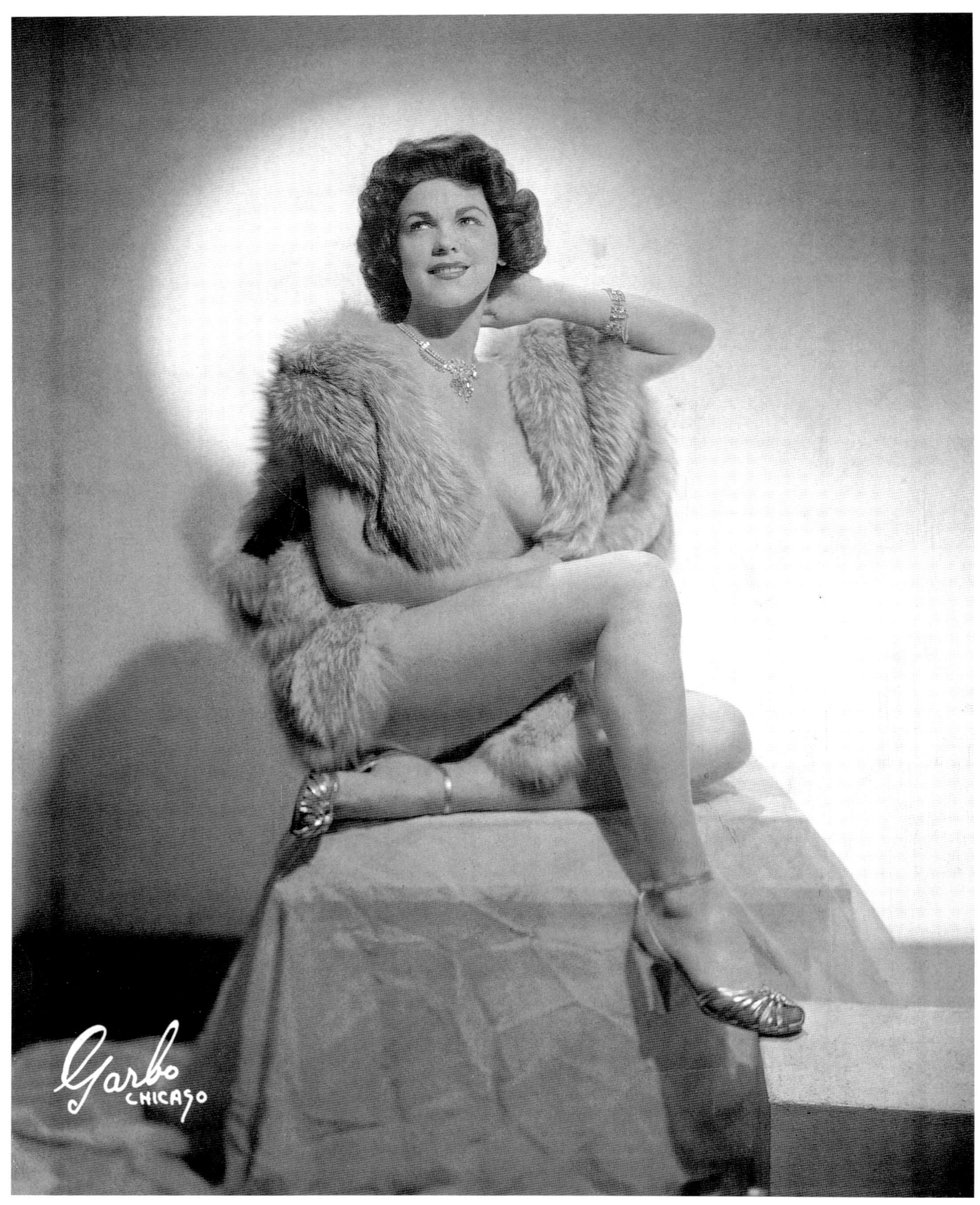

Marian Russell

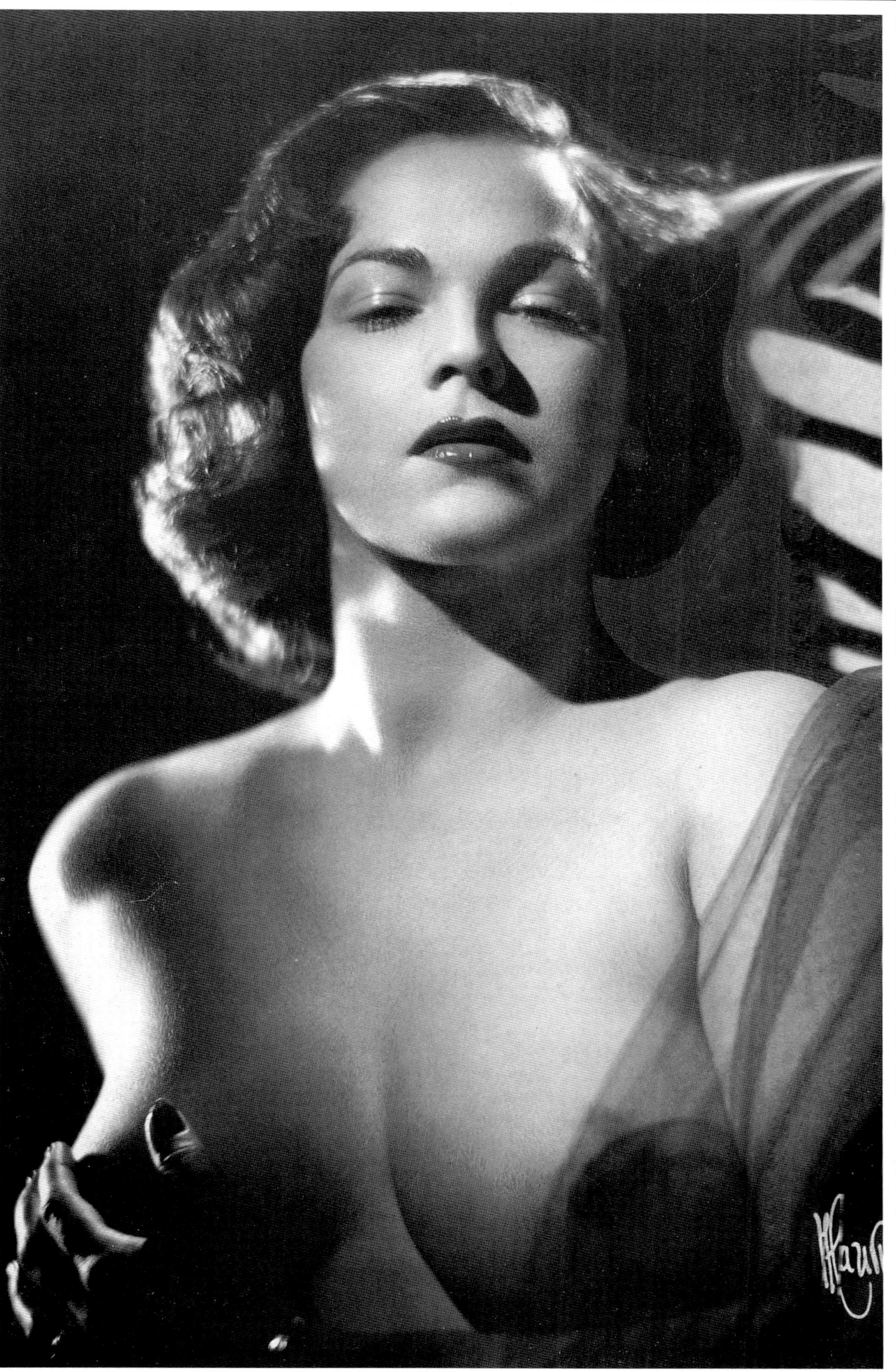

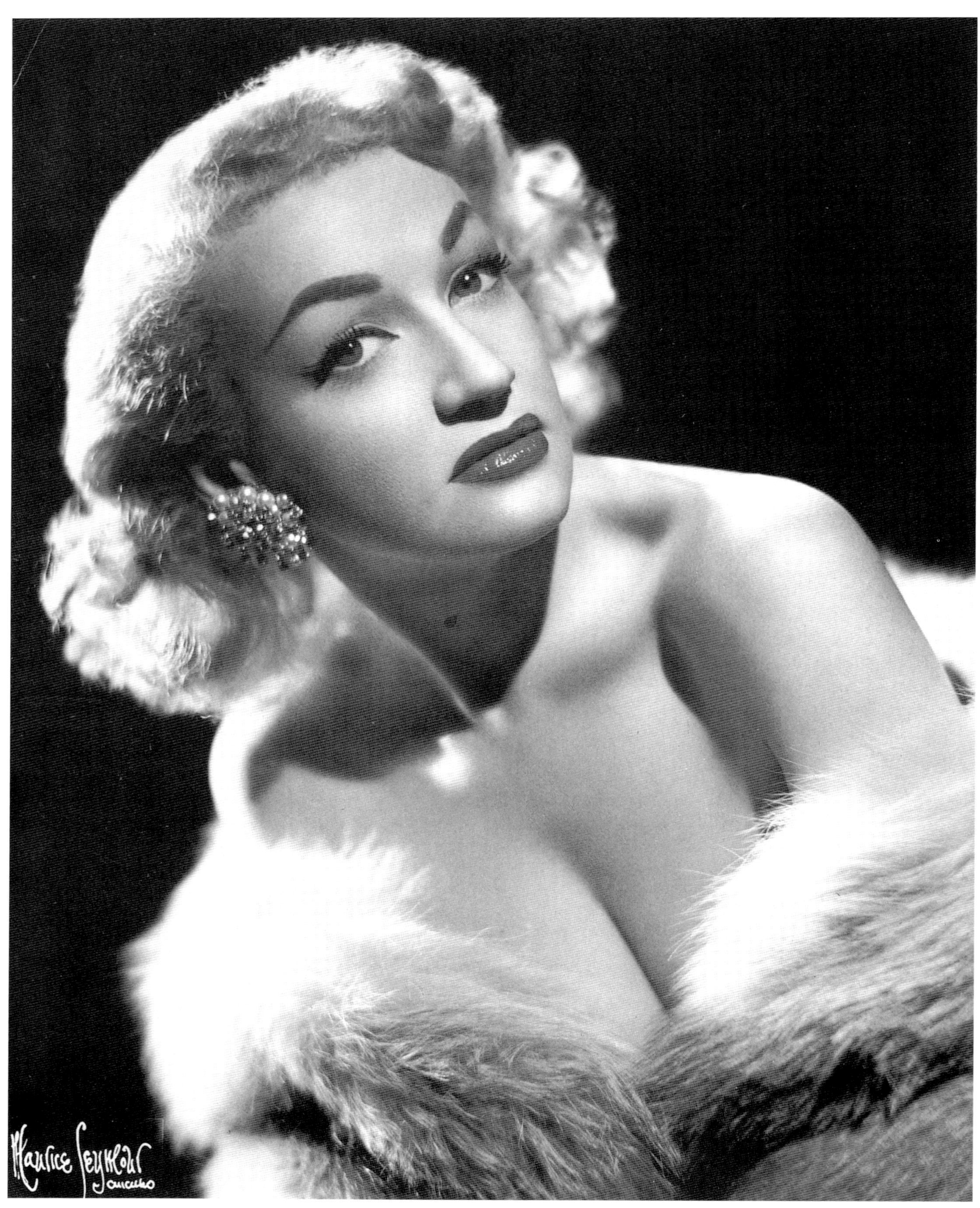

Sheila Ryan
Sheila the Peeler

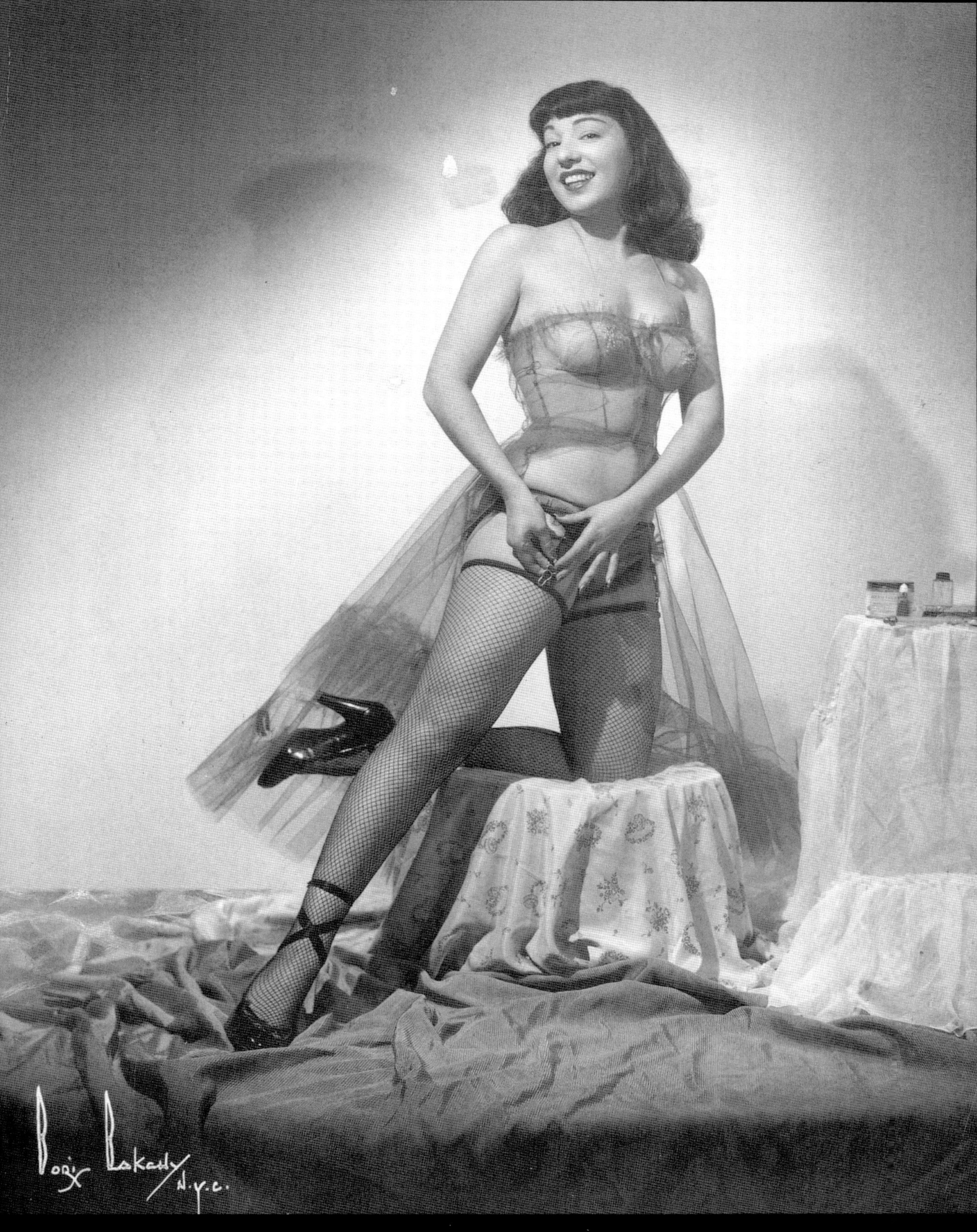

Judith Sargent
The Body of France

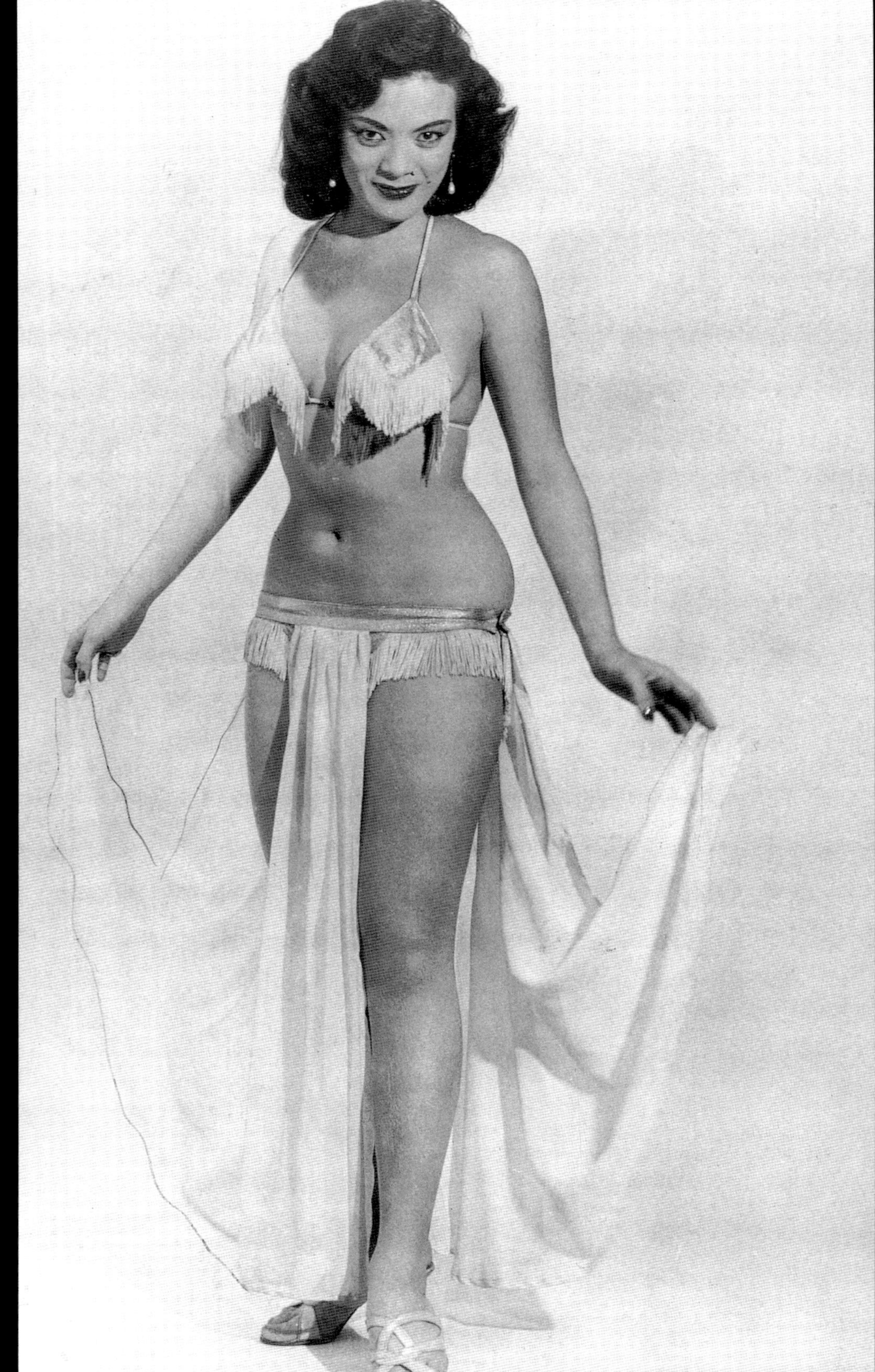

Tura Satana

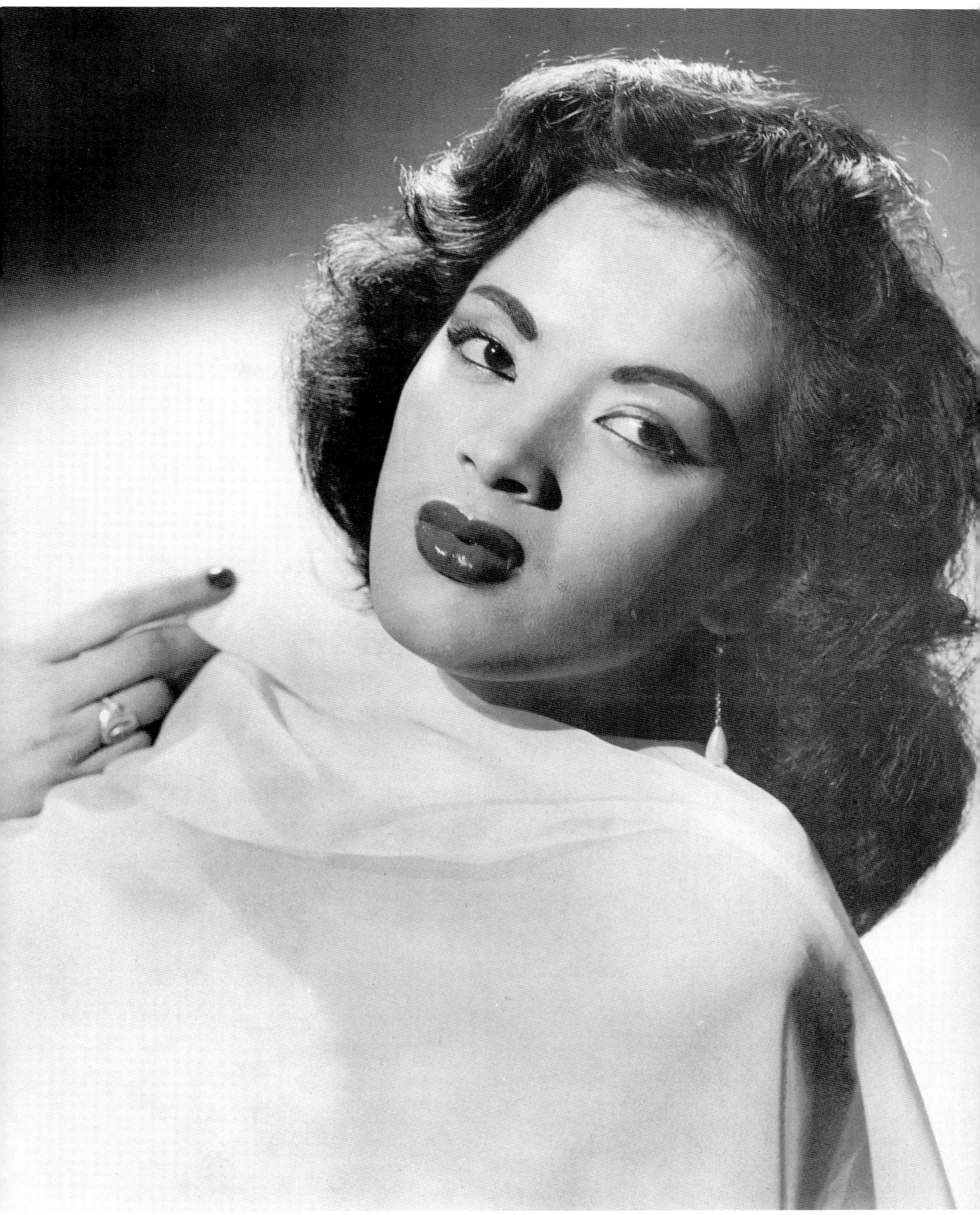

A new art form had been created. The striptease artist had to first develop a walk which would establish the character she was creating for the audience.

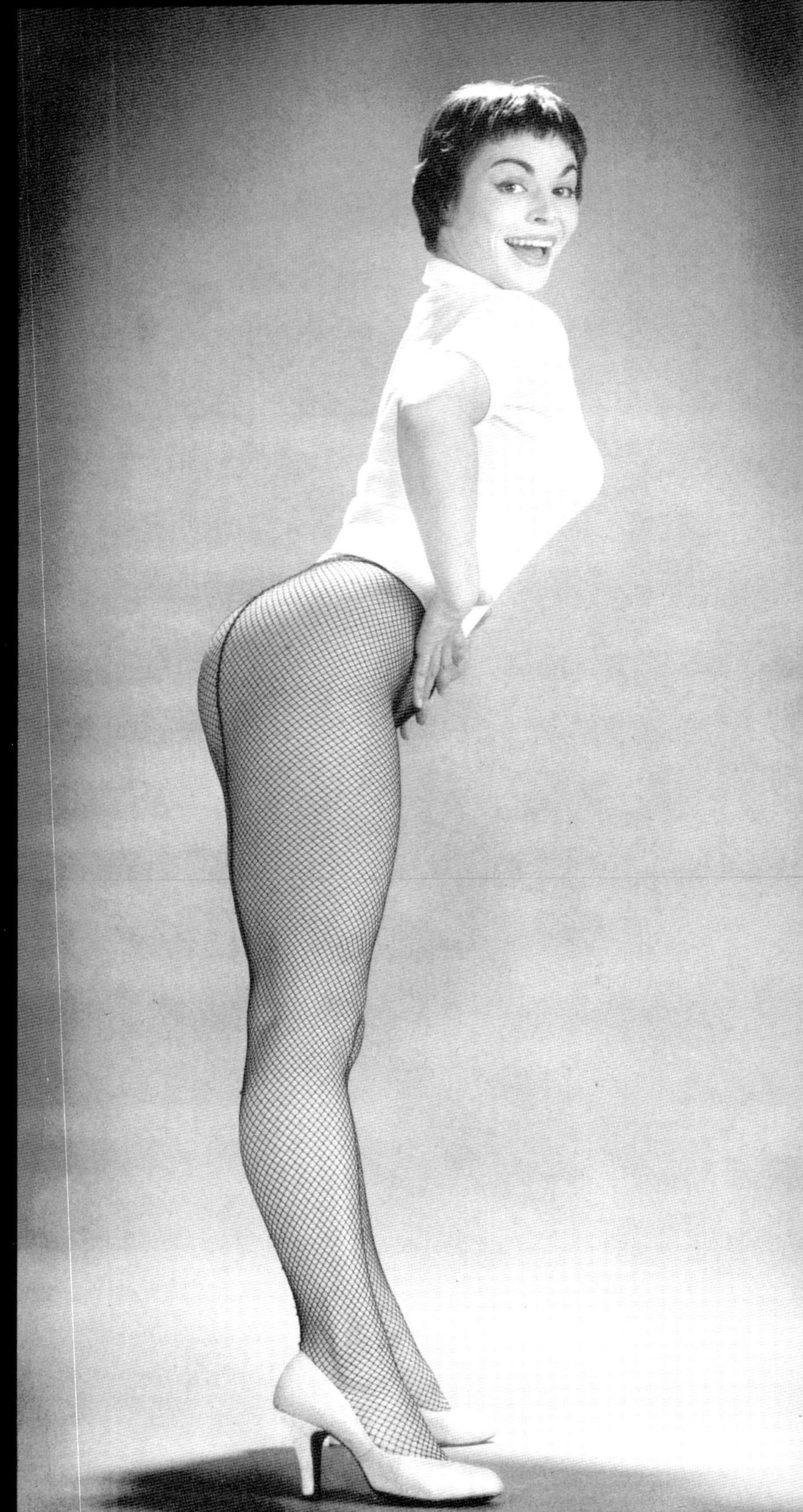

Sparkling...
Sequin
Beauty to the 4th Dimension

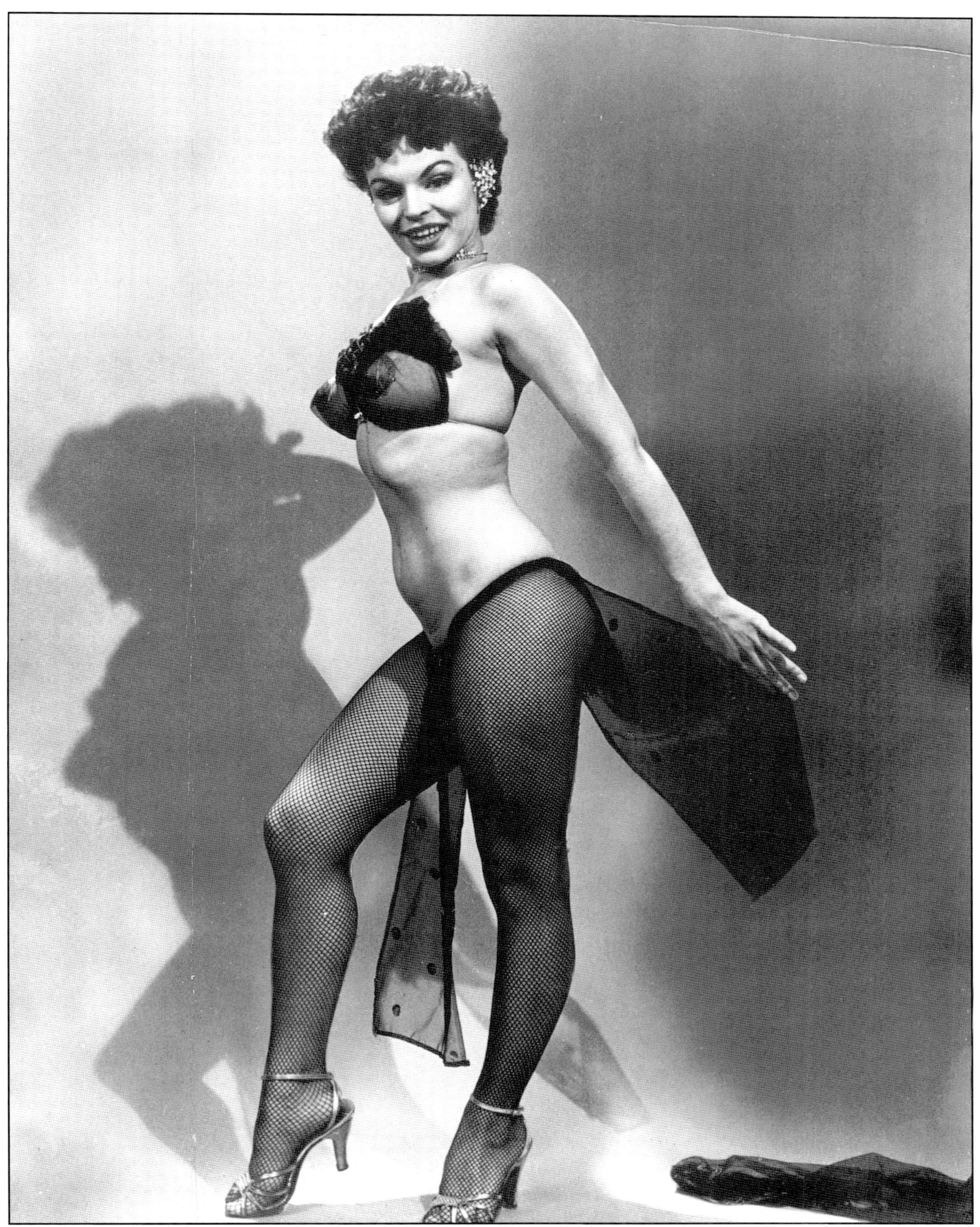

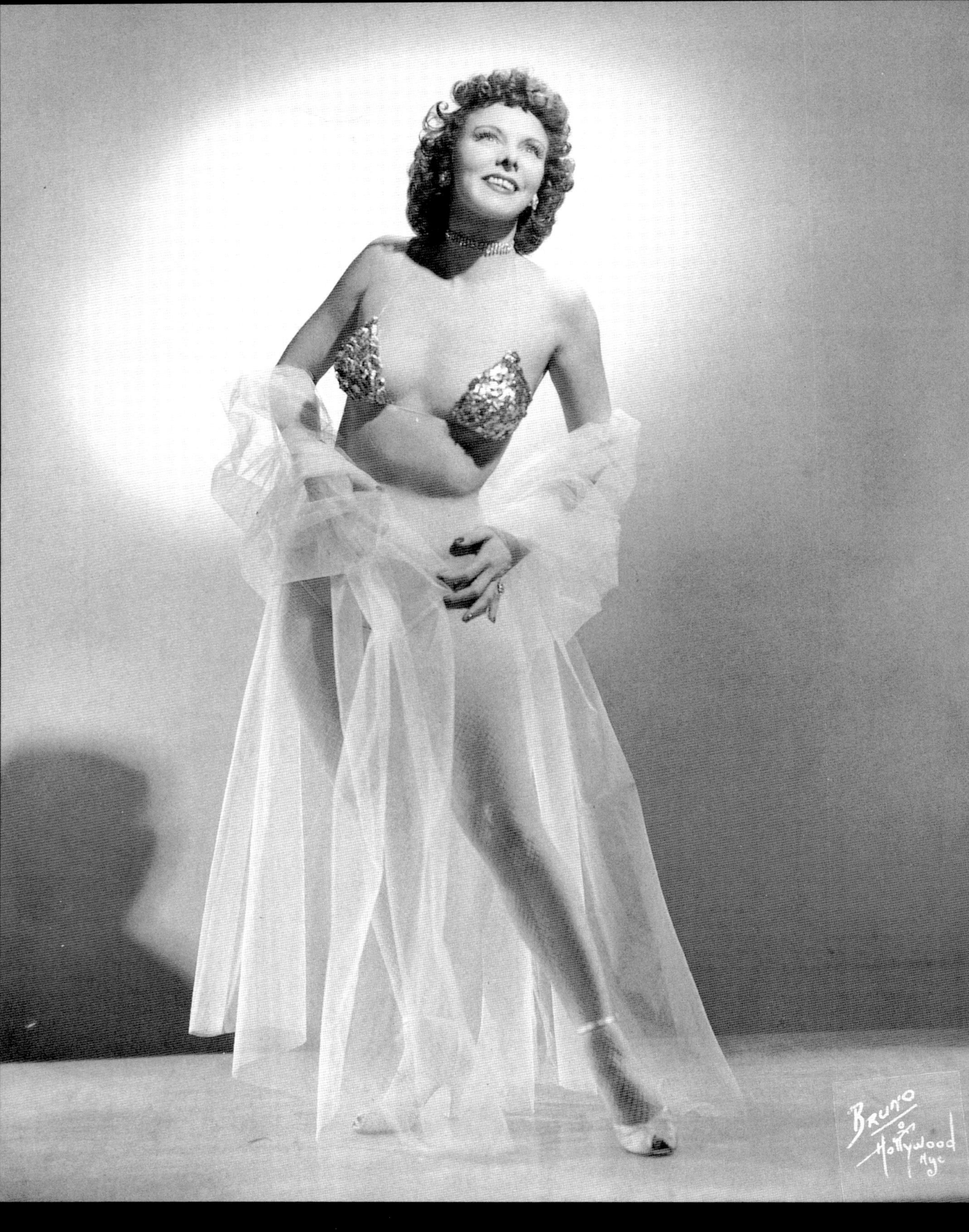

Georgia Sothern

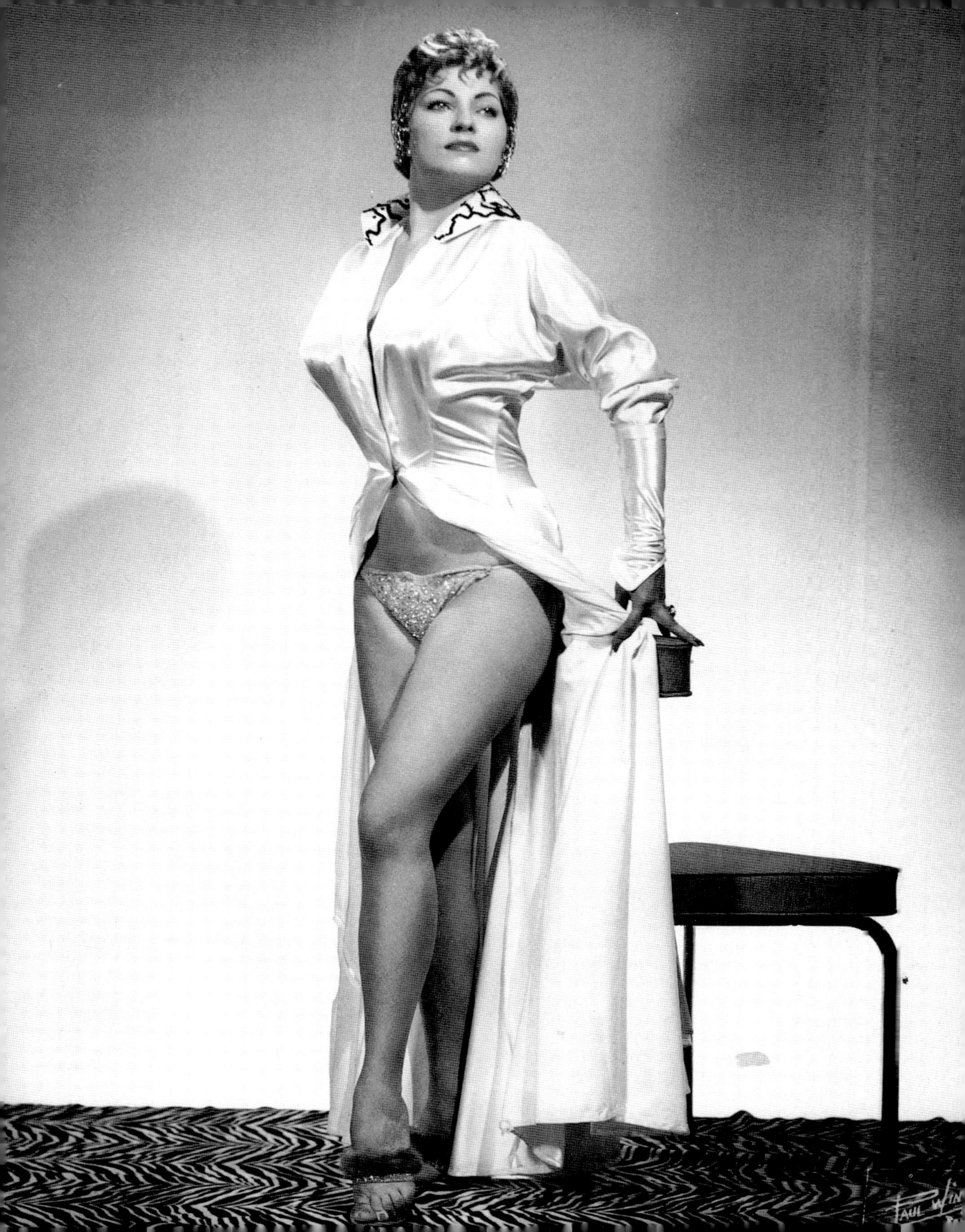
PAUL WIN

...she had to know exactly when to take off what; how much to take off; how much to leave on and what to do for an encore. The way she held her hands was important, they had to be graceful, but not too much so. The thing was the tease. . .

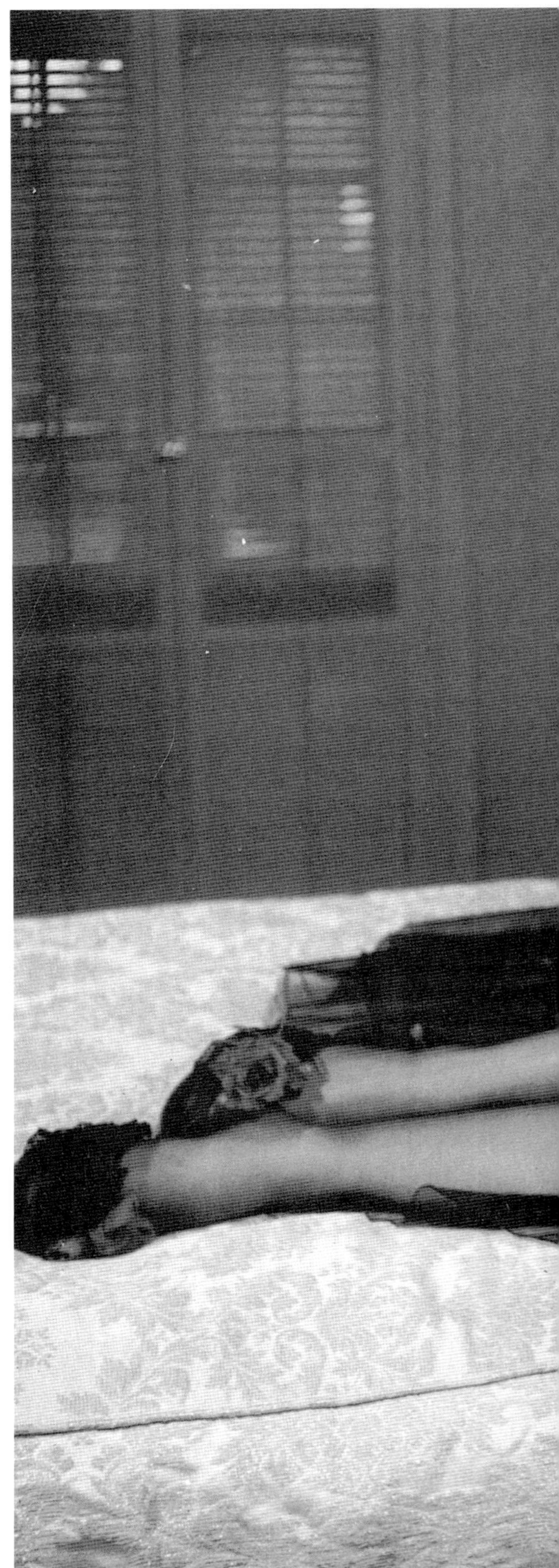

Lili St Cyr

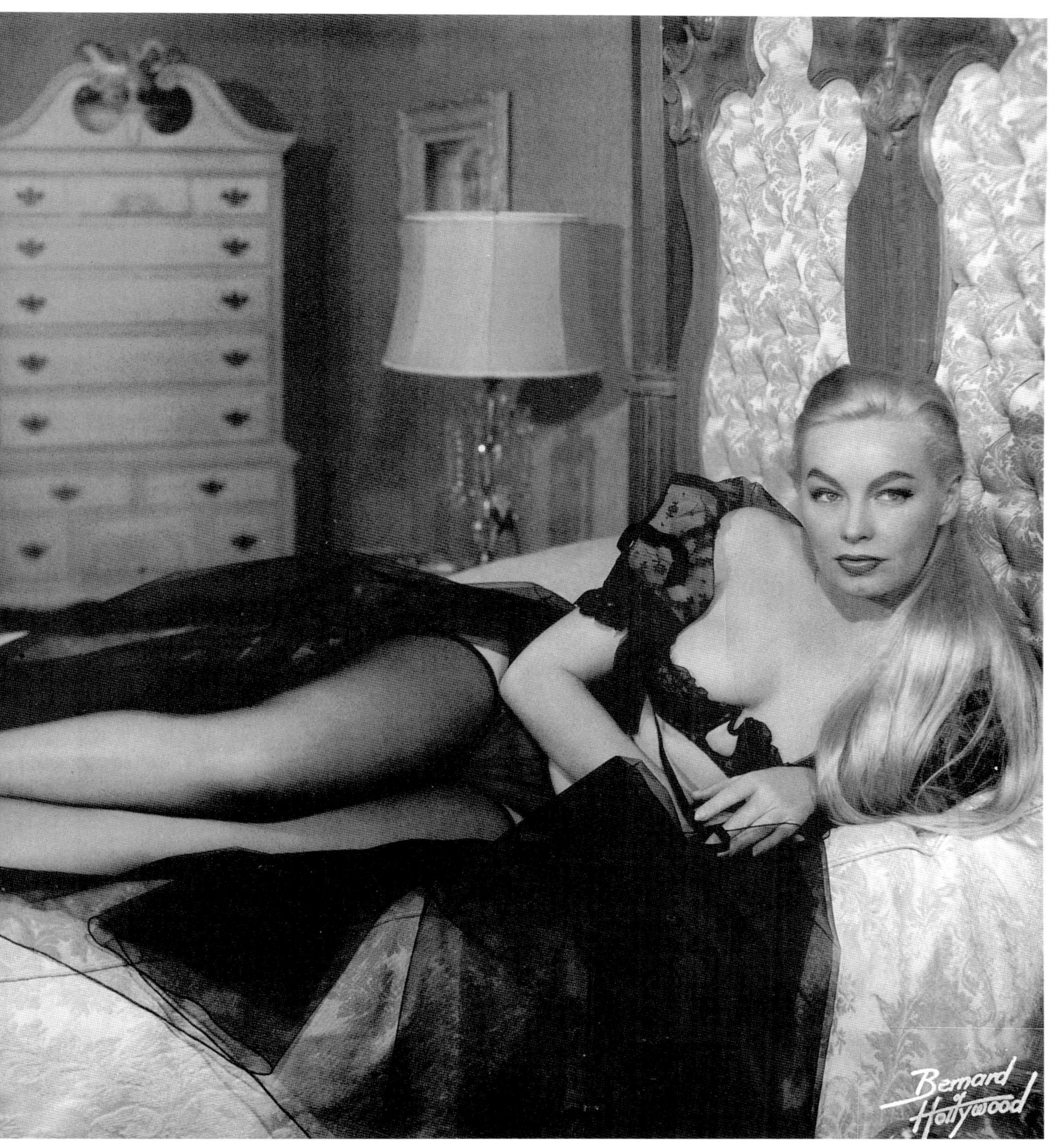
Bernard of Hollywood

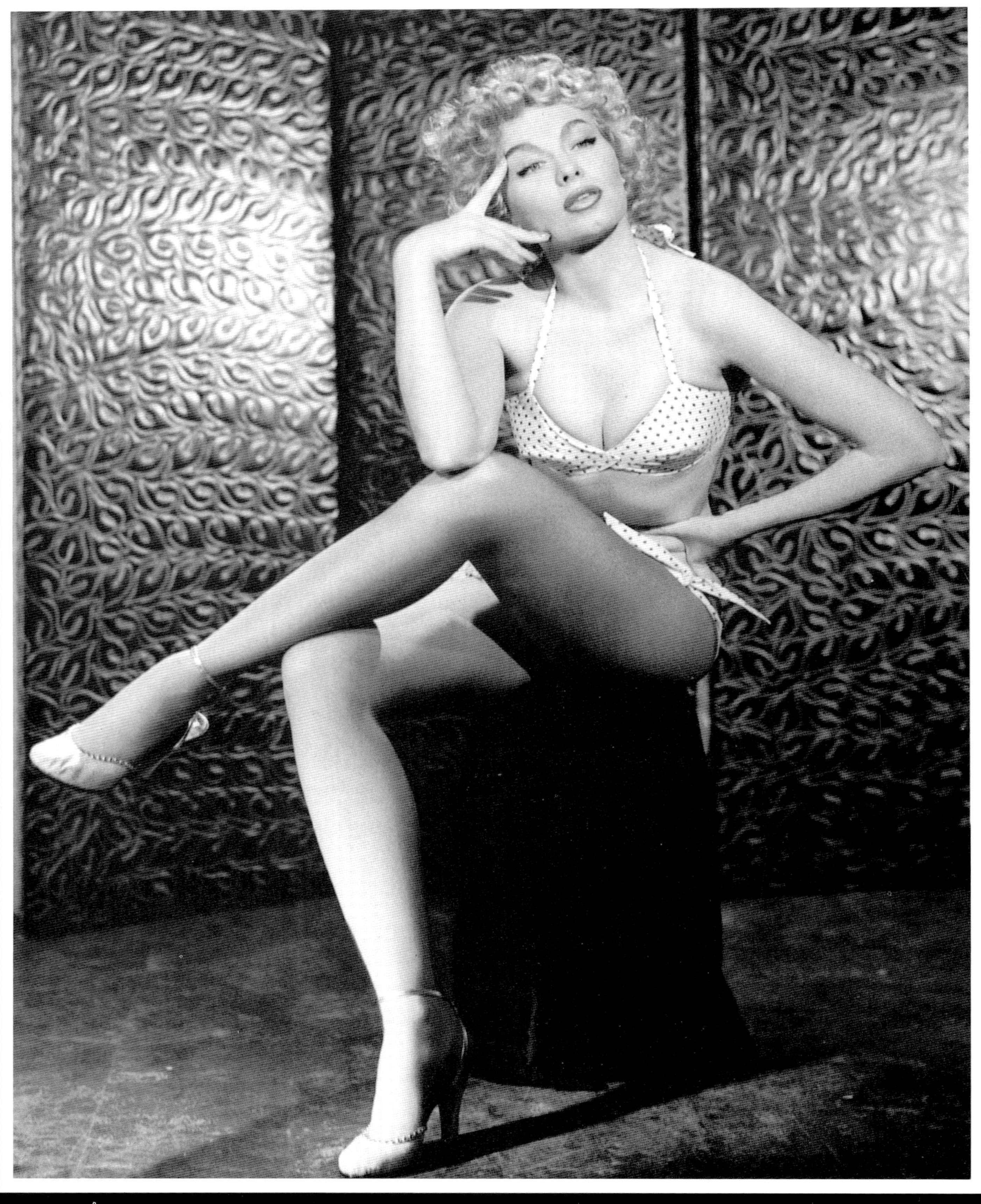

Lili St Cyr

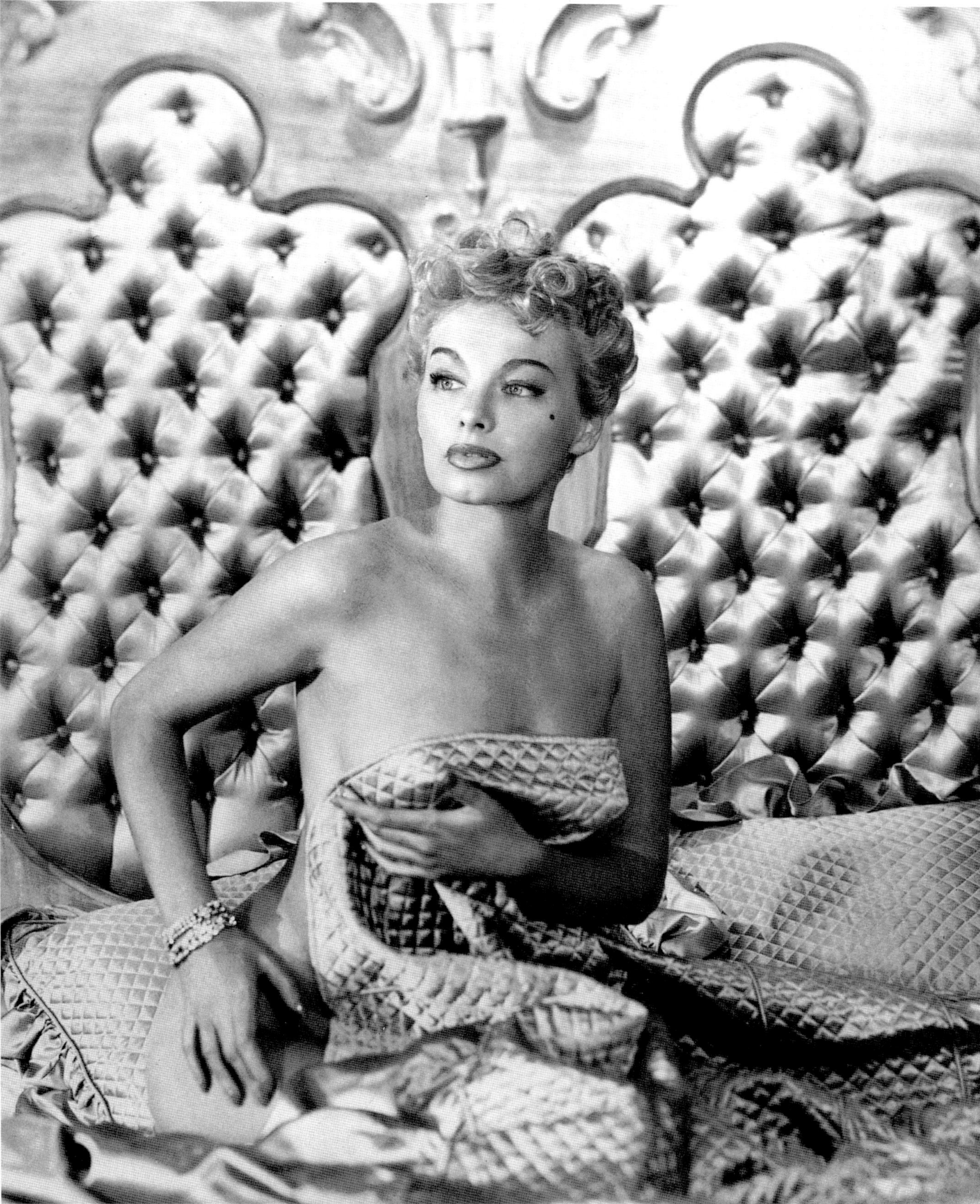

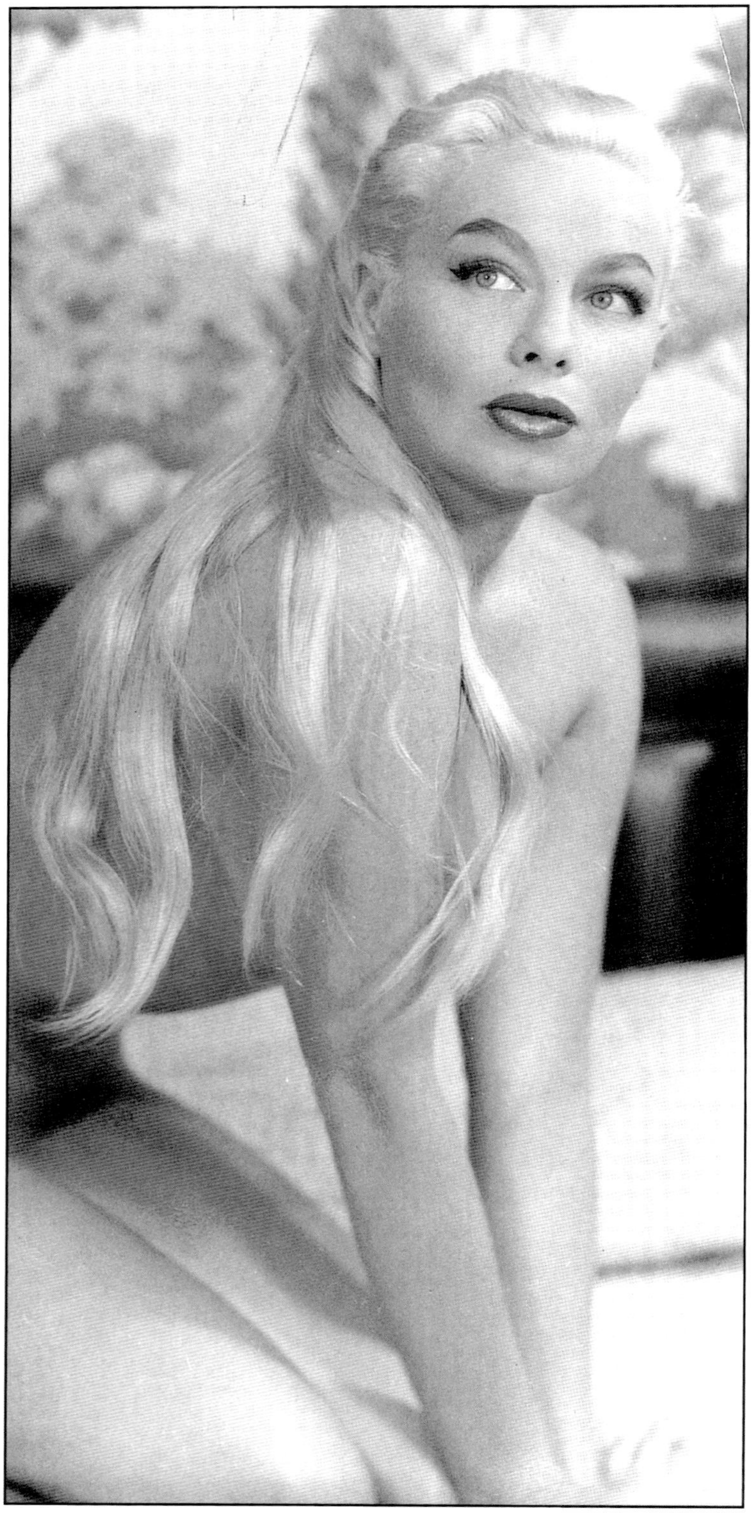

Lili St Cyr

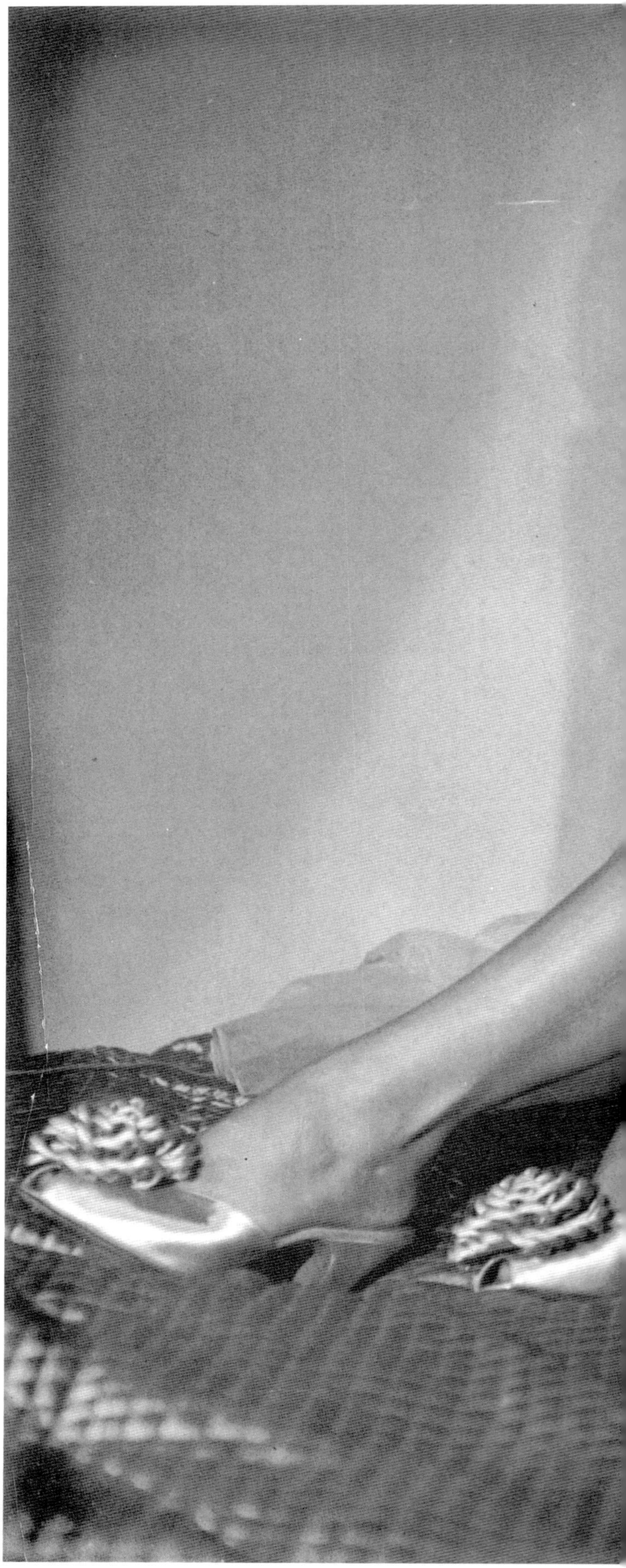

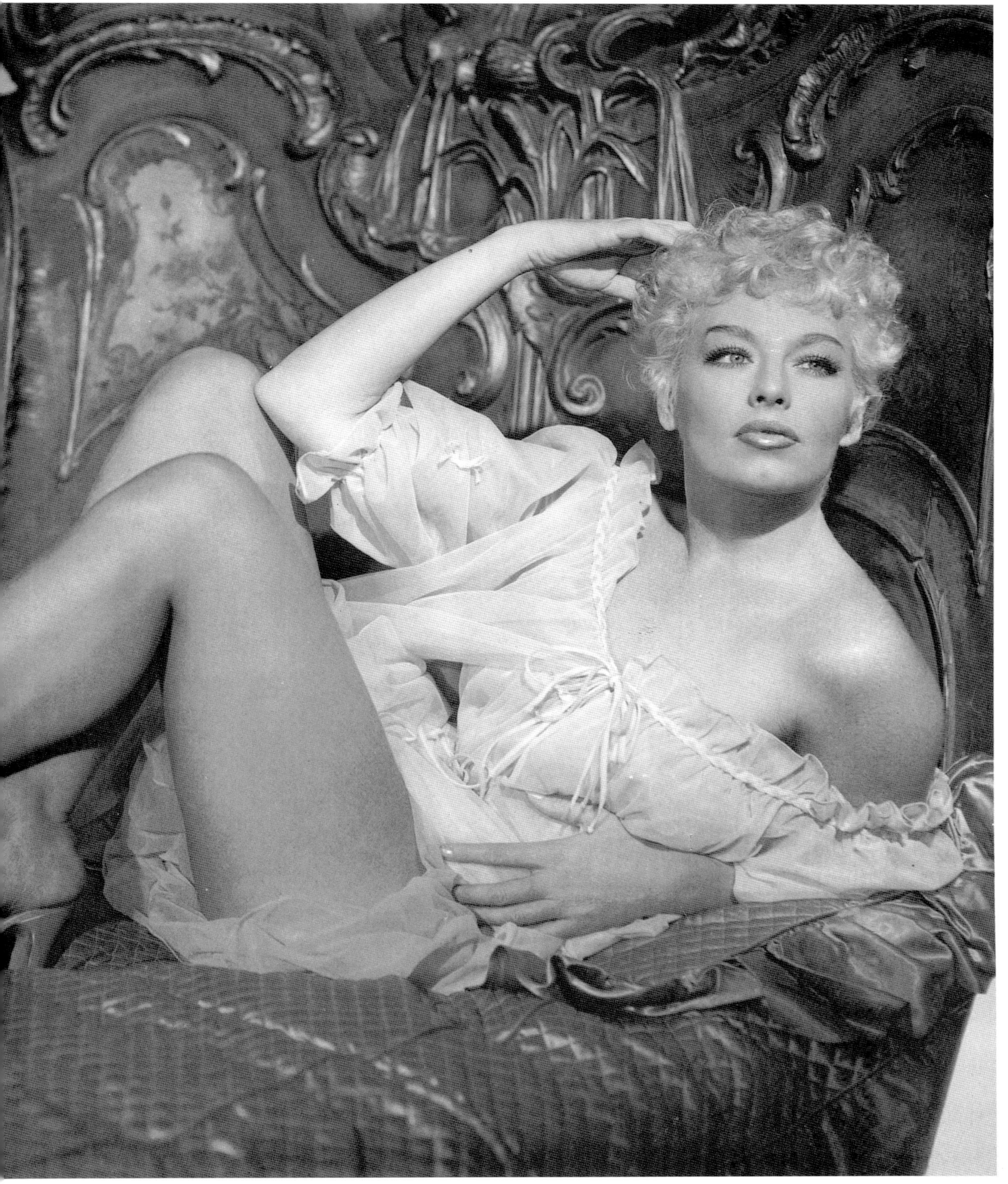

As an Art Form

But burlesque was far more than just chorus girls, comics, and striptease artists. It showcased exceptional talent, brilliant humor, sparkling originality, clever double entendre that made you think, and most of all the magic and genius of having you see what was not really there.

An example of the parody of Burlesque was displayed when Earl Carroll opened his theater with the show *Murder at the Vanities*. The Minsky theater countered with their show *Slaughter at Minsky's*. Among the countless satirical acts created by Minsky were: *Anatomy and Cleopatra*, *Julius Teaser*, *Panties Inferno*, *She Stripped to Conquer*, *The Sway of the Flesh*, *Dress Takes a Holiday*, *Desire Under the El*, *The Shame of La Boheme*, *Follies Brassiere*, *A Broad at Home*, *Boy Needs Girl*, *Tease For Two*, *Wake Up and Give*, *Mind Over Mattress*, *Her Strip Abroad*, and *Strip! Strip! Hooray*, to name but a few.

The typical burlesque show followed a standard format. After a full orchestra played music to hush the anxiously waiting audience, the curtain would open to a sprightly chorus line of dancing and kicking cuties. Their performance would be quickly followed by a comic team doing a familiar bit, to again bring the raucous house under control. Next, and catering to the more erudite in the audience, a serious singer, usually with an operatic selection, would add to the show. Before the audience got too upset with the serious interlude, a *cooch dancer* (one who could do contortions or gyrations) or, in some cases a *shimmy dancer* would remind the crowd of what was yet to come. A short dramatic sketch would again slow the pace before the exuberant chorus girls did another routine. This was an appropriate introduction for the *soubrette*. A comedy scene next made the audience quiet down so as not to miss any of their laugh lines. The first half of the show would usually end with a team of acrobats demonstrating what amazing feats the male body was capable of.

After an intermission, the second-half began, pretty much following along the lines of the first-half, but shorter. Now, instead of the *soubrette*, the headline stripteaser gave the audience approximately seven minutes of sheer art and fantasy. This performance would seem like a minute or two to the audience, so great was their pleasure. This was what the audience had come to see, judge, and fantasize about, until the next week's performer changed their minds.

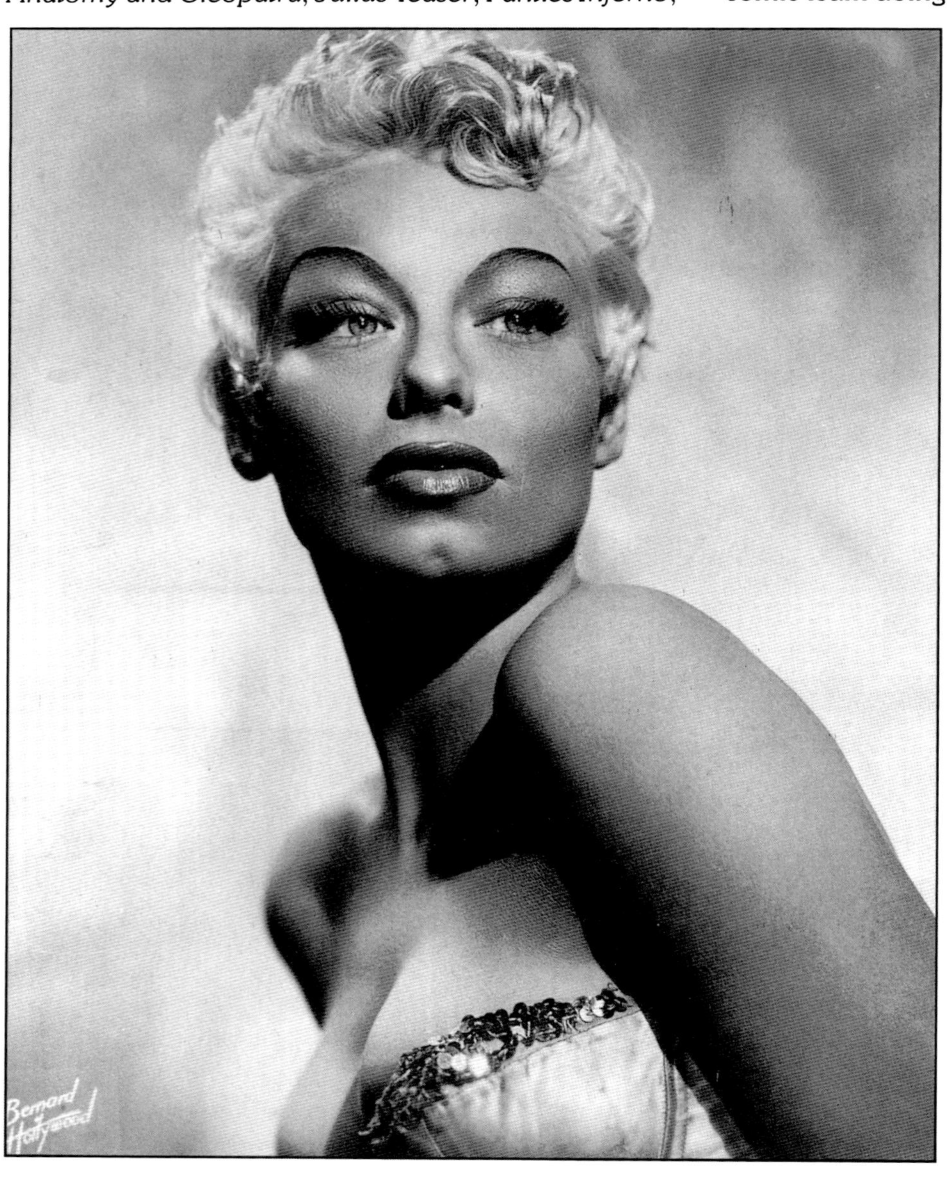

Lili St Cyr

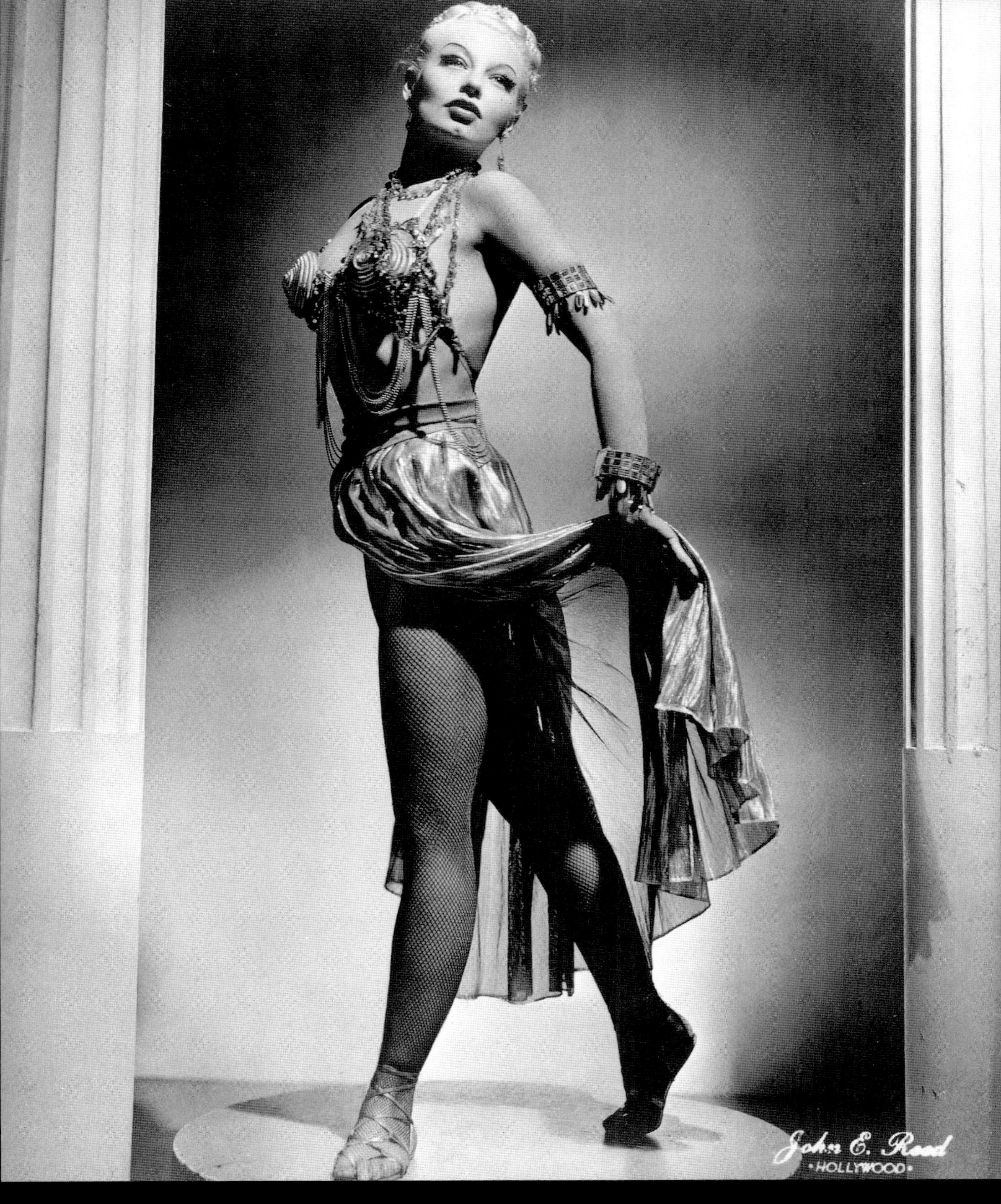

Lili St Cyr

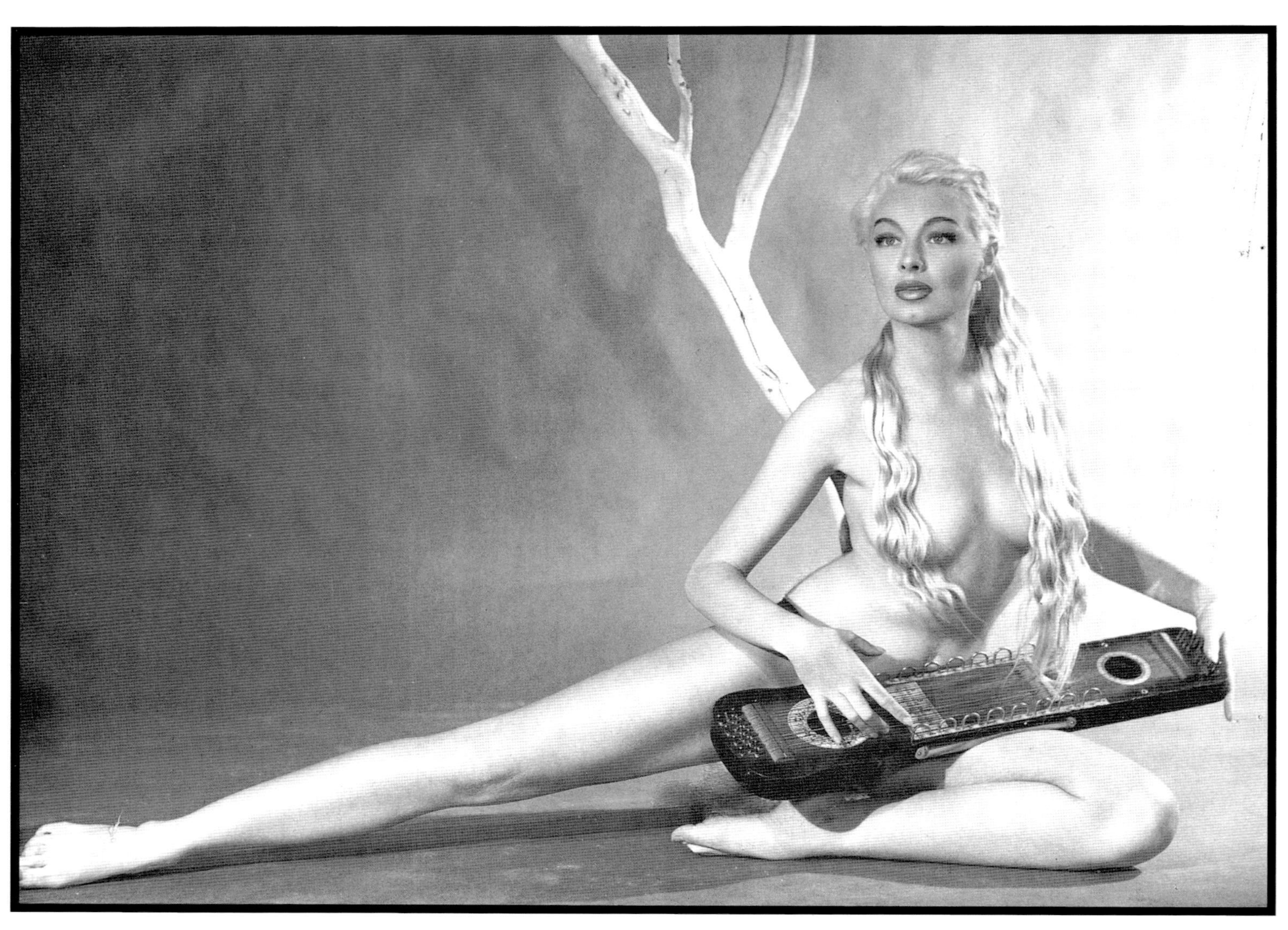

Lili St Cyr

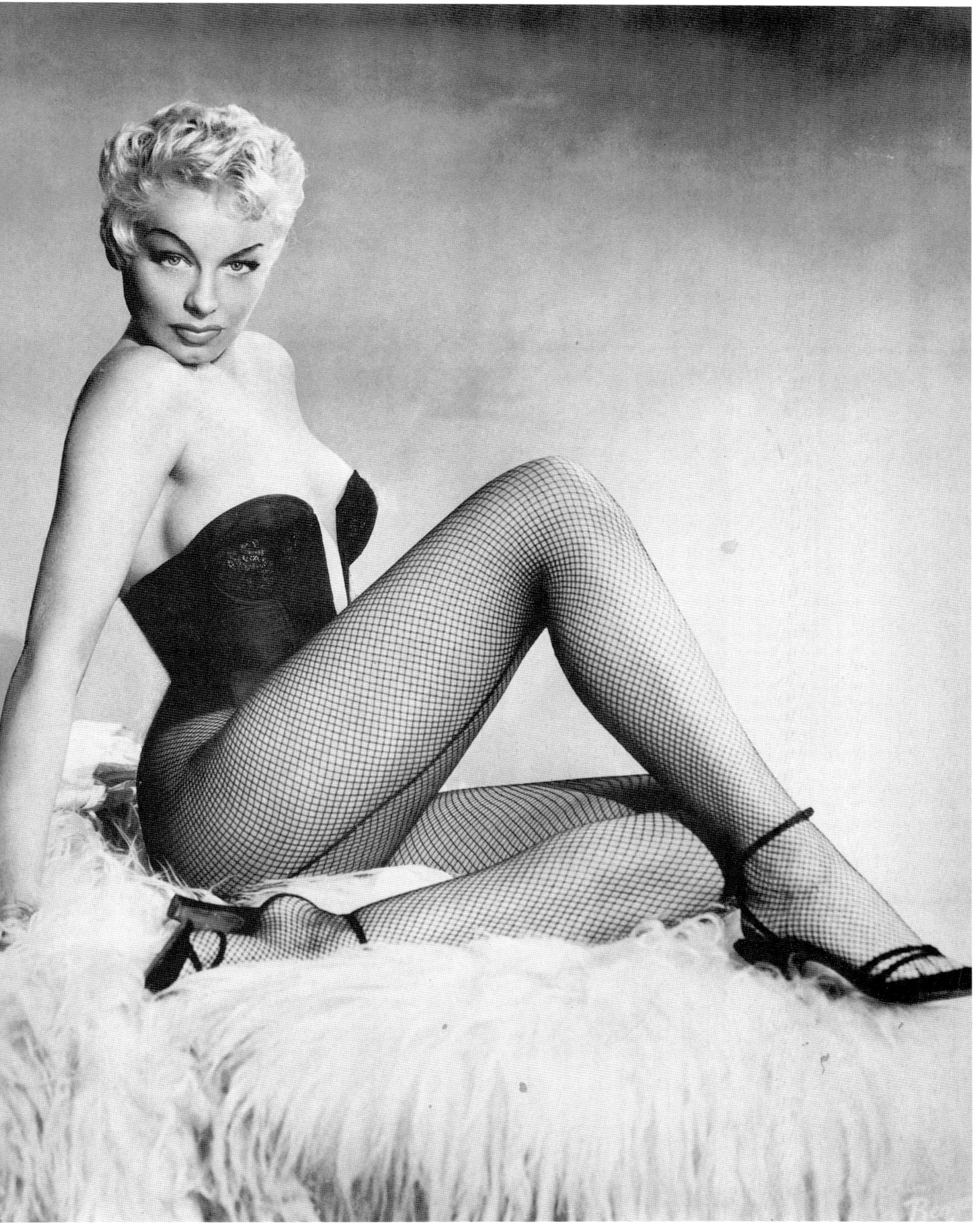

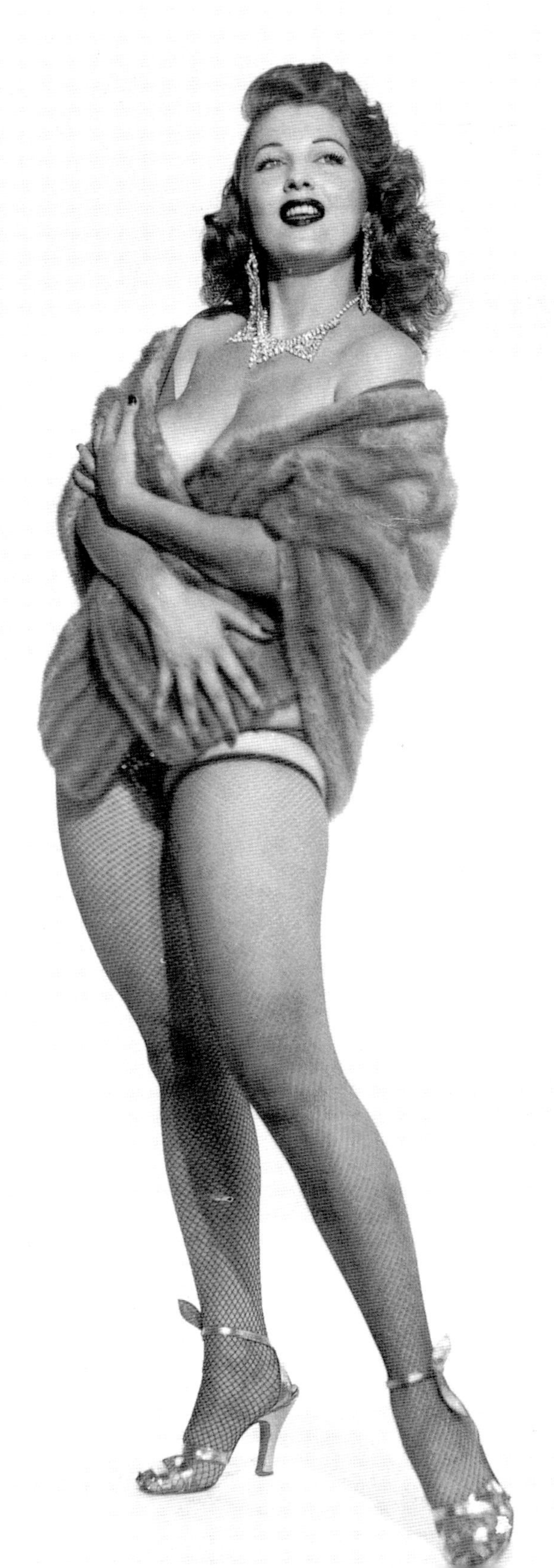

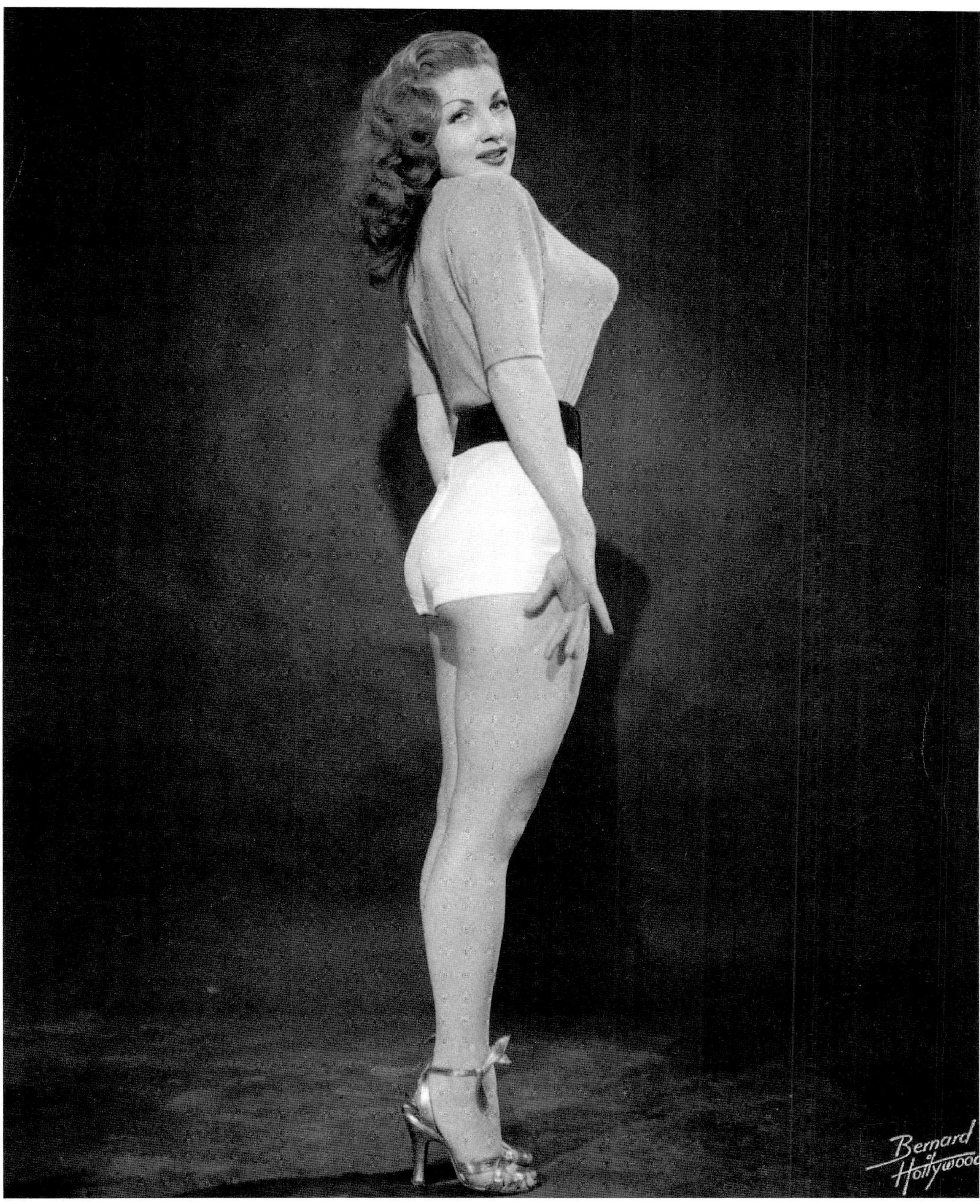
Bernard
of
Hollywood

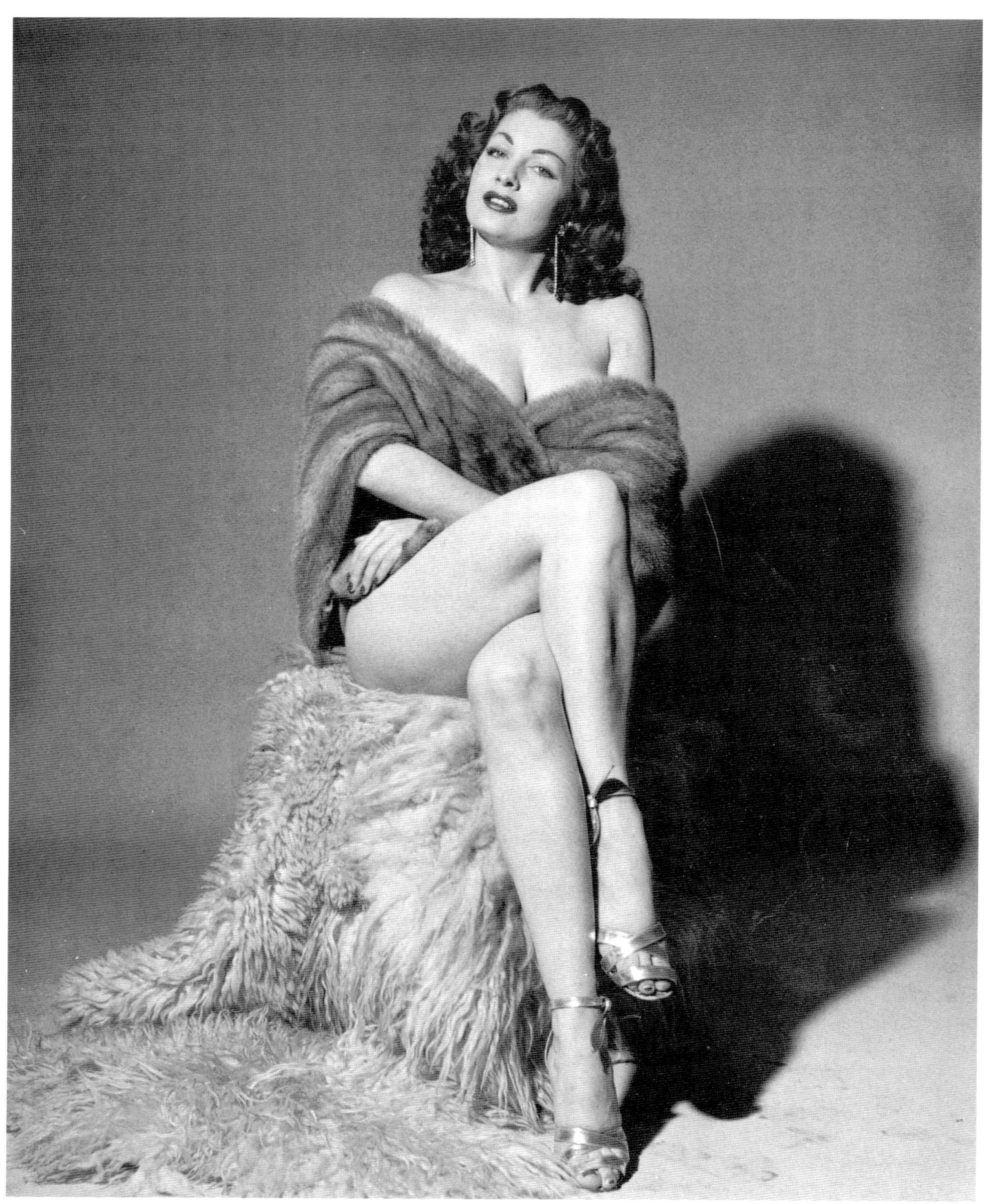

Tempest Storm

...the headline stripteaser gave the audience approximately seven minutes of sheer art and fantasy. This performance would seem like a minute or two to the audience,...

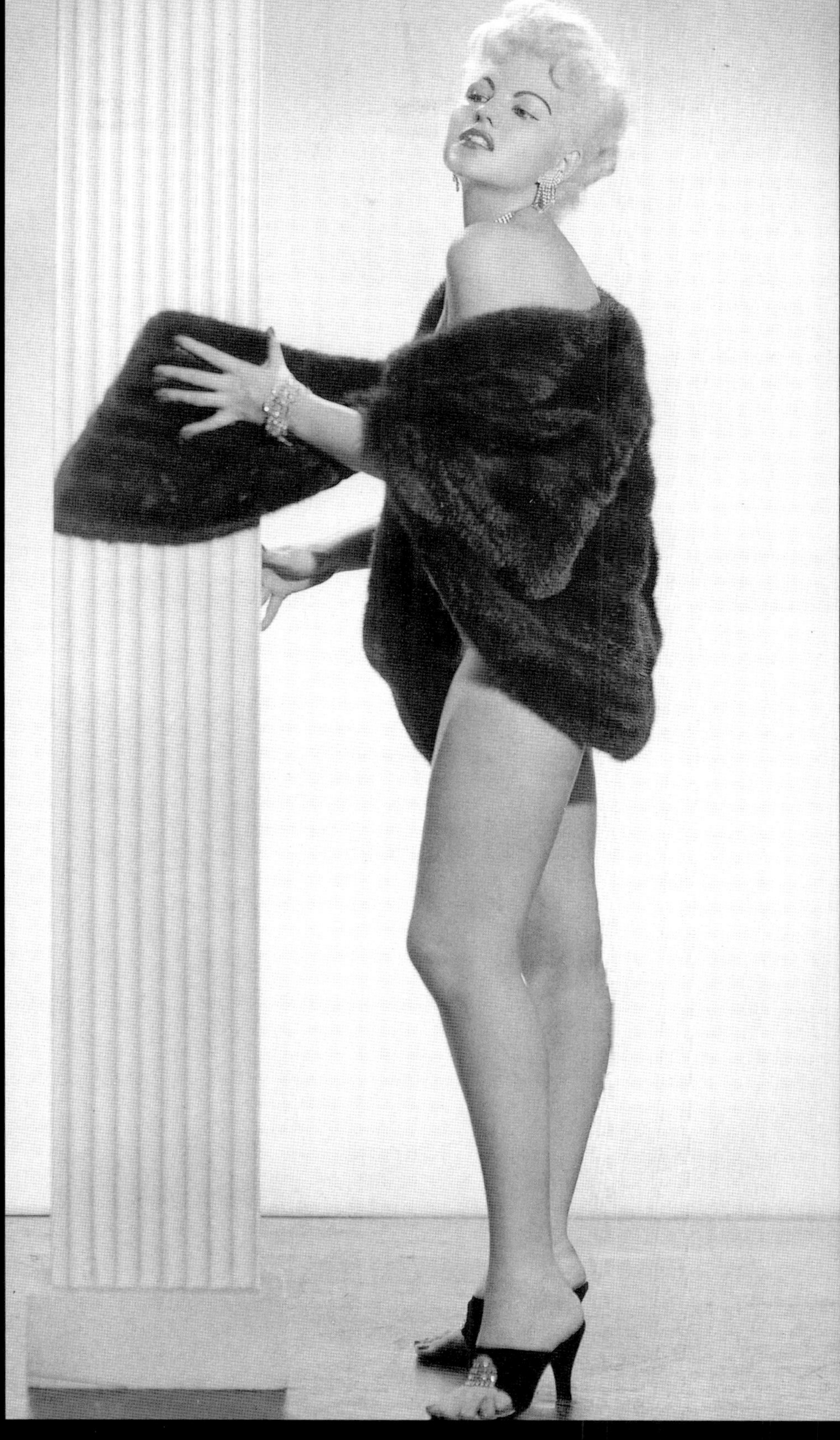

Robin Sweet
The Newest Body in Burlesque

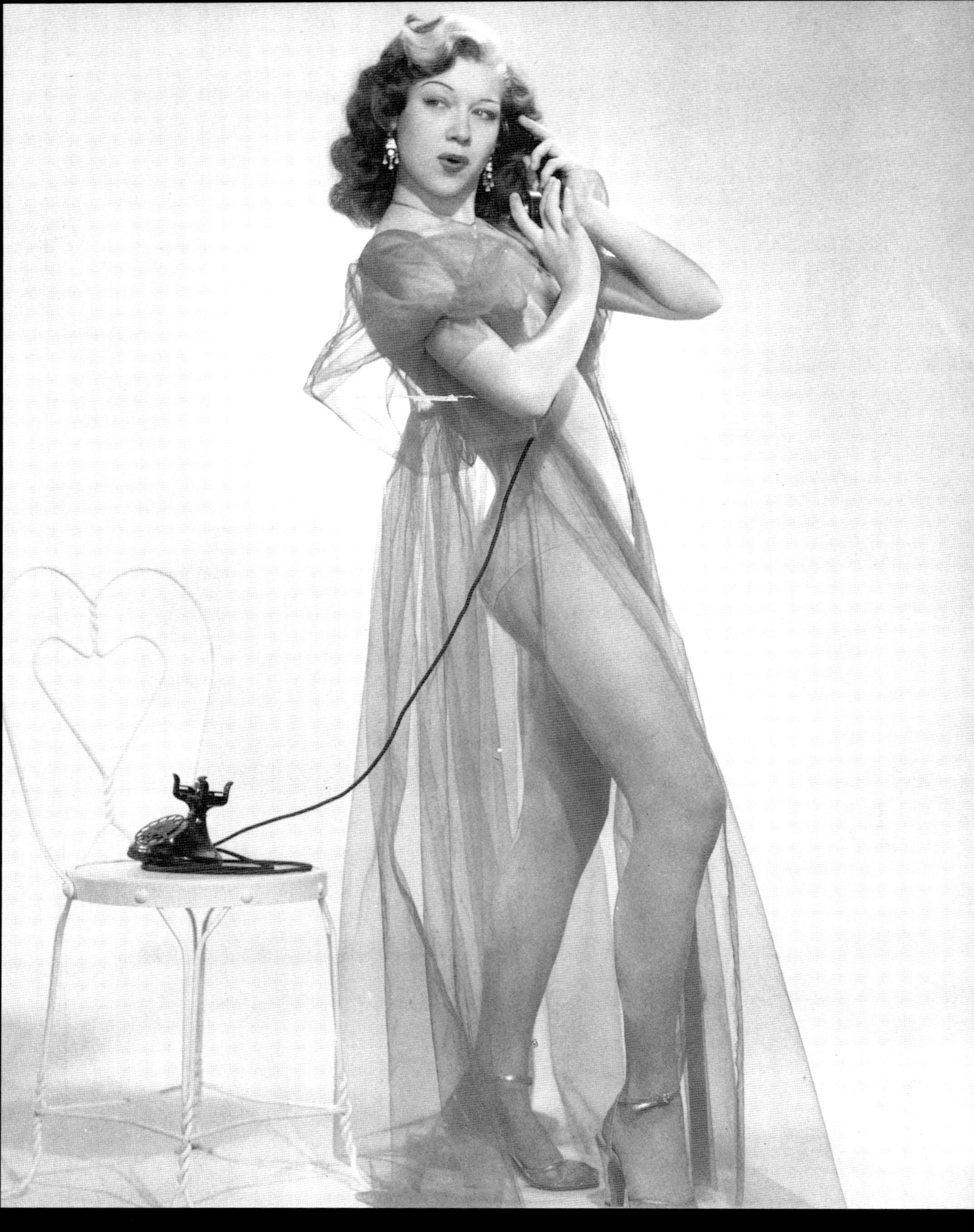

The Sultry Siren of...
Thunder

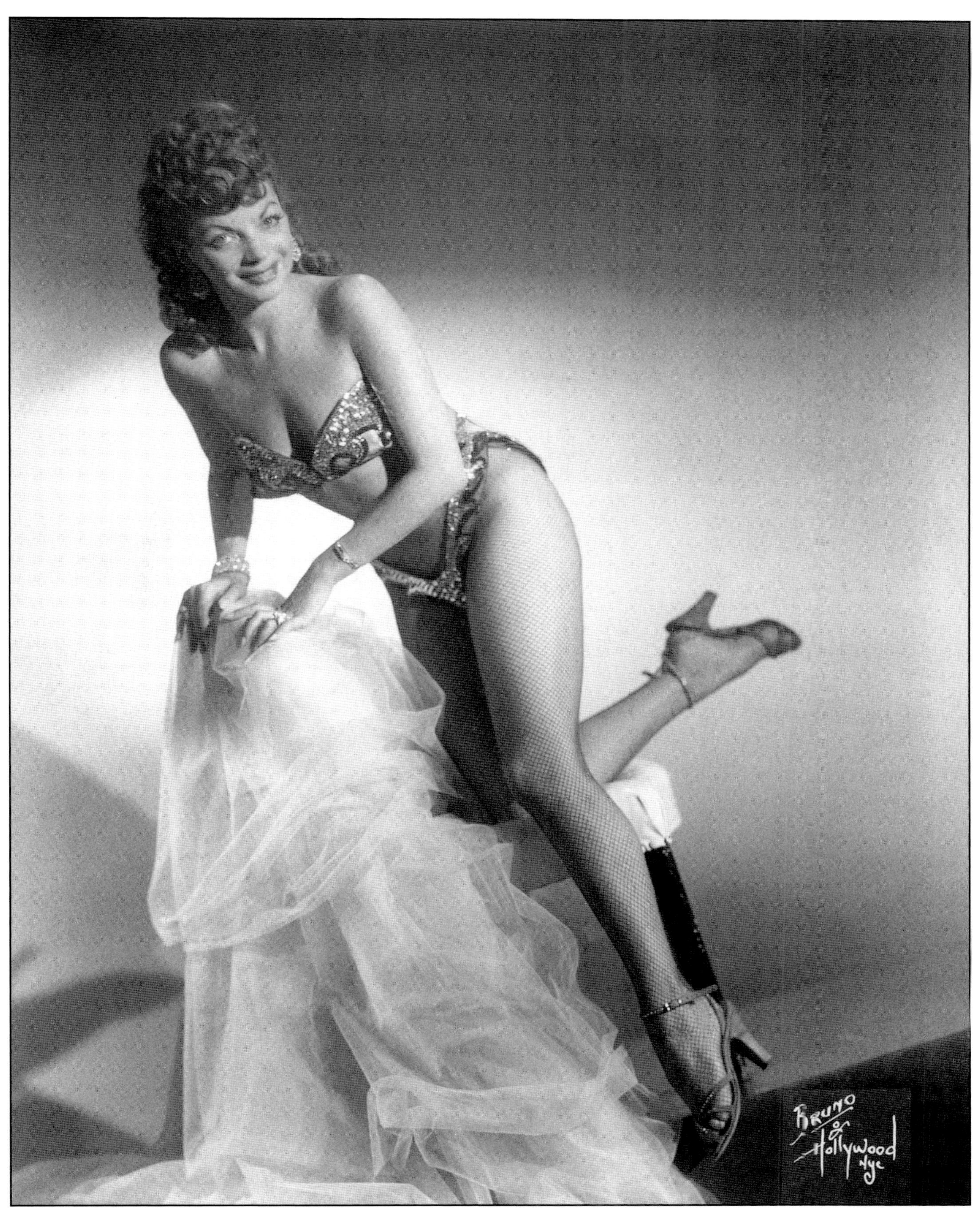

Trudine

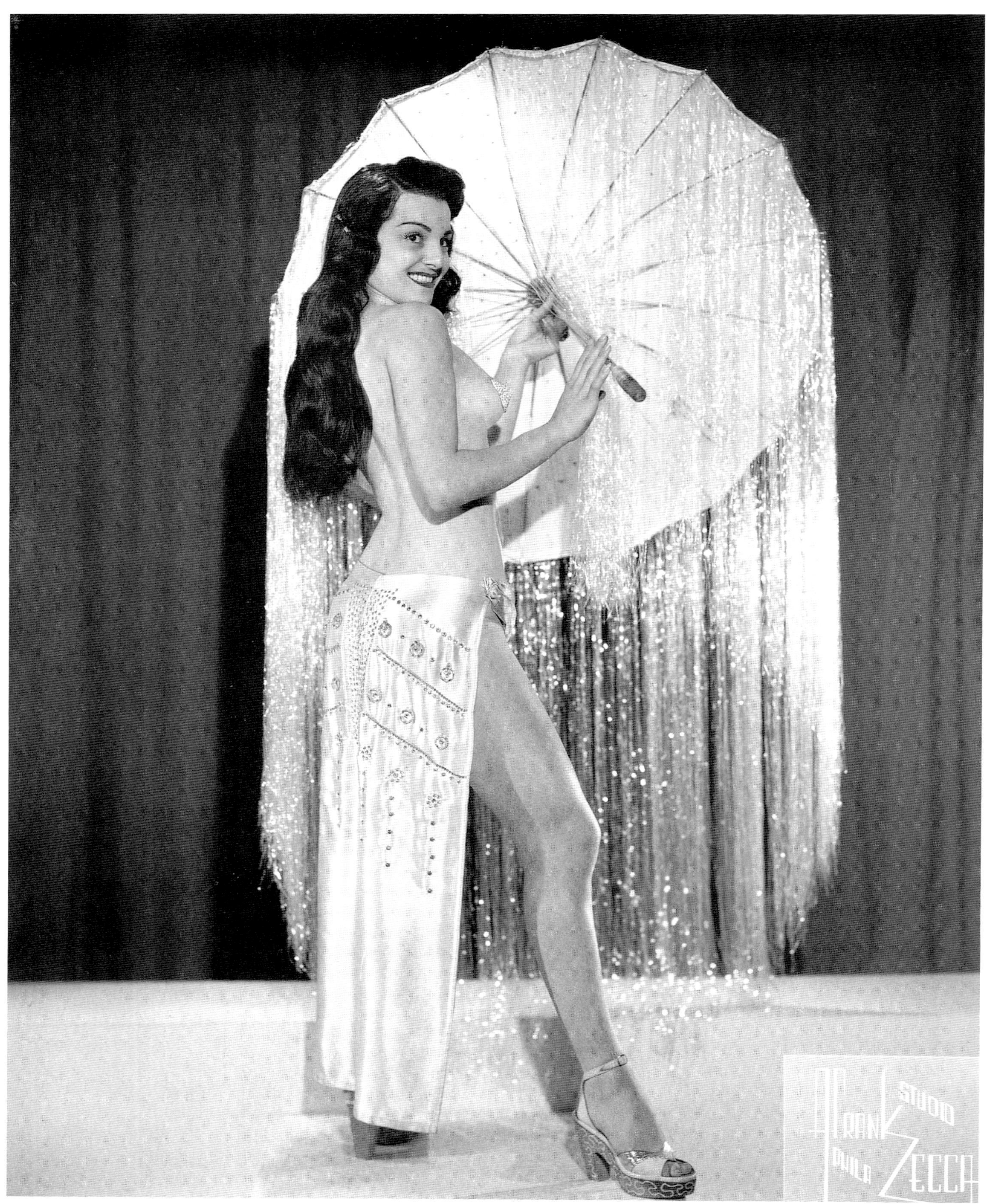

Jan Tiffany

Socially Speaking

Time and circumstances played a large part in the bare truth about Burlesque. The American government's prohibition of the sale of alcoholic beverages had proven to be the great leveler of the classes in America. Rich "uptowners" began coming downtown for their "kicks," mistakenly believing they would not be seen by their upper-class friends. But their friends were also "slumming" (going down to the slums), which was the common thing to do and Minsky 's theater was the place to meet the people they formerly tried to avoid. Some of the best "speakeasies" (illegal bars for illegal alcohol) in the city were only a few hundred yards from Minsky's theater.

While the Prohibition era and the Great Depression were both creating the social conditions of the 1930s, average people had an awful lot of free time on their hands, very little money, and little pleasure in their life. Thus, Burlesque entertainment and cheap booze became the escapes they sought from the cruel, hard world outside the bars and theaters. It was a world in which there were no jobs to be had, breadlines stretched for blocks, apple peddlers were on every corner, and depressed men walked the streets day and night. Where, but at Minsky's, could you see four hours of continuous entertainment with comics, sex, and sometimes even a movie for a seventy -five cents? Broadway shows, at the time, were charging $5.50 for less show.

This was a time when the words "hell" and "damn" were considered offensive, and the classic novel by James Joyce, *Ulysses*, was banned for being immoral and obscene, and was called unfit for American readers.

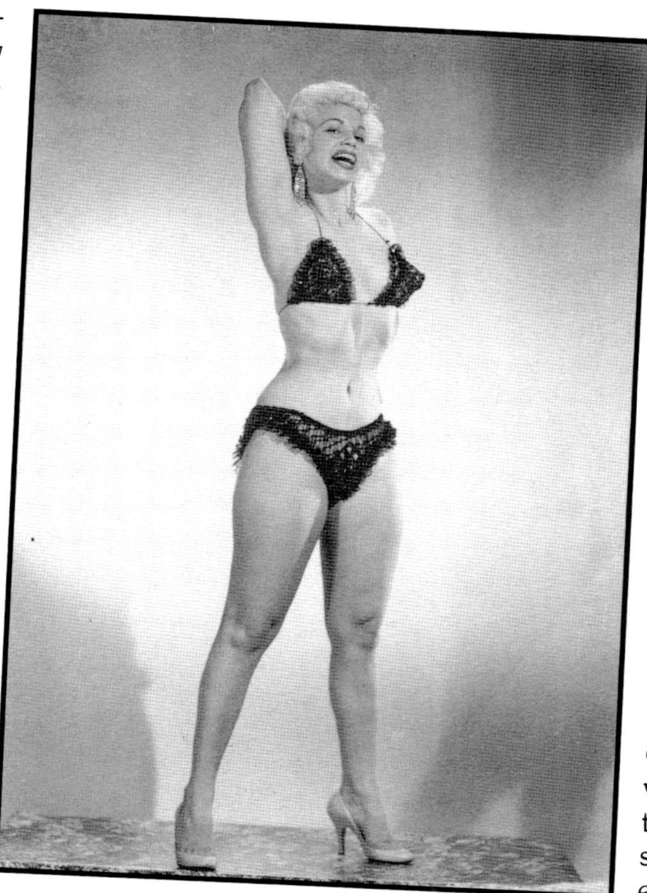

Diamond Carol

The Bare Truth about Burlesque is that it was a lot less nude and raw than what we can see today on Broadway or Off-Broadway, in the movies or on television. Burlesque used the promise of nudity, plus a lot of suggestion and illusion to titillate but never showed full frontal nudity. Striptease, was first a part of the story in the opera *Salome*. Today, you see more of the female body on any beach in America than you could see at the "indecent and immoral" burlesque houses of yesterday. Occasionally we are reminded of our moral heritage. Ever since the first Puritans came ashore at Plymouth Rock, with deep religious fervor, the code of morality for Americans has not been determined by the people, but by both their religious leaders, who wished to enforce their standards of taste, and by politicians, who feared that condemnation by religious leaders would ruin their chances of getting re-elected. Hypocrisy runs rampant throughout our moral history. Self-appointed critics and censors, who practice apparent propriety and conventional morality in their public lives, often practice a different standard of morality in their private lives. History has taught us what one era considers filthy another considers barely suggestive.

The astute writer H. L. Mencken, in an *American Mercury* article in 1934, described the situation well when he wrote, "If you get three Americans in one place, two will get together to reform the morals of the third."

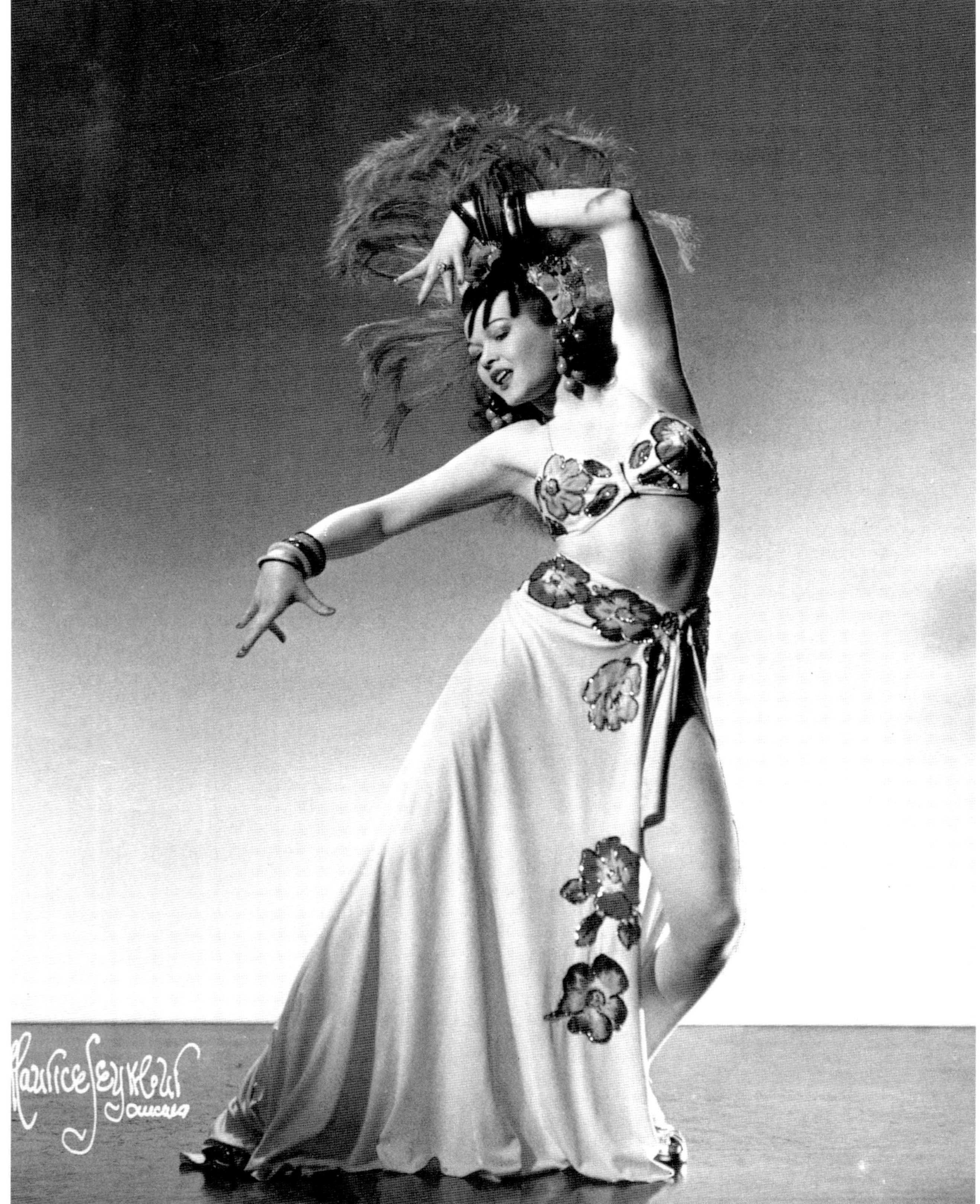
Maurice Seymour

This was a time when the words "hell" and "damn" were considered offensive, and the classic novel by James Joyce, *Ulysses*, was banned for being immoral and obscene...

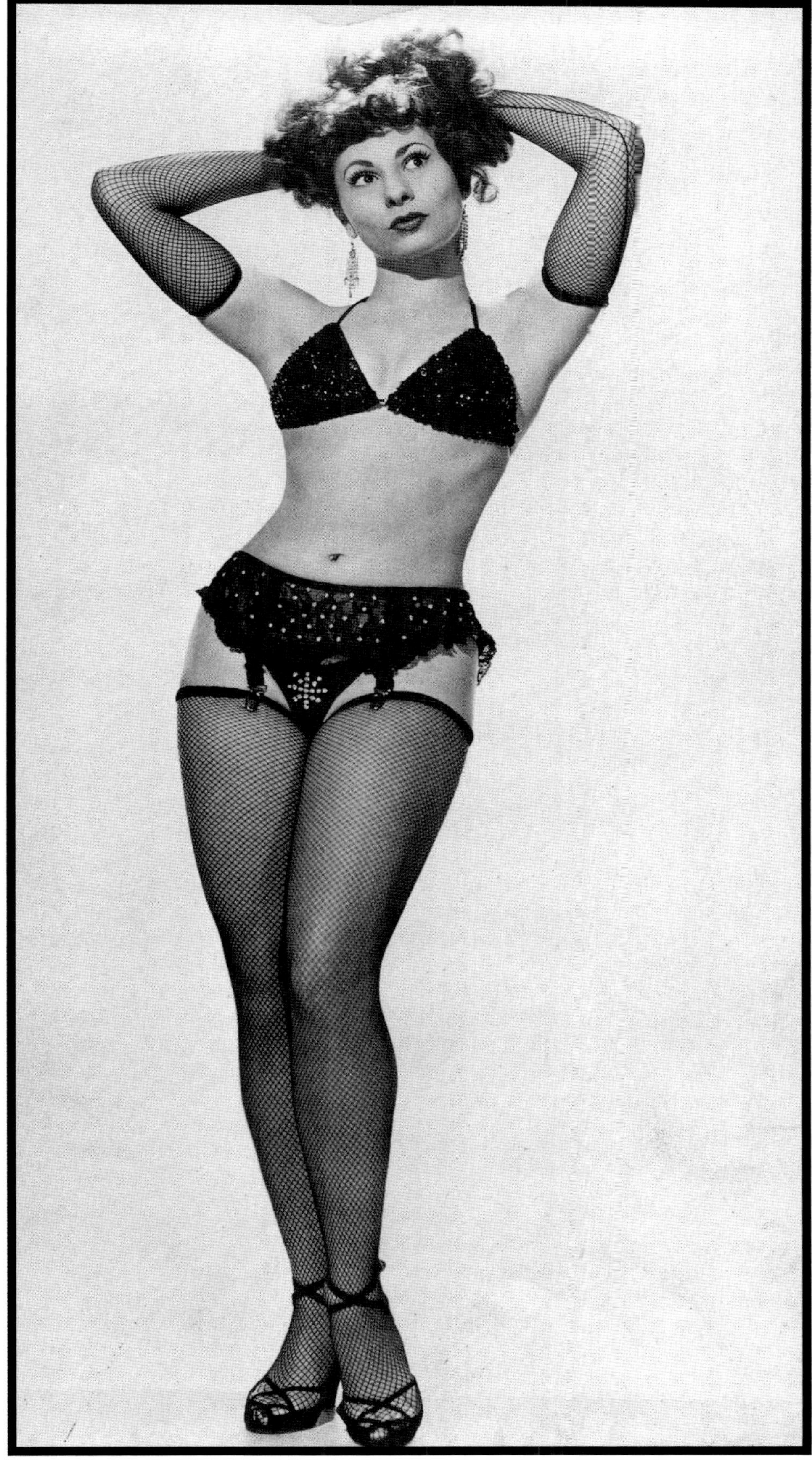

Patti Waggin

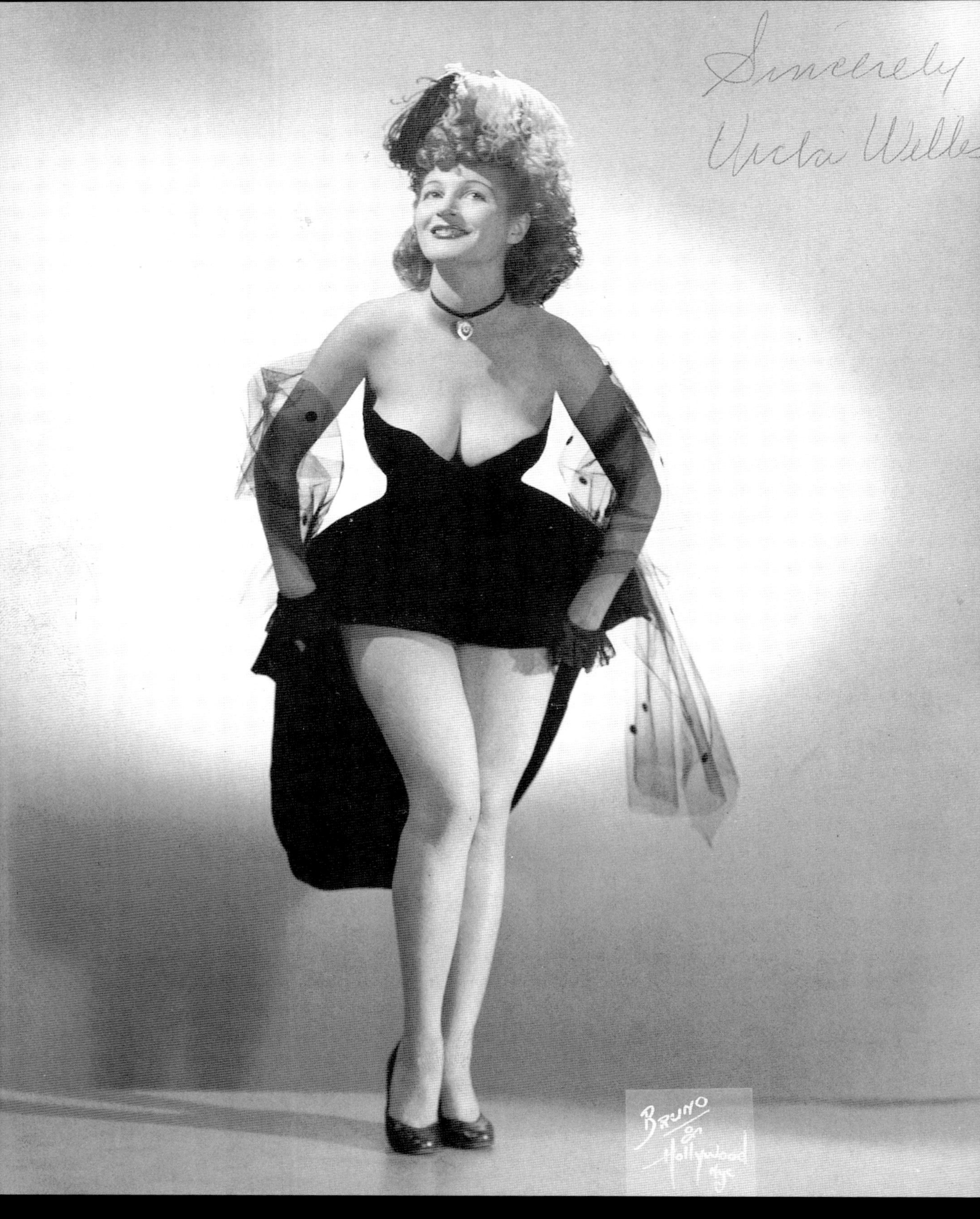

Vicki Welles
(Autographed)

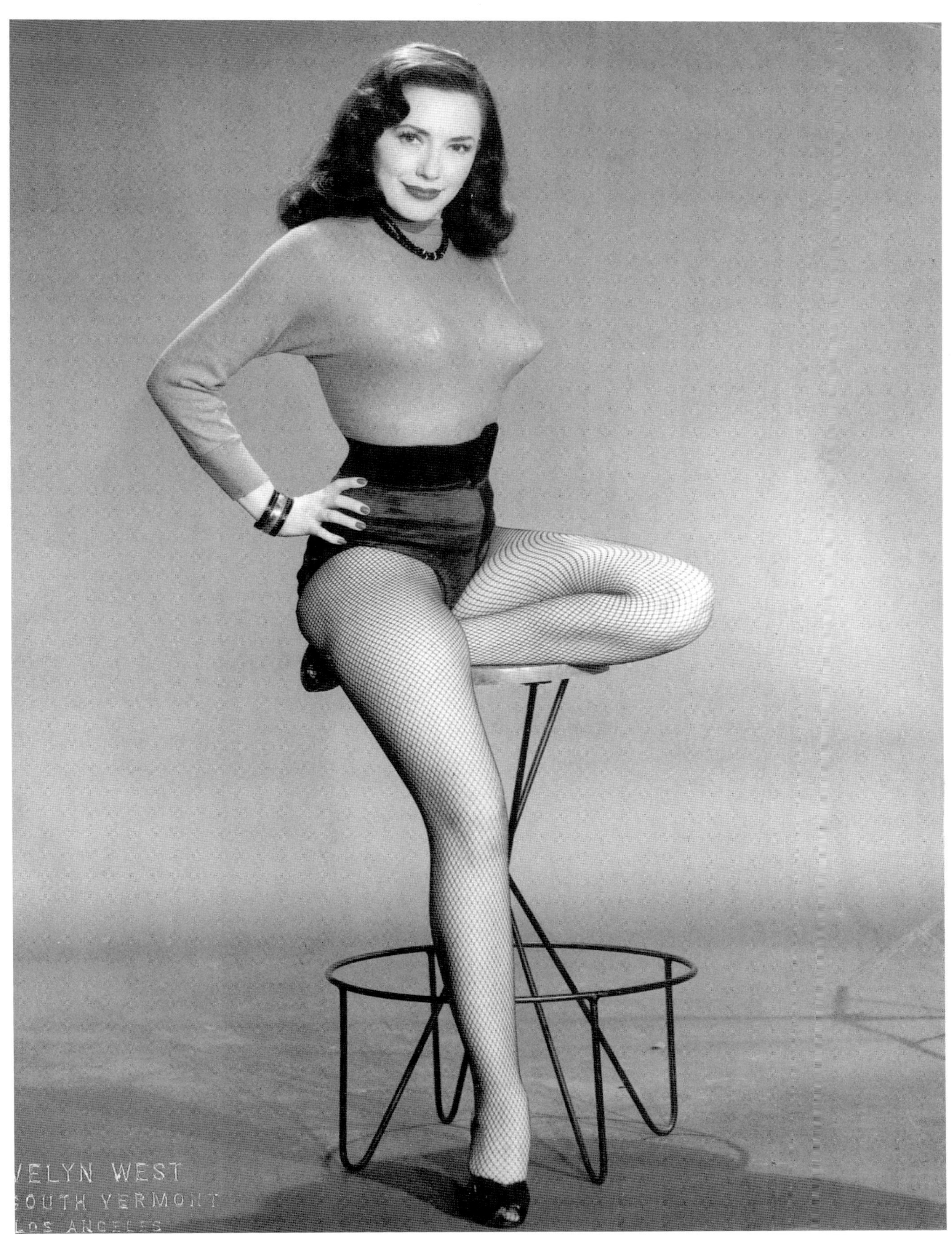

Evelyn West

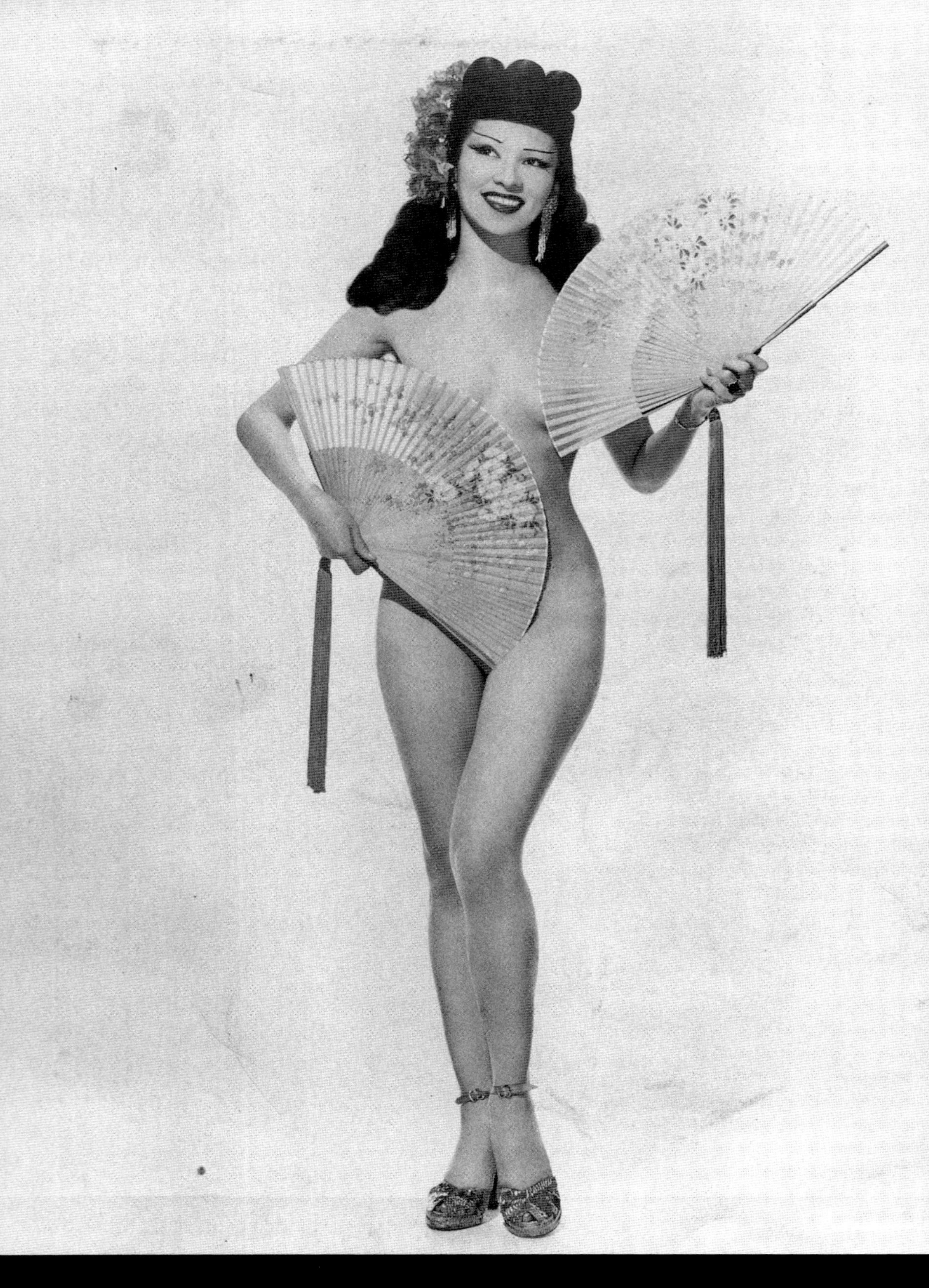

Barbara Yung-Ying
The Tempestuous China Beauty

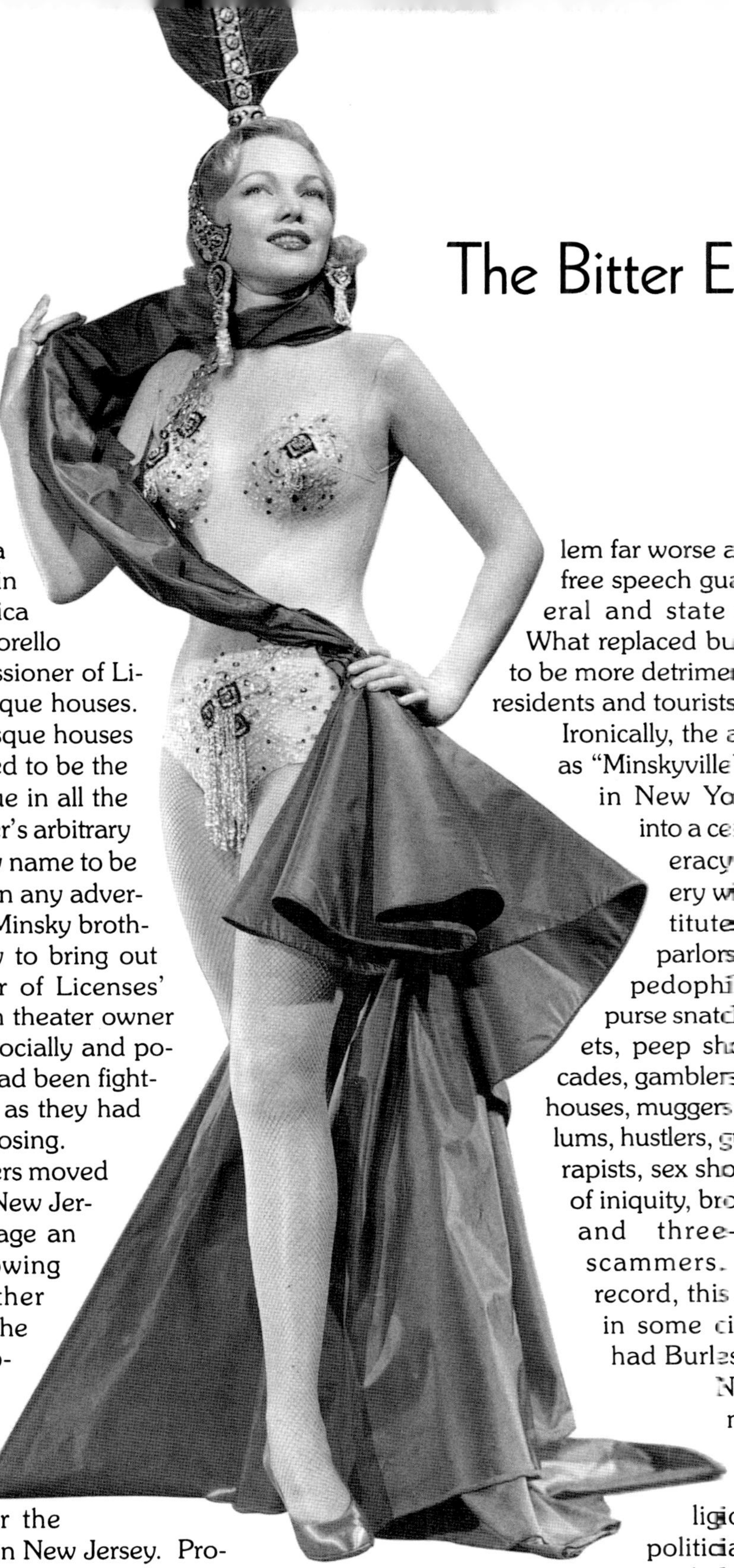

The Bitter End

Even though burlesque was a popular form of entertainment in virtually every major city in America in 1937, New York City Mayor Fiorello La Guardia, ordered his Commissioner of Licenses to deny licenses to Burlesque houses. His action forced all of the Burlesque houses in the city to close and this proved to be the beginning of the end of Burlesque in all the country. Part of the Commissioner's arbitrary ruling even prohibited the Minsky name to be used with the word "*burlesque*" in any advertisement or on a marquee. The Minsky brothers were denied the opportunity to bring out the fact that the Commissioner of Licenses' brother was a competing uptown theater owner who, along with other equally "socially and politically connected uptowners," had been fighting to close burlesque for years, as they had much business to gain from its closing.

Therefore, the Minsky brothers moved their Burlesque show to nearby New Jersey, where they continued to wage an on-going fight against the growing forces of censorship for another twenty years. However, once the illegal precedent had been established in New York City, constant harassment, costly fines and endless lawsuits (one lasting seven years) eventually made it unprofitable for the Minskys to continue their battle in New Jersey. Providing buses to shuttle the masses of people, who still clamored for this form of adult entertainment, across the river, failed to save this form of entertainment.

If the reformers who "rid the cities of sin" believed they had put an end to the moral problems of the country, they soon found they had actually made the problem far worse and violated the free speech guarantees of federal and state constitutions. What replaced burlesque proved to be more detrimental to the city's residents and tourists.

Ironically, the area once know as "Minskyville" on 42nd Street in New York, developed into a cesspool of degeneracy and debauchery with pimps, prostitutes, pornograph parlors, drug pushers, pedophiles, pederasts, purse snatchers, pick-pockets, peep shows, penny arcades, gamblers, X-rated movie houses, muggers, beggars, hoodlums, hustlers, gun-toting gangs, rapists, sex shops, S & M dens of iniquity, brothels, con men, and three-card monte scammers. Just for the record, this also happened in some cities that never had Burlesque.

Not until the mid-1990s, almost sixty-years after religious leaders and politicians "saved" the people from themselves, did the old Minsky neighborhood again begin to change. Then it was not due to legislation, but economics and a populace that had had enough of hard times. There is a valuable lesson to be learned from the story of Burlesque, and this, too, is the bare truth.

...the Minsky brothers moved their Burlesque show to nearby New Jersey, where they continued to wage an on-going fight against the growing forces of censorship for another twenty years.

Zorita

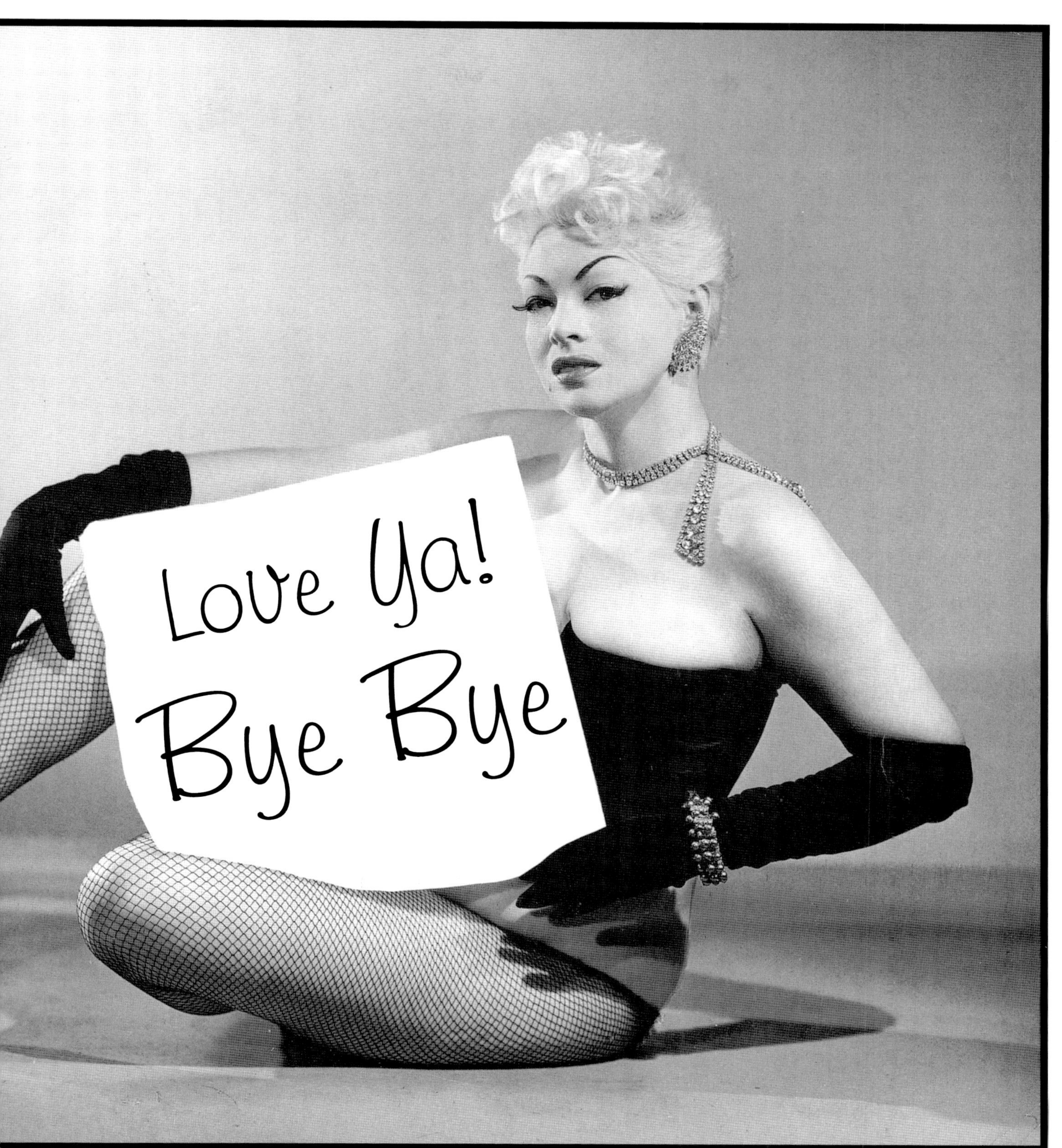
Love Ya!
Bye Bye